CAPITALISM AND SOCIAL THEORY

CAPITALISM AND SOCIAL THEORY

THE SCIENCE OF BLACK HOLES

Rajani Kanth

M.E. Sharpe Inc.
Armonk, New York • London, England

Copyright © 1992 by M. E. Sharpe, Inc.
80 Business Park Drive, Armonk, New York 10504

All rights reserved. No part of this book may be reproduced in any form without written permission from the publisher, M. E. Sharpe, Inc.

Available in the United Kingdom and Europe from M. E. Sharpe, Publishers, 3 Henrietta Street, London WC2E 8LU

First Printing 1992

Library of Congress Cataloguing-in-Publication Data

Rajani Kannepalli Kanth
    Capitalism and social theory: the science of black holes / Rajani K. Kanth.
        p.   cm.
    Includes bibliographical references and index.
    ISBN 1-56324-069-6 (c). — ISBN 1-56324-070-x (p)
    1. Capitalism—Social aspects.   I. Title.
HB501.R224   1992   91-36533
306.3'42—dc20   CIP

Printed in Canada
The paper used in this publication meets the minimum requirements of American National Standards for Information Sciences—Permanence of Paper for Printed Library Materials, ANSI Z 39.48—1984.

JD 10 9 8 7 6 5 4 3 2

For Cory, Antara, and Indrina

CONTENTS

Capitalism and Social Theory:
The Nexus of Praxis: An Introduction xi

ONE *Capitalism & Social Theory: Marxism and Pluralism* 1

    1 ~ Marxism and Pluralism: The Fateful Marx-Weber Encounter 3

    2 ~ Max Weber and Rationalization: A Critique 17

    3 ~ Bureaucracy, Power, and Domination: A Commentary 25

TWO *Marx & Political Theory: Theories of State, Class, and Power* 45

    4 ~ The Iron Law of Oligarchy: A Critique of Michels 47

    5 ~ The Ruling Class: A Critique of Mosca 57

    6 ~ Classical Marxism, NeoMarxism, and the State: A Retrospective 67

THREE *Political Economy & Policy: The Foundations of Classicism* 81

    7 ~ The Riddle of Laissez-Faire: Tales of Ricardo 83

    8 ~ The Demise of Ricardianism: Some Theses on Ricardo 93

    9 ~ Political Economy and Policy: The Malthus-Ricardo Embroilment 103

FOUR *Economics & Epistemology: Toward Materialism* **123**

    10 ~ The Foundations of Economic Analysis: Toward Realism **125**

    11 ~ Science, Class, and Theory: The Elusive Anatomy of Social Discourse **145**

    12 ~ Political Economy and Philosophy: Tensions in Orthodoxy **183**

FIVE *EuroMarxism & Third-Worldism: Toward Autonomism* **197**

    13 ~ Euromarxism and Dependency: A Portentous Disjunction **199**

Bibliography **211**

Index **221**

About the Author **228**

Acknowledgments

This book is a compilation of various vignettes, of the vital fragments that have made up my intellectual life, in a journey begun in more hopeful times a full twenty-two years ago at the Delhi School of Economics, in whose superlative department of Social Anthropology I first made acquaintance with social theory on a scale, and with an intensity, since unmatched. From there, I moved to the Jawaharlal Nehru University, another unpretentious salon of real learning, this time at the opposite end of the classroom as a teacher, ostensibly in the sociology of politics. And then it was on to Columbia University, New York, and finally to the New School for Social Research, a student again in a town that epitomizes, at least to this alien observer from afar, the very antipodes of the intellectual life, a sordid gutter of urban waste, glitz, and dementia where, all but unknowing, I went through a collapse of the senses from which I am yet to fully recover. At any rate, in that blight, in that rank and venal ethos, sexist, racist, and misanthropic as it was, I studied political economy—in the library, and in the street, cursing the madness that had made me give up the fair messuages and pleasances of New Delhi for the cacophonic nightmare of Manhattan. Since then, the parched but peaceful mountains of Utah have been my muses, in airy contrast to the septic vapors of the East Coast; in turn, now, in this haven of quiet, I was to add philosophy (a stint in Oxford putting me on to the genius of Roy Bhaskar) and feminist theory to my researches—both as phenomenally revelatory areas of inquiry as my early excursions in Marx, Freud, Levi-Strauss, and (later) Derrida. This book must bear bemused witness to all of these extended lucubrations. Homage is due, however, to the founts of faith sustaining such labors: firstly, to the rich intellectual life of New Delhi whose uncompromising qualities nurtured my early beginnings, nourishing the conviction that truth was beyond care or compromise; and secondly, to all of my students, toadies, humbugs, and gems inclusive, from New Delhi to New York to Salt Lake City, who have been, for me, almost, the happiest family I have ever been proud to call my own in all of these long, harsh years of exile. In a different key, I offer humble appreciation for the utterly selfless, and loving, care and concern bestowed upon this work, above and beyond any call of duty, by the truly inimitable Barbara Thayer of M.E. Sharpe—may her tribe increase!—and for the generous license granted by Richard Bartel, who first saw virtue in my efforts at a very preliminary stage. Finally, grace is owed my wife, Cory, who sat verily like patience on a monument, smiling at the many griefs of this tristful enterprise.

Rajani Kanth

Capitalism and Social Theory: The Nexus of Praxis
An Introduction

Today, it is the resilience of capitalism that has attracted the attention of thoughtful intellectuals in the face of the dramatic self-dissolving collapse of East Bloc socialism, assisted as much by the plain facts of current history as by the cacophonic barrage of procapitalist propaganda meted out by the various governmental and parastatal organs devoted to such matters by either overt or covert official definition. The critics of capitalism, socialist or not—especially the less secure among them—are either on the verge of—or have already taken the plunge into—capitulation, looking rather shamefaced in the discovery of having, in their own minds, lived the *Big Lie* for so long. Votaries of socialism are in retreat, each spilling into the other, rewriting their own failed programmes, and discovering new lesions in Marx that would have been heresy to admit but ten years ago. The Left has taken a tumble and the disarray is both disheartening and pathetic to behold.[1]

To those who take the longer view, however, recent events are far less climactic, and a lot less definitive of the shape of things to come. In the celebration of the post-war boom (the so-called Fordism of academic jargon), it might be recalled that similar joys were expressed with more than mere carelessness by scholars who might have known better; Daniel Bell's prediction of the end of ideology (or Charles Reich singing of the greening of America) being only a notorious example or two from a whole field of such sprouts, the beatific visions exploded only by the unbelievable outbreak of revolts against world capitalism worldwide that marked the later sixties. Of a sudden, the buoyant system took ill and the reckless party was over by the time the seventies rolled in. Reports of the demise of anticapitalist struggle proved hopelessly premature and the capitalist roller coaster slid off the rails in more than one situation, in both the first and third worlds.

Equally reminiscent—and instructive—is the earlier epoch of growth and high jinks (the twenties) and then crisis (the thirties), when the exhilaration of the roaring twenties turned abruptly into the dismay of the tumbling thirties with only a worldwide conflagration providing the stirrup for a renewed bout of accumulation. The point couldn't be simpler: *to judge capitalist success—or failure!—(materially or ideologically) by its marginal performance is to surrender judgment to the vagaries of the present situation.* The system is infinitely changeable (crisis prone) and success is not necessarily followed by more of the same. Social theory of the more unreflective kind, right or left, accordingly, will find itself unsupportably molded by altering historical experience, reflecting every twist and turn of empirical events to a point of incoherence. Both vulgar Marxism and bourgeois ideology share this same glaring weakness of being both ahistorical and altogether empiricist in their pronouncements. The simple truth is quite otherwise: neither has capitalism succeeded—the unemployment figures of Britain, Germany, and the United States currently bear ample and healthy warning—nor has socialism failed except for certain variants never established by popular consent. All we are seeing is a profound restructuring of both in response to challenges both internal and external to each. The East-West struggle is far from having ended; and indeed the North-South struggle is only just beginning[2]—with European civilization (exclusive of the former USSR) apparently having temporarily sewn up its breaches and achieved closure.

So the epoch has not transcended—but is only living up to—its Marxist possibilities (the recent turmoil in the Middle East being singularly premonitory). The papers presented in this volume all testify to this ordinary, but overlooked, apprehension: to the continued relevance of all genuine Marxian categories to an analysis of power, wealth, and ideology—or, politics, economics, and social theory, respectively. The essays are infused with a critically inspired historical materialism, faithful only to the realist content in Marx, and not to the many errors and elisions contained therein. They apologize neither for socialism nor capitalism, nor do they, with the expected sectarianism of standard academic discourse, fall into any premeasured school (which usually takes its answers as given, and then asks dissembling "questions") of either radical or

INTRODUCTION

Marxian theory. *All of them aim at the demystification of reality, the expungement of ideology, and the revealment of that nucleus of emancipatory possibilities that is vested in every epoch.* The papers necessarily possess another characteristic, that of not recognizing (let alone honoring) the traditional boundaries between various social science "disciplines"— boundaries that are sacrosanct to the typical career academic with a corporate ethic and a given territory to uphold and defend, respectively. Finally, the papers point to the primacy of praxis in social life, the sole reference point to which all theory ultimately must return; for social theory, as we know it today, could not but evolve in close conjunction with the changing form of Capitalist realities.

~

The Ideological Moment

More often than not, Marx had a negative concept of ideology—seeing it as an unreflective reflex of reality (where we cannot help believing what we do)—rather than a positive concept of ideology, which is more akin to what we would understand today as propaganda. However, in the intellectual response to Marx, it was a very self-conscious (i.e. class-conscious), motivated pleading that was the prime mover. In many ways, one could see all of modern-day social science, especially its dominant, Anglo-American variant, as the great ideological rejoinder to the Marxian challenge. In this enormous intellectual crusade the only real *bourgeois* who could meet the measure of Marx was Max Weber, whose sophistication in this regard has never really been surpassed even up until now, in these energetic times when propaganda has attained the status of science.

Far from taking Marx head-on, Weber simply sidesteps him by melting down his critique of capitalism into a pluralist peatbog where all manner of odd distillates are conceivable. Historical materialism is seen merely as an accent on life by an interested observer; another might well "read" reality differently. By giving equal weight to any and all perspectives on society, Weber sought—desperately—to relativize social truth such that despotism, domination, and exploitation could all be seen as idiosyncratic ways of viewing the world, reflecting different epistemologies rather than any measurable ontological entities. Where Hegel had written that the truth was the whole, Weber stood him on his head, suggesting that the whole could never be ascertainable by human social endeavor since subjective locations, in neoKantian epistemology, got in the way of perception of an individualist ontology.

Weber's conservatism, though not particularly enamored of capitalism (the romantic-conservative movement, of which Weber was a part, hearkened to the past: Weber was, in fact, a German Imperialist), nonetheless had to accommodate it, since it purported to be an all-encompassing theory of structures of (inevitable) domination. In this context, Weber's theory of *bureaucracy* is quite politically revealing since he made little effort to conceal his admiration for its efficient virtues (or, better still, its virtues of efficiency) despite the fact that bureaucracy was a "paradigmatic form of domination," not susceptible to overthrow except by a great charismatic interruption. Transmitted in designedly unreadable form into U.S. social science by his faithful disciple, Talcott Parsons, Weberian ideas became the mainstay of official social science, wedded to a neoconservative social agenda of containing dissent, and calming revolt both domestically and abroad.

The papers in Part I establish the true ideological lineage of Weber, situating him unambiguously as *the ultimate capitalist answer to Marxian dialectics*. To this day, the only reasonably consistent (even if fundamentally misconceived!) response to the Marxian critique, within a Eurocentered discourse, remains the pluralist one. The papers in Part I provide a critique of Weber's confrontation with Marx, and some highlights of that classical encounter in the study of capitalism.

~

The Political Moment

Politics is about power and domination. The correlates of power in a class society are the latent—though often disruptively manifest—struggles between the ruling and ruled classes over the biased rules of the game. Marxian theory locates politics within the domain of class struggle, in a nonunilinear developmental context that takes into account the existential possibilities presented by productive forces, means of social control, extent of repressive apparati, and the depth and efficacy of political consciousness and political organization on the part of the subaltern orders.

INTRODUCTION

It is not the *outcome* of the political struggle that is predetermined, only the struggle itself that can end in defeat, victory, or simply stalemate for either side. The great advantage of the ruling class is its near-monopoly of the machinery of state, legitimizing, through force or fraud, depending on the "political formula" in use, class domination over social property. But even near-invincible states can—and do—succumb to popular revolt when the "time is right," when the forces and relations of production are in irreconcilable conflict. So runs the classical Marxist argument.

For generations, since it was first publicized by anarchist and Marxist traditions in the nineteenth century, conservative theorists have battled this simple revealment—the "disenchantment," in other words—of the agenda of power. Their response, seeking a more benign "political formula," to keep the masses in soporific stupor, has taken two very separate forms. One response was disarmingly frank and reactionary: thus, elitist theory spoke easily of the inevitability of minority rule, the futility of mass aspirations for democracy, and the operation of the "iron law" of oligarchy, all based either upon ineffable social realities or on more invidiously indefeasible aspects of "human nature." Pareto, Mosca, and Michels thereby provided the ruling orders with vital ammunition to debunk both socialist and democratic theory. Their continued success is reflected in the sheer continuity, within the current political votaries of capitalism, of the ideological framework sanctifying elite rule and the apathy of the masses (its vital precondition) as twin requirements for the ideal polity. Nowhere is this more apparent than in the property-owning, corporatist, authoritarian political ideology of the United States.

A second response, more "liberal"—i.e. more sophisticated—came in the work of Max Weber, by any count the greatest revisionist of Marx, and the pluralist tradition he so successfully inaugurated. Against the all too visible scaffolding of power (conjoined to wealth) erected by Marxist theory, he counterposed other categories of social stratification, such as wealth, status, etc., to obfuscate their clearcut interconnections as presented by Marx. The science of wealth was to be carefully separated from the science of power, in an ideally bourgeois division of labor, leaving capitalist reality completely befogged and impenetrable. Weberian pluralism did not deny Marx outright—that was to be left to lesser minds—rather, it sought to contain his critique by erecting a dozen other hierarchies parallel to class stratification. One way to shroud the Eiffel Tower, one might say, is to build a dozen other towers of equal height around it: and that was precisely the Weberian object—to nullify and neutralize the power of Marx's unyielding critique of capitalist domination.

Part II provides a critique of these anti-Marxian theories of domination together with a commentary on more recent "neo-Marxian" efforts to travel "beyond Marx" in the construction of a "theory" of the state.

~

The Economic Moment

Ever since the triumph of Ricardian political economy in the first third of the nineteenth century, economics has itself become the crown jewel of the hegemonic ideology of industrial capitalism,[3] a tool, simply, to elaborate endlessly the virtues of *laissez-faire*, the exhortation now meaning only to leave the capitalist division of property untouched by any public or social intervention. For all the nuanced differences between the Ricardian and Jevonian systems, economics until this day—in its dominant Anglo-American variant—has striven only to defend and rationalize—and to apologize for—unfettered capitalist enterprise.

In this disingenuous undertaking, neoclassical economics has excelled as the ideology, *par excellence*, of capital; so deep rooted is this tendency that, entirely unaided, economics has become, theoretically, *the science of nothingness, a science of silence, a science of black holes*. Apart from its operational side (where it functions as *praxiology*) pertaining to control and regulation on behalf of capital, which survives in blissful ignorance of—indeed contradictory to!—all neoclassical axioms (a schizophrenia introduced by Keynes into the discipline), the tautological blankness of neoclassical theory must count as one of the most impressive monuments to pure ideology ever erected.

Ideology, of course, may not be countered by its own kin, by a counter-ideology; in this regard, all theoretical critiques of neoclassicism (including my own paper on Realism) must remain, ultimately, quite ineffectual, though necessary. Neoclassicism will never give way or bow down to the force of criticism alone (as the Sraffians discovered to their naive dismay in the famous "capital" controversy): this ideology will vanish only when the social relations it sanctifies are changed or modified; and the way that things look now, there is no immediacy to the prospect of a withering away of neoclassical conceptions of society. However, the obvious source of strength of the neoclassicals—the fact that the apparatus of capital is on their side—actually only weakens their *intellectual* "case" in general, the mediocre (the "hired prizefighters" of Marxian vintage) descending to naked apologetics, while the brilliant[4] escape into a rarefied stratosphere where intellect and conscience can be concurrently appeased. Suffice it to say (and no other critique could be quite so damaging!) that a person who studied *only neoclassicism* in his/her life would be, without mistake, the most errant fool (or knave!) the world has ever seen.

The papers in Part III explore the classical, Ricardian basis for capitalist ideology—where it was first laid, securely, in a period where economics was to become the hegemonic philosophy of social life, generally.

~

The Philosophical Moment

Bourgeois epistemology, taking its lead from neoKantian, Weberian social theory, has always shown a penchant for epistemological pluralism coupled with a *feigned agnosticism* about the nature of reality. Of course, this ontological skepticism did not flow from any progressive, reasoned intellectual insecurity about the limits of the knowable; rather, it was garnered of a conservative fear of radical exposure. In this feint, capitalist reality is best concealed from unsympathetic eyes that might see it for what it is: for the disenchantment of the world had, after the French Revolution, as Burke, Kant, and Weber had noticed, already gone too far—hence the denial of a reliable ontological quotient, and the popular view that somehow, we each (and all!) construct our *own* reality as we choose. A bourgeois default initially, it was turned into an even more disgraceful *Marxian* elision by the postAlthusserians, Hindess and Hirst in the United Kingdom, and Wolff and Resnick in the United States, respectively. In more academically oriented economics, the irrealist tendency is possibly best represented in the recent work of Philip Mirowski. Almost invariably, varieties of irrealism drift toward analytic philosophy, deserting the dialectical historical terrain of Marxism in the name, sometimes, of superior "science," a rather poor misnomer for an arguably mistaken philosophical error.

Against this wave of irrealist philosophy has been the fast rising tide of *transcendental realism,* as presented by Oxford philosopher Roy Bhaskar, restoring the primacy of *ontology* in the study of both society and nature. The papers in Part IV explore the value of this perspective in developing the idea of a philosophical basis for political economy that must exist regardless of any explicit consciousness of it. The simple Bhaskarian suggestion, echoing Marx, that *a real ontology limits and constrains epistemological possibilities* in human society, is used to develop a critique of both Ricardian classical economics and neoclassical economics—defending, incidentally, the proposition that, despite the fact that nature is opaque and our viewpoint not innocent, the activity of "science" is still possible in the context of society.

~

The Anthropological Moment

Classical Marxism couldn't help but be Eurocentric; Marx was the heir to the European enlightenment and remained limited in his own understanding of things nonEuropean by the state of European knowledge of such matters (neither broad nor deep in this regard) in his time. Witness, for instance, his easy plagiarism of Hegel's passage on Indian village communities[5], still represented, in the late nineteenth century (!), as isolated rural entities unincorporated into larger structures of political economy and domination. Even more spectacular is the easy digest of the so-called "Asiatic" (!) mode of production, built on hydraulic principles, and purporting to capture the essence of nonEuropean, precapitalist societies. Asia constituted the silent *Other*[6] and Marx's was the *European Voice* that spoke on behalf of both.

However, whatever Marx's limitations of time and place, the current heirs of *EuroMarxism* cannot be so absolved of responsibility for their more unabashed and self-justifying errors. It is axiomatic in EuroMarxist discourse—as in Brenner's work[7]—that the European colonies in the third world had nothing to do with Europe's take-off into industrial maturity (thereby gainsaying the importance of *primitive accumulation* to capitalism). Compounding this insult is injury, in fact, when it is suggested that, correspondingly, the European world had nothing to do with the creation of third world poverty, degradation, and general socio-economic

INTRODUCTION

regression. Finally, EuroMarxism has turned into *a defeatist discourse of subservience and obsequiousness toward capitalism,* with its politics of selective adaptation to the system, and its awestruck fetishism of the almighty *forces of production* extant in the latter; the typical EuroMarxist today is more likely to be an art connoisseur, or a postModernist literary critic, than a political economist—an armchair academic, rather than a mover or shaker of political life, either on or off campus. The divarication between any manner of popular movements and Marxism is almost totally complete within this smug and sectarian discourse, becoming more alien, by the day, from both the spirit and the letter of classical Marxism. The old morality of identifying with the oppressed, such a distinguishing feature of classical Marxism, is now debased into a reification of technique, process, and structure as in the studies of the most cynical neoclassical and his/her calculus of profits and progress, where people, once again—a century after Marx!—appear as disembodied "factors" of production. Where Marx had seen production as a regrettable necessity, forcibly imposed by an antagonistically organized class society, latter-day neoMarxists turn productivity itself into an ethic: how else could Geoffrey Kay[8] have maintained, in EuroMarxist arrogance, that the workers and peasants of the third world had not—amazingly!—been exploited enough!

Aside from celebrating European bourgeois civilization, EuroMarxism has become a bigger apologist for capitalism than even neoclassical theory (as in the work of Warren), seeing imperialism as the choice bearer of civilization to the nonEuropean world. Here, latent *racism* blends with capitalist apologetics to deliver the medicine of imperialism in the name of the classical Marx, rather a stereotypical case of the devil quoting scriptures to invidious effect.

Today, happily, the *Other* is not quite so silent anymore, and the lone paper in Part V speaks to this egregious default in western Marxism, pointing out some rather obvious dangers and the need for a radical reform—soon—of its degenerating orientations.

~

The great, enduring strength of Marxism, as reflected in these papers, lies not in its alleged *predictive* capacities (touted usually by the ignorant, unaware that society is an open system where invariant regularities simply do not obtain) but in its explanatory vigor, resting on the basic thesis of historical materialism: that ideational systems can only be deciphered and understood (and, ultimately, overcome) in the systematic specification of the material social conjuncture—i.e. that the social theory extant *within* capitalism is the social theory *of* capitalism serving to rationalize and uphold its ever changing form. Indeed, even Marxism—in its role as the *Great Rejection*—is ultimately a creation of capitalism in that its bounds are set by the system it opposes. Put differently, as Sartre once suggested, Marxism can only be overcome when society—if ever— becomes ready to move beyond capitalism; until that fateful conjuncture there is no possibility of Marxism losing either its value or its relevance. Viewed thus, Marxism is the *Final Critique* of capitalism which must prevail (if not over capitalism)—through absorption—over all other radical critiques of the system.

The reason for this explanatory vitality is rather simple: Marxism captures the real ontology of capitalism in all its various potentially transformational moments like no other system. In this regard, any realist appreciation of capitalism must bend toward Marxian insights, almost involuntarily. Marxism at its best, therefore, is Realism, and the good Marxist is one who keeps reality in focus as the determining factor of theory, rather than the texts of Marx, which can easily be turned into a pseudo-ontology of the Word (as in vulgar Marxism and some dominant trends in EuroMarxism) where reality may only be captured through the filtering lens of "theory" thereby inverting, as in *theology*, the materialist method so central to the entire enterprise. *The primacy of ontology over epistemology must remain the fundamental Marxian axiom of social theory*, in contradistinction to all forms of bourgeois ideology and all tendencies within neoMarxism that stress the spurious notion that it is consciousness that designs—and discovers—existence all by itself. All the papers in this collection stress this social truth as they explore the various ways in which bourgeois social theory has evaded for over a century a prerecognition of the real structures of capitalism.

Notes

1. The 1990 issue of the *Socialist Register* betrays, in one volume, almost all of these tendencies.
2. The recent Gulf conflict is an early and ominous sign of the incipient "New World Order" referred to by President Bush in his capacity as Commander in Chief of the *North as a whole*.

INTRODUCTION

3. For a complete statement of this thesis, see R. Kanth, *Political Economy and Laissez-Faire: Economics and Ideology in the Ricardian Era*, 1986.

4. Scholars such as Kenneth Arrow would be representative of this ilk; about the other variety, perhaps the less said the better.

5. It is, perhaps, not generally known that Marx had plagiarized his entire description of these alleged entities from Hegel's *Philosophy of History*; at any rate, the depiction of Indian rural society under the title of "The Future Results of British Rule in India" remains one of the most anthologized of Marx's writings.

6. See Johannes Fabian, *Time and the Other*, 1983, for elucidation.

7. R. Brenner, "The Origins of Capitalist Development: A Critique of Neo-Smithian Marxism," *New Left Review*, 104, 1977, pp. 25-92.

8. G. Kay, *Development and Underdevelopment*, 1975, p. x.

ONE

~

Capitalism And Social Theory: Marxism And Pluralism

~

> ...I will concentrate first on the ontological question of the properties that societies possess, before shifting to the epistemological question of how these properties make them possible objects of knowledge for us. This is not an arbitrary order of development. It reflects the condition that, for transcendental realism, it is the nature of objects that determines their cognitive possibilities for us; that, in nature, it is man that is contingent and knowledge, so to speak, accidental.
> —Roy Bhaskar, *The Possibility of Naturalism*

1

Marxism and Pluralism: The Fateful Marx-Weber Encounter

It might well be claimed, with considerable assurance, that Marx and Weber originated the very field of modern sociological analysis of political power, in traditions that are current to this day, albeit in modified, diverse, and sophisticated forms. It has also often been suggested that Weber's theoretical formulations were no more than a conscious reaction to the startling thrusts of Marxian ideas; ideas that threatened to upset, and indeed continue to upset, most traditional interpretations of how society is supposed to exist, function, and change. And, while it is certainly true that Weber advanced several major conceptions of his own invention in the field of social science, it can hardly be denied that he had quite an acute perception of how they stood, critically, in relation to the Marxist framework of social thinking.

To be sure, in his own private political life and pronouncements, Weber affected no special sympathies with either socialism or socialists ("I am a member of the bourgeois classes, I feel myself as such and I am educated in its views and ideals"—Weber, 1967, p. 26). In fact, his personal conservatism, when pressed, was on the borderline of even more dangerous, and culpable, "intuitions"; contrasting the Orient to the Occident (to the detriment of the former, naturally,[1] an old European pastime), Weber attributes the "difference," in all seriousness, to "heredity": "The author admits that he is inclined to think the importance of biological heredity very great..." (Weber, 1958, p. 30). And this, not too far in time from that all-German renaissance of yet stronger theories of "heredity" that were subsequently to shake the world, critically exposing the fragile foundations of European civilization. At any rate, judging from his private opinions—quite aside from the overall *oeuvre* of his studies—therefore, there would seem to be some basis for the accusation that he was quite the "bourgeois Marx" who attempted, not always successfully, to stand Marx on his head.

In another rendering, one which usually passes for the truth in mainstream discourse, more compliant critics deny that Weber's theories were meant to be a total repudiation of Marxist thinking, asserting that he only attempted (successfully) to round off and complement Marxian historical materialisms with political and military materialism, for instance. In this interpretation, Weber's work is seen as a genuine *synthesis*, an attempt to chart, in (scholarly) detail, those areas of social life (elisions) that were not explicitly covered by Marx's (implicitly programmatic) writings—in an effort to fill in the blanks, so to speak. As one scholar observes:

> Weber regarded Marx's methodological approach as one of fundamental importance and his own as supplementary to it. In no sense was Weber developing a method in opposition to Marx. Insofar as any refutation of Marxism was intended, it was of certain naive and mechanistic interpretations of Marx's theory held by some of his followers.[2]

In this portrayal, Weber is almost characterized as a preeminent Marx scholar, ingenuously complementing Marxian theses with some original ideas of his own (as Therborn puts it, "...Weber was clearly interested in, appreciative of, and influenced by, the work of Marx."—Therborn, 1980, p. 276—and yet, in contradiction, he goes on to argue that, "...Weber's remark proves that in fact he knew and cared little about Marxism."—Ibid., p. 289). Certainly, evidence may be adduced to suggest that Weber did hold several of Marx's many social propositions in great regard, indeed grafting them onto his own work quite readily, as either working or workable principles. However, on review it would seem that such a belief stems more from the often contradictory assertions in Weber's writings than from any real structural similarity between them and Marxism. And, certainly, if Weber did not consistently deny Marxian ideas, it could also be, perhaps, only because they were very often undeniably true. At any rate, the thrust of Weber's writings, in their entirety (as might be gleaned from a careful reading), could hardly be said to be aimed at consecrating the intuitions of Marx, but rather to point to their lapidary shortcomings; interpreted thus, it would be quite fair to maintain that Max Weber may well have been, to date, the greatest *revisionist* of Marx.

The most arresting piece of analysis revealing the true divergence between Marx and Weber is, of course, Weber's thesis on the Protestant ethic, wherein the classic materialist argument is sought to be "reversed" so as to demonstrate the force of "ideas" in history—something, Weber felt, was ignored by "economic materialism" (his, and others', preferred term for Marxism). Weber, in a passage toward the conclusion of the essay, indicates that the study was undertaken precisely to reverse the economic causation attributable to Marx, and to demonstrate, on the higher level, that all social perspectives are necessarily partial and one-sided—including, of course, his own. As he put it, "Each is equally possible..." (Weber, 1967, p. 83). In point of fact, however, the Weber thesis doesn't quite "work," actually, on its own chosen grounds: one can argue, far more convincingly, that the great split in church ideology, expressed in the rise of Protestant thought, was itself a forced reflection of the fast-developing bourgeois social relations in production in late-renaissance Europe, thereby easily reversing the causal priority favored—and furthered—by Weber.

Nevertheless, Weber sought to grant Marxism partial legitimacy as only one way of constructing reality—a concession that is, of course, immediately withdrawn by the announcement of the "axiom" that there can never be a complete explanation of social life and behavior from any single point of view. (This denial of an apprehendable "totality" separates the Marxians, ontologically, from the neoKantians such as Weber. While the implied ontology of society may be debatable, the implications for politics for such a pluralist relativism are far less opaque: by vesting the critic of domination with the same legitimacy as the defender of it, it is the struggle for emancipation that is forever shortchanged and devalued. In this sense, Weber's ontology is necessarily conservative in its political implications). It is also argued that Weber was "repelled" by vulgar, dogmatic, monocausal Marxism, which is certainly entirely possible; but, so astonishing is his ignorance of dialectical thinking, it is equally possible that he simply mistook the latter for Marxism itself, and indeed knew of no other form of the latter.

At any rate, to return to the Protestant ethic thesis: unless a serious misappreciation of the Marxian problematic is involved, it did not require a Max Weber to demonstrate the "force" of ideas in history as a "counter-claim" to the Marxian historical materialist thesis; it is, in truth, Marx who unambiguously stated that ideas, once they capture the imagination of the people, can indeed become "material" forces. Such arguments would have been better, and more fruitfully, directed against vulgar materialism, which so often passes, quite disingenuously, for the "official" view of Marx; but, even so, Weberian pluralism, in origin and development, has since remained an ideological—and theoretical—countercurrent (as in the work of his best known popularizer in the English language, Talcott Parsons) to the subversive revelations of Marxian social science, no matter what its original intentions (so when Therborn writes that Weber's sociology "did not develop as a critique of historical materialism..."—Therborn, 1980, p. 276—he is obviously not taking cognizance of its ultimate impact, a rather startling error from a fairly hidebound, orthodox Marxist), and in spite of several efforts to conceptualize it as simply an original "extension" of the structural materialism of Marx (i.e. as a "positive" critique of the materialist conception, as Therborn would have us believe).

Just as revealing is the variance between Marx and Weber in the realm of analysis of the systemic links between political structures and other social structures. For Marx, categorically, the state remains the critical agency of class domination, located primarily in the arena of poli-tics, no matter what its ancillary functions. It arises, in the first place, at a particular moment in history when the class division of society is complete and class differences have become irreconcilable, and it disappears, or so Marx implied, at another moment in history, when class society is itself abolished.

There have therefore been societies without the state in the past, and it is conceivable that there might be societies in the future which are similarly organized. The state is thus a political *variable*, a creature of specific forms of economic organization, and the class struggle extant therein, whose principal concern is to guarantee a given form of property relations, and the domination of those who benefit from them. If there is a logic to its "function," it is the need-specific of a society characterized both economically and politically by class domination—it is, by no means, a universal, functional requirement of all societies.

Marxism and Pluralism: The Fateful Marx-Weber Encounter

The transformation of terrain in Weber's analysis, radically altering the hierarchy of relations, is quite significant, if not always readily apparent: he defines the state as a political association which has a monopoly, or near-monopoly, of the means of violence, considered "legitimate"—in disparate, if doubtful ways—by those whom it seeks to dominate, or at least by the majority of those whom it seeks to dominate. Of course, at least on this one aspect of the state, Marx and Weber seem to be in accord: the state is not, for either theorist, by any stretch of the imagination, primarily a benevolent association, as in the vulgar liberal view that is current to this day (although, it might well perform benevolent functions, when required, out of a regard for system preservation). But, matters are more complex than this would imply; the domination referred to in Weber is not specifically *class domination*: it is, instead, the domination of the state over society, the latter described by Weber as a diffuse conglomerate of the undifferentiated masses (quite similar to the radical dualisms of "elitist" theory). In other words, there is no necessary coincidence, in Weber, between political economy and political sociology: the dialectical and dependent relationship between the economic structures, taken as a whole, and political structures is not understood developmentally across history, in transformation and transition, as in Marx. Their relationship is assumed rather to function arbitrarily, in a series of temporary compromises—there being no necessity, in Weber's thinking, for a logical trend in their mutual relations.

A fundamental notion in any political theory, the concept of the "legitimacy" of the political order is an important one for Weber. However, substantive clarity is undeniably lost (a corollary of his vaunted "value-free" claims for science) when the investigation, quite singularly, fails to distinguish (indeed makes no effort to distinguish) between false and true consciousness of a given factual situation—between popular ideology and material reality, in other words—in his concept of the legitimization of domination, be it traditional, charismatic, or "rational-legal." Whether the "consent" of the people is obtained through coercion or chicanery, manipulation or outright fraud, so long as it holds true for the majority, the domination involved is considered "legitimate": here, then, is a blanket justification (how *wertfrei* can one get?) of most classical, European forms of despotism that come to mind—slavery, feudalism, etc., to say nothing about more contemporary forms of tyranny. One explanation for this sociological cynicism is, perhaps, the possibility that

Weber, akin to the elitist school, had a theory of power distribution involving the belief that all societies, past, present, or future, are likely to split into the same divide between those who are dominated and those who dominate, regardless of how this domination comes to be "justified"—and so perhaps Weber, too, viewed this as an immutable historical fact, treating it accordingly.

In this charged field of discourse, Marx's position ranges far distant from that of Weber; we are cautioned that, just as we could not accept, uncritically, a man's (or a woman's) opinion of himself (or herself) as truth, so too should we never evaluate a historical period on the basis of its own consciousness. Marx's elucidation of the role of ideology in society (alone amongst all the classical social theorists, Marx is the only one who offers us a theory of ideology: i.e. a *theory of theory*,[3] by virtue of the notion of "false" consciousness)—a ruling ideology often being nothing other than the ideology of the ruling class—makes it apparent that it is the scientist's charge to strip away the veil of false consciousness masking reality. This essential scientific enterprise is often thwarted by the fact that the scientist himself (or herself) is not immune to the ideological processes prevailing in a given context; but, at the very least, the definition of the problem is, itself, the first step toward guarding against popular falsifications. Not only is this a necessary scientific task, *it is in fact the scientific undertaking itself*—for if appearance and reality coincided, says Marx, there would be no need for science (*society is not transparent, runs the argument, nor is our contemplation necessarily innocent*), and certainly no need for a social science. Applying this critique to Weber, it becomes apparent just how questionable it is to refrain from calling attention to facts on the ground that this involves value judgments, especially when the facts are themselves undeniable; indeed even more so, when a political philosophy or a value judgment is implicit in the very posture of a nonjudgmental study, whether this is made explicit or not. On the question of method, therefore, Weber succeeds only in tying himself up in some rather untidy knots; but, fortunately for him, he manages to extricate himself, usually, by recourse to the time-honored practice of quietly ignoring his own injunctions as to procedure. As W.G. Runciman observes:

> It is a frequent accusation against Weber that he fails to follow his own recommendations about method. To some of his critics this is a good

thing rather than otherwise, but it is either way hard to dispute that Weber's historical writing is less wholly free from subjective interpretation than his own remarks about method might suggest.[4]

It would appear that Weber's analysis of the legitimacy of the state, as noted already, seems to enjoy currency quite regardless of the substantive question of the nature of the political system at issue—a value-loaded affirmation far from immune to a Marxian disavowal. But this assertion is not peculiar only to Weber's political sociology: indeed, it follows from the first principles that he had laid out in his complex methodology for the social sciences. Fundamental assumptions, Weber believed (*sic*), are always arbitrary—the point, however, even so, being to follow up such pre-analytical predispositions, as rationally and scientifically as possible, in the ensuing analysis. This follows, also (for Weber), because a subject becomes significant to us only when it is "value-relevant" to our subjective fancies—but this does not, or should not, preclude the possibility that subsequent scientific investigation can proceed in a "value-free" manner.

It is indeed quite apparent that Marx and Weber are apart not merely on ontological issues, but in their epistemics as well; as Giddens suggests:

> ...the most important respect in which Weber separates his views from those of Marx concerns the broad epistemological standpoint which underlies the whole of Weber's writings. The radical neo-Kantian position which Weber accepts takes as its premise the complete logical separation of factual and normative propositions.[5]

The implication, then, is that science is not culture-free (of course, the converse proposition is never considered by Weber: is culture, for instance, necessarily *"science-free"*?)[6] and that, structurally, all scientific explanations are, on first principles alone, incomplete, fragmentary, and one-sided, since the initial choice of terms is itself arbitrary, as is their prior definition. All that is revealing in a scientific inquiry is the limit of our own outlook and orientation ("No amount of historical research is going to make a Catholic and a Freemason agree in their interpretation of religious history...", says Runciman, 1969, p. 156). It would thus appear that the very first step in social science is based on a purely private belief: irrational, nonempirical and nonnegotiable (yet, somewhat inconsistently,

Weber allows for *Wertungsdiskussionen*, a rational debate over "values"). If this were the only triumph of pluralism that ridicules science itself, it would be a sorry triumph indeed. At any rate, applying such socio-logic to the field of political philosophy, we get, as Runciman puts it:

> ...a position very similar to that put forward in T.D. Weldon's notorious *Vocabulary of Politics* (1953). A political philosophy to Weber almost as much as to Weldon, is like a matter of taste. One can only state one's taste and go away—there is no point in arguing.[7]

Marx's stance on the question of political philosophy, expectedly, is infused with both discernment and penetration. Scientific assumptions, as much as private beliefs, in the Marxian rendering, appear far from arbitrary once the overall social provenance of prevailing orientations is carefully exhumed. And far less contingent is a political philosophy or ideology: such ideas are always based on the structure of material interests—and the contradictions therein—operative in a given context, and can, at the very least, be related to them in a significant and meaningful manner. For Marx, nothing that exists and functions in the social milieu is entirely meaningless or haphazard: there are always structural rationales and connections, these being quite easily discerned once the effort is made to probe deeply enough into social causation—*and away from phenomenal forms to generative, causal mechanisms*. Or, to put it another way, beliefs and philosophies may well appear to be "arbitrarily" held, but their consequences are always definite, irrespective of the self-awareness of the individual. But since Weber, at least as far as his arguments on method are concerned, denies that science can provide answers to the question of "meaning," he classifies the content of political philosophies as outside the domain of scientific investigation, and inside the realm of private opinion and belief. As Gerth and Mills put it:

> In his writing on method, Weber rejects the assumption of any "objective meaning." He wished to restrict the understanding and interpretation of meaning to the subjective intentions of the actor. Yet, in his actual work, he is no less aware than is Marx of the paradoxical fact that the results of interactions are by no means identical with what the actor intended to do. Thus the Puritan wishes to serve God, but he helped to bring about modern capitalism.[8]

On the ontology of social relations of capitalist society there are, to be sure, some items of overlap between Marx and Weber: property relations are the central and elemental determinants of the class structure, and Weber concedes the usage of many terms specific to Marxian analysis, such as class consciousness, class interest, and class conflict, although they are not conceived as the sole determinants of political activity. In fact, not unlike Marx, Weber does characterize capitalist society, unwaveringly, as a structure of social domination. However, Weber's specific contribution in this area is often supposed to be the interjection of other necessary protocols besides the decisive control of key economic resources (normally assumed to be stressed in Marx) such as dominion over the means of political administration, violence, and scientific research, imperative to the capitalist structure of social domination (the last-mentioned particularly, as the work of Foucault, emphasizing the systemic coupling between power and knowledge, suggests).

Implicit in this interpolation is the assumption that Marx, through some oversight, had disregarded the importance of these institutions. It is quite true, of course, that Marx wrote no treatises on the functioning of these parastatal structures, per se; but there is no denying that he was well aware of their overall *logic* (within the mode of production), indeed specifying this logic emphatically in the classic texts of historical materialism. And if the political moment is seen as constituting a "superstructure" (which is far from a disparagement of the importance of the political, as is sometimes believed), it nevertheless is regarded as vested with independence and autonomy precisely so as to perform its important, and varied, political duties the better.

Quite instructively, however, where Weber is impressed by the manifest "rationality" of the capitalist social enterprise, Marx is struck by its profound irrationality and its serious, even catastrophic, internal contradictions. Stated differently, Weber is well aware of the difference between formal and substantive rationality, and yet chooses to dwell, in benign detail, upon the former in his discussion of the state apparatus, bureaucracy, etc.; whereas, in Marx, it is the critical irrationality of the state in capitalist society that always, relentlessly, occupies center stage. Indeed, the notion of retrograde relations of production, defended by state power, placing reins on the galloping forces of production, so central to the Marxian schema of social change, spells out the specific moment of "irrationality" of antagonistic modes of production quite unmysteriously and palpably. Arguably, then, the difference between them is not attributable to differing political philosophies and personal values, as might be imagined—i.e. to different epistemologies (as in a Weberian interpretation!)—but to radical differences in their relative appreciation of capitalist ontology. Weber fails, in other words, to observe the real historical process of the evolution of social structures, having, thereby, a less than adequate theory of social development and causality, within an all-too comfortable "structure-functionalist" vision of social integration. Or else, it is difficult to see why he steadfastly underestimates the possibility of institutionalized resistance to capitalist domination on the part of social forces that do not accept either its "legitimacy" or its "rationality." But, of course, this elision is given in the prior Weberian divarication of both political economy and history from the study of political power.

The specification of the notion of a status hierarchy, in contradistinction to, and set apart from, class stratification, is another Weberian accomplishment, quite popular in certain forms of contemporary political sociology, where it is treated as a useful antidote to the traditional considerations of class (as in certain variants of the study of the social institutions of India, where *caste* may then be counterposed to class in a rival theory of "caste-conflict," without relating the "caste" hierarchy meaningfully to other material struggles, and so on), which Marxists are prone to put forward (be it) with monotonous regularity in discussions of political conflict. It would be, of course, quite foolish, aside from being quite unreal—and certainly un-Marxist—to use class orderings to negate status orderings, and *vice versa*, since they dwell in different domains, and since the relationship between them must be investigated empirically, in given cases, if they are to be related at all—it being as ridiculous to interpret the Russian Revolution as a status conflict as it is to use social class to explain why a mother's brother has a higher status than a father in certain tribal organizations. In fact, it is not clear whether Weber himself intended the one term to displace the other—at least if one is to believe Weber himself on the subject:

> The way in which social honor is distributed in a community between typical groups participating in this distribution we may call the social order. The social order and the economic order are, of course, similarly related to the 'legal order.' However, the social and economic order are

not identical. The social order is, of course, conditioned by the economic order to a high degree, and in its turn reacts upon it.[9]

With only a few amendments, this statement could quite easily be made to conform to some of the major tenets of historical materialism. The social and economic hierarchy, or, for that matter, the economic and political hierarchy, are not necessarily identical; in fact, a certain healthy overt separation of the economic from the political, formally speaking, may well be the best safeguard for class rule—which is why Marxists tend to think of democracy as a sort of ideal form of capitalist rule. As Marxists often point out, the (political) governing class and the (economic) ruling class need not coincide—in fact, a safe distance between the two may well be the best guarantee of a popular mystification of their real connections—far from the common vulgarizations to the contrary, amongst both vulgar Marxists and their critics, tending to misrepresent the Marxist position on the subject. Status has an existence both inside and outside of class—but far from it that the discovery of a status hierarchy, or a power hierarchy, overrides the class factor altogether. To quote Runciman:

> To assume, as some commentators do, that whenever a factory worker buys a spin drier or stops wearing a cloth-cap or fails to vote Labor at a parliamentary election he is therefore motivated by the quest for status at the expense of traditional class loyalties is frankly absurd. After all, as Lockwood puts it: 'A washing-machine, is a washing machine, is a washing machine.'[10]

Weberian analysis is perhaps most tantalizingly inadequate on the problematic of socio-political change and the dynamics of development and transition in historical society. The closest it comes to elaborating anything approaching a trend is in its treatment of the transcendent process of rationalization of all social structures across history, continually extant, despite frequent checks, and reversals, to the inexorable movement produced by "*charismatic*" challenges that temporarily impede the process of "disenchantment"—only to surrender, eventually, to the logic of "routinization."

There is ample evidence that Weber deplored this process of bureaucratization characteristic of contemporary society—succumbing perhaps to some values of his own—indeed placing his faith in the monumentalized individual (reminiscent of the Carlylean "hero") to rescue society, temporarily, from such inevitable, if stultifying, "progress." Weber's ideas on social change are quite apparently predicated upon the irrational and the unpredictable: the notion of *charisma* which, periodically, rocks society out of its ossified routines. Astonishingly, in a sociologist of such perspicacity, social change has little to do with the correlates of social production, technology, or class conflict, or even with the dynamics of political power—all of which, of course, are the preeminently crucial factors in the Marxian model of social revolution. In the latter analysis, the social revolution (revolutionary, as opposed to incremental, in essence conservative, change) is possible only when the objective and subjective factors are both present and mature; when there is an irreconcilable contradiction between the forces and relations of production; and when the subaltern social classes are politically conscious, organized, and willing to struggle openly against the manifest irrationality and iniquity of the system: at least, so runs the Marxian script.

But perhaps the most radical, and telling, dissonance between the two investigations resides in the fact that the Marxian system incorporates both *theory and practice, being ever aware of their interconnections and interdependencies*—whereas Weber assumes the royal posture of the classical (or perhaps not so classical!) professorial scholar who is, apparently, willing only to analyze and interpret the social world from afar (confident that official social science can be neutral and unbiased), but not, necessarily, to engage in changing it. From the perspective of the Marxist, of course, Weber does not sacrifice value judgments for the sake of objectivity, as it might appear, but rather, precisely, *vice versa*. Weber did succeed, however, quite resplendently, within the general neo-Kantian tradition that he inaugurated, in "modifying" Marx, at least in mainstream discourse, purging its critical vocabulary of its revolutionary content, and thus assimilating an emasculated Marxism into the mainstream of conservative social science—where it continues to maintain an assured, if largely token, presence. Ultimately, of course, Weber (an avid fan of German imperialism, no less) could hardly have apprehended the real meaning (to use Weber's favored *verstehen* idea) of Marxian discourse—except negatively. Marxism intends, quite self-consciously, to be *a critical "science" of emancipation*; the "knowledge" it generates is with a view to radical social amelioration—it can never devolve into a charter for a passive study of an essentially static "reality," despite tendencies within it, especially of the contemporary *EuroMarxist* variant dominant in academe, that process their tools toward such self-serving ends. It can, accordingly, never be the academic sociology that neoWeberians, in their pluralist manifest, and neoMarxians, in their revisionist credo, would like to turn it into.

Notes

1. For a true statement of Weberian ignorance of Oriental intellectual achievements, see his ideas on the "uniqueness" of western civilization in Andreski, ed., *Max Weber on Capitalism, Bureaucracy and Religion*, 1983, pp. 21-29.

2. Irving Zeitlin, *Rethinking Sociology*, 1973, p. 125.

3. For the full complexity of Marx's theory of ideology, see Jorge Larrain, *Marxism and Ideology*, 1983.

4. W. G. Runciman, *Social Science and Political Theory*, 1965, p. 55.

5. A. Giddens, *Capitalism and Modern Social Theory*, 1971, p. 195.

6. See in this regard, the interesting discussion offered by Roy Bhaskar, *The Possibility of Naturalism*, 1979.

7. W. G. Runciman, op. cit., p. 156.

8. H. H. Gerth and C. Mills, *From Max Weber: Essays In Sociology*, 1958, p. 58.

9. Ibid. p. 181.

10. W. G. Runciman, op.cit., p. 143.

2

Max Weber and Rationalization: A Critique

The tendency toward bureaucratization, or rationalization, in the evolution of social structures (particularly, of course, in the Eurocentered context of European history, to remind ourselves of a long ignored, but simple, fact), is a central tenet of Max Weber's philosophy of history. The concept itself bears resemblance to the more romantic interpretations of the disenchantment of the world (Schiller), referring essentially, in appropriate sociological translation, to the demystification of social reality. It is significant that Weber attached, in spite of his much vaunted "value-free" commitments, a negative evaluation to this inexorable historical process, clearly not overly enthusiastic at the relentless secularization of socio-political structures that was taking place within his time—and of course he was far from being alone in voicing dismay at its content and pace.

From the Enlightenment onward, critical thinking in social philosophy had disturbed the self-assured stability of feudal privilege and aristocratic power, culminating—alongside other material conjunctions—in the great French Revolution of 1789, which struck, in Continental Europe, the first momentous political blow against feudal absolutism. But, in the aftermath of that revolution, Europe witnessed, in what has come to be termed Romantic-Conservative thought, a major historical counteroffensive launched by reactionary ideologists to suppress social criticism and banish critical social philosophy. The subversion of popular consciousness through the dissemination of dangerous political ideas was sought to be prevented in a variety of ways; the tactics employed ranged from appeals to the sanctity of tradition to religion, positivist science, and positive philosophy—all simultaneously on display in the works of Comte, Saint-Simone, Kant, and Burke. But with the dramatic rise of Marxian and affiliated social ideas, all of the old spectres that had struck horror in the heart of European reaction were to be resurrected. Once again the stability of the new ruling classes was threatened (or so ran the perception) by the immediate possibility of mass revolt. Marx's political ideas were specifically sought to be contained by newly sprung elitist ideology, best exemplified in the works of Mosca and Pareto, and by the more seemingly democratic "pluralist" social science, best illustrated in the grand sociological conceptions of Max Weber.

Socialist theory exposed the rational—and material—political content of social domination, demonstrating the hidden interconnections between seemingly unrelated social institutions. It had laid bare the machinations of ideology and the mystifications of religion, stressing the determinate linkages between politics, economics, and religion. The magical shell in which society was securely ensconced was suddenly being stripped away, and the old ideological smoke screens that had performed such yeoman service in the past were now proving ineffective against the new radical political economy that challenged, as never before, the established authority of the nineteenth century.

Small wonder that Marx became the whippingboy of all subsequent "sociology" (as he remains to this day) with the discipline of sociology itself becoming the chosen vehicle for the rejection of the intransigent philosophy of materialism. Such was the nature of the process of "rationalization" taking place in European society in the nineteenth century. Quite a few besides Weber and the social interests accommodated by him were nostalgic for the good old days.

Of all the social theorists that took up the challenge of Marxian ideas, few stand serious comparison with Max Weber, whether in the breadth of his historical research, or the range of his sociological investigations. In the opinion of some commentators, in fact, his work has been seen as an effort to round out the monist implications of historical materialism; and certainly in his own writings Weber claimed to be in substantial agreement with the conception of economic determinism (representing Weber's understanding of Marxism)—which he considered an invaluable sociological insight—while the Marxist historical method itself was construed as an equally important heuristic principle. But the rounding out had other objectives and implications as well.

The concept of rationalization, in effect, was to become almost a parallel theory of socio-historical development (in relation to Marx) in spite of assertions to the contrary. Rationalization was evident not only in the fixation of clang-patterns in music, but also in Weber's typological sketch of world religions, where his comparative studies focused on the extent to which religions are predicated on rational world views. Western civilization was thought to be peculiar in the sense that the disenchantment, rationalization, or what you will, is claimed to have been carried out more thoroughly than elsewhere. Weber believed that western culture, in its entirety, had undergone this process, of which modern science was said to be the preeminent example. But other spheres of human conduct were also regarded as having been subjected to the same quality of mentality and organization that made possible rational and purposeful conduct predicated upon the predictability of human behavior. However, it is in Weber's analysis of capitalism, of course, that rationalization finds its most detailed application: capitalism is compelled to fundamentally rationalize all spheres of social life, including technology, capital accounting, law and administration, and politics and authority.

It is here, however, that problems arise in his interpretation of the transhistorical process. There is the undeniable suggestion that this historical process is sort of an immanent trend in society, unrelated in its impetus and development to concrete institutional patterns and arrangements. The implication is irresistible that it is this mysteriously evolved, but all-embracing, principle that, of its own accord, transposes social structures by superimposing itself upon them—an almost perfect equivalent to an idealistic, Hegelian pure reason that marches triumphant through history in order only to realize itself. Marx had already demonstrated, in the case of Hegel, the folly of ignoring, in favor of transcendental explanation, the substantive social forces involved in social change; in his own studies, Marx clearly demonstrated that the social forces making for the secularization of social life sprang from understandable changes in both the organization and technology of social production: social development is not to be explained through abstractions, wrote Marx, but indeed *vice versa*.

At one stage, Weber, in spite of himself, is forced to acknowledge that very identifiable social basis of rationalization:

CAPITALISM AND SOCIAL THEORY: MARXISM AND PLURALISM

> Today it is primarily the capitalist market economy which demands that the official business of administration be discharged precisely, unambiguously, continuously and with as much speed as possible...

Elsewhere, too, Weber leaves little room for doubt, at least to the insightful student, that it is indeed "capitalist" rationality that demands the separation of the worker from his means of production, the administrator from his means of administration, and the scientist from his means of research (as every untenured academic knows, or should know!). It is, therefore, not some meta-historical or mysterious process of rationalization that is at work, rather the specific rationality demanded by a specific social formation.

More so than any other theorist of capitalism, it is in Max Weber that the idea of rationality finds its real resting place—for the modern bureaucracy (an institution that preoccupied him extensively) was to be viewed by him as, par excellence, the very epitome of formal rationality in social enterprise ("...the most rational known means of carrying out imperative control over human beings." Weber, 1947, p. 337). The bureaucratic apparatus is said to function more efficiently than any legal enslavement of the functionaries, far cheaper than formally unremunerated, honorific service (it is, therefore, more rational—efficient—than comparable institutions under slavery or feudalism). At the same time, bureaucratization is stated as going hand in hand with the concentration of the means of production and management; it is, without reservation, a structure of domination, which, in the absence of a restriction of the principle of a free market, makes for the "universal domination of the class situation."

On the other hand, there are many specific virtues of bureaucracies (which, no doubt, critics of bureaucracy itself would deny unreservedly): precision, speed, unambiguity, continuity, discretion; unity, subordination, and, above all, calculability. It is a structure that seems to become, by eliminating emotional and irrational elements from the business of doing business—another ideal requirement of capitalism—more perfect the more it dehumanizes ("...*sine era et studio*" Weber, 1947, p. 340). It is fascinating to observe how Weber, while concretely relating almost all the functions of bureaucracy to the objective needs of capitalism, as specified by Marx much earlier, still preferred to view bureaucracy as an autonomous structure not subject to the social forces of capitalism. Although it has been suggested by commentators that Weber was acutely aware of the class character of such imperatively coordinated associations, there is no explicit mention in his writings of either the class nature or the class content of the functions of bureaucracy in capitalist society. Instead we see the congruence of two separate logics, the logic of capitalism and the logic of bureaucracy:

> ...capitalism in its modern stages of development strongly tends to foster the development of bureaucracy, though both capitalism and bureaucracy have arisen from many different historical sources.[1]

This becomes all the more inexplicable when we realize that Weber does not deny the class character of capitalist society—in fact, quite to the contrary, he acknowledges all of the classes of capitalist society fundamental to Marxian analysis: the bourgeoisie, the working class, the intelligentsia, the petit-bourgeoisie, etc. Moreover, he also acknowledges that property and the lack of it are the crucial bases of class situations. The difficulty is cleared when we turn to Weber's political sociology, which steers a fairly autonomous course from his political economy: it is in this crucial separation of the two that he, in all subtlety, turns away from Marx.

The basis of coordination of socio-political activity is not necessarily social class, we are told, but rather distinct constellations of interests in solidary groups, with the political struggle itself defined as a struggle for domination between individuals and organizations—yet another immanent principle opening the way, perhaps, to even Freudian explanations of power. Groups and organizations rather than social classes therefore become the basic operational units of a political sociology. Accordingly, the bureaucracy is not, as in the Marxist conception, a subagent to the ruling classes of capitalist society, but rather a structure of domination unto itself, vis à vis the masses.

It is clear that Weber has very little to say about the substantive goals (ends) of the system he is describing, and how those criteria define the nature of the system itself. Virtually all of the conditions for the existence of a bureaucracy that he gives us turn out to be the historical conditions for the emergence of capitalism, be it monetization or the development of productive resources, et al., and yet the bureaucracy is not, much like capitalism itself, explained in class terms.

There are other contradictions in the analysis as well. Bureaucratic organizations are said to come into power on the basis of a leveling of economic and social differences—a statement that fails to convince, unless capitalism, somehow, is seen as the historical agency of social leveling—the evidence for a claim that, in the late twentieth century, still remains to be shown. In the very same discussion, however, run the explicit, and yet contradictory, suggestions that bureaucratic organizations have led frequently to cryptoplutocratic distributions of power, an intimation that might well be nearer the mark in terms of the empirical record of inequality.

There is more than a hint of sophisticated eclecticism in the Weberian analysis. The Marxian propositions are all claimed to be empirical possibilities, while remaining, in some disjuncture, theoretical half-truths; thus, for example, a class may well be an instrument of capitalist domination, and property may well determine power. This springs from (if it does not actually instigate) Weber's rather complicated rules of sociological method—rules which he freely ignored in his own work. Weber held a rather generous perspective of sociological pluralism, where any and all explanations are equally true or untrue, since social reality can never be comprehended in its entirety.

Here is, then, an almost Kantian rejection of scientific truth—all scientific perspectives being culturally relevant—and a return to the remystification of a society that, on first principles, can never be grasped in its totality. Weber, in fact, even held that all fundamental assumptions were essentially arbitrary, whether private belief or political philosophy—for it is only a "hairsbreadth" that separates science from faith. Herein, one finds the restoration of the irrational in grand form, constituting, it might be noted, a rejection of that very process of rationalization which he had commented on so extensively.

The contradictions in Weber's ideas (not to mention an abiding irrationality) is fully appreciated when we learn of his faith in "charisma" as the prescription antidote to the process of rationalization. For Weber it is the charismatic leader who is the real hero of history, who defies rationality and restores the vanishing properties of myth and magic to the world. Social change, in a radically transformational sense, and in direct contradistinction to the dialectic of Marx, is born out of the profoundly irrational and unpredictable—history made by outstanding individuals who themselves escape structural determination: by outsiders, essentially, to both history and society.

Weber ignores, at will, the historical dialectic between political administration and the organization of production—i.e. he divorces wealth from power—and abstracts transhistorical tendencies such as rationalization, treating them as independent processes without reference to the totality of social causation. But norms and values, as Weber might have known, do not operate irrespective of the socio-historical formations in which they are generated, and to which they bear a structural relationship. He fails to grasp the possibility that the most rational of structures may conceal the most irrational of contradictions, leading to a violent overhaul of the original structures when certain historical suitabilities are in place. His somewhat deliberate failure to link economic exploitation with political domination, formal rationality with substantive irrationality, and class structure with social consciousness, leads him to statements of partial truths and abstract tendencies that, far from explaining the totality of social transformation, need to be explained by it.

Notes

1. Max Weber, *The Theory of Social and Economic Organization*, 1947, p. 338.

3

Bureaucracy, Power, and Domination: A Commentary

The study of bureaucracy, conceived of as a modal form of the modern state apparatus, is necessarily part of an inquiry into the larger problematic of political power, and forms of social ownership of productive resources, within whose parameters bureaucracy occupies a definite ontological space. Unquestionably, power and superordination in hierarchical, antagonistically organized society are replete with political specificities, or "relative autonomies" in classical usage, which cannot be gainsaid. But it does not follow that they are, of themselves, irreducible data, for it is far from impossible to underscore the articulated permutations between political power and institutional property relations, i.e. the ascertainable and manifest links between the domains of political sociology and political economy. If these links are sustainably rational and real, then the attempt to understand—and to overcome—bureaucratized state forms must necessarily rest in an analysis of the structural basis of societies in which it functions as the instrumental mode of administrative domination. Arguably, it is easier to assert these links than to deny them; but their precise mode of articulation is obviously open to specification. In this, Marx and Weber in fact constitute the contrasting extremes, with others occupying only intermediate positions.

At any rate, this structural delineation of society must specify both the location of the ultimate rationale of power, and the more immediate instruments through which it is exercised and institutionalized. In this regard, given the modal predominance of putatively "capitalist" and "socialist" modes of social organization (including the nouvelle "ex-socialist" societies of Eastern Europe, and notwithstanding the more hybrid, intermediate forms), such studies may only be conducted with these empirical examples as the necessary referents. Stated differently, an examination of the real rationale underlying and underpinning the modalities of state power becomes imperative in order to comprehend their dynamics of existence, functioning, and decay, with the existing experience of capitalist and socialist societies providing the ontological data materially undergirding the analysis.

While modern political sociology might well be thought to have originated with Karl Marx, if only in the negative sense of being provoked into mainstream revision of his theses, it is Max Weber (Weber, 1947) who is usually credited with the accolade of being the comprehensive theorist of bureaucracy. The tendency toward *"bureaucratization"* and *"rationalization"* in the evolution of social structures was a central tenet of Weber's philosophy of history, postulates held to abide in the European historical context, underscoring the essential *monocentrism* of his conceptualization (indeed, it would be fair to suggest that his considerable knowledge of nonEuropean civilizations well matched his equally impressive ignorance in that area. See Andreski, ed., 1983, pp. 21-29, for a sample of Weber's views denigrating the achievements of the *Other* relative to the Occident), the concepts bearing some affinity to the more romantic notion (à la Schiller) of the *"disenchantment"* of the world, i.e. the demystification of social reality. It is significant that Weber, not overly enthusiastic at the relentless secularization of the socio-political functions and structures in evidence in Europe, at least since the French Revolution, attached an identifiably negative evaluation (despite his "value-free" protestations) to this inexorable historical process. For him, western civilization was distinct, unique, and peculiar—in the sense that this disenchantment was being carried out more thoroughly than elsewhere, a pattern exemplified as much in the fixation of "rational, harmonious music," for example, or in the "rational use of the Gothic vault as a means of distributing pressure," as in the manifold "rational" demands of modern science. At any rate, the process of "bureaucratization" differs conceptually from bureaucracy itself, the latter being only one manifest embodiment of the much larger process extant in capitalist evolution.

All spheres of social conduct were conceptualized, within this ongoing process, as being subject to the same quality of mentality and organization that made purposeful conduct rationally predicated upon the essential predictability of human behavior. And it is in capitalism that the process finds its most detailed application, for it is this form of society that fundamentally rationalizes the entire range of social life, from accounting and economic organization, to law and administration—and even, according to Weber, politics and authority. The concept of rationality finds its real resting place, a sort of a permanent roost as it were, in the organization of bureaucracy in capitalist society: for the modern bureaucracy is presented as the very epitome of formal rationality in social enterprise, public or private.

The bureaucratic apparatus is alleged to function more effectively than any "legal enslavement of functionaries," while being more economical than formally unremunerated, honorific service (being, thereby, more "rational" than comparable institutions in slavery and feudalism). Over other arrangements, the superiority of bureaucracy is seen as consisting in a number of (far too) easily assumed virtues—precision, speed, unambiguity, continuity, discretion, subordination, and, above all, of course, calculability. It is altogether curious that common knowledge of the workings of bureaucracy, expressed routinely in popular outrage, rarely confirm these "ideal-type" representations; it would seem to follow that these generous attributions must largely be the invention of those seeking to perpetuate the bureaucratic form, rather than those engaged in mere dispassionate study. Be that as it may, for Weber, the alternative to bureaucracy is amateurism, bungling, and chaos. In his words:

> For the needs of mass administration today, it is completely indispensable. The choice is only that between bureaucracy and dilettantism in the field of administration.[1]

Bureaucracy, indispensable in structure and function, becomes ever more perfect (i.e. rational and relevant) the more it depersonalizes and dehumanizes the human element—persistently eliminating from business those crippling emotional and irrational elements that are deemed so dysfunctional for healthy capitalist advance. This "impersonality," in fact, becomes almost praiseworthy; for, Weber tells us, it enables the conduct of business to be *sine era et studio*, everyone, democratically, being subject to "formal equality" (Weber, 1947, p. 340). And yet, simultaneously, if somewhat incongruously, bureaucratic development does go hand-in-hand with the increasing concentration of the means of production, management, and coercion, making for the "universal domination of the class situation."

Weber leaves little room for doubt that it is capitalist rationality that demands such forced alienations: separating the worker from his means of production, the administrator from his means of administration, and the scientist from his means of research. As he puts it:

> ...capitalism in its modern stages of development strongly tends to foster the development of bureaucracy...conversely, capitalism is the most rational economic basis for bureaucratic administration and enables it to develop in the most rational form...[2]

In the same vein, Weber frankly acknowledges the antithesis between bureaucracy and democracy, and the fact that the strengthening of bureaucracy may "often" reinforce support for a "crypto-plutocratic" distribution of power. In sum, modern bureaucracies are said to derive from an identifiable, unilinear, historical tendency, independently given, with obvious, and far from benign, implications for property, class, and domination—but without being specifically structured by them.

Weber's obvious admiration for the efficiency of capitalist bureaucracy is nurtured, again curiously, alongside an educated, if acutely fatalistic[3] lament that the process, for all its offensive attributes, is quite definitely irrevocable. Permanent remedies being ruled as unavailable, some checks to the process are, even so, admitted. For one thing, effective political leadership of "working parliaments" (as apart from merely babbling ones!) is held up as a corrective to the pretensions of bureaucracy. For another—although an antidote perhaps more dubious than the poison—we are given *charisma*, that irresistible demigod of antiroutine, which shakes society out of its slumbers when the entrenched bureaucracy is too impotent to move of its own accord.

The weaknesses in this discourse, holding its strengths constant, are legion. For one thing, the idea that Parliament (be it an active, "working" one) and bureaucracy may well share a common interest vis à vis the people is not allowed to obstruct the optimistic perception of an effective, political restraint on bureaucracy—the analysis being wholly within a constitutionally defined "checks and balances" problematic, hardly flattering to a penetrating social analysis. Actually, while such constitutional, i.e. formal, checks are far from being unimportant, as evidenced by the profound implications of their absence in East Europe, contemporary capitalist societies nonetheless are also abundant witness to the fact that such structures may easily become the tools of more cohesive, interlocking interests. On the other hand, to treat another issue in the late twentieth century, faith is surely to be found flagging in mysteriously evolved, all-embracing, immanent principles that, like Hegel's pure reason, march triumphantly through history realizing themselves. For rationalization is arguably a transcendent principle, metahistorical, and possibly also metaphysical (aside from the strong hints as to its uniquely European, ethnocentric consummation; of course, Europe's "special destiny," common to Eurocentered analyses, was one of Weber's pet historiographical themes).

Moreover, the fact that specific bureaucracies can be resisted is given us in fairly recent history. At least initially, for instance, the Czarist bureaucracy was quite effectively dismantled by the Bolsheviks; and the history of Weber's own Germany between the two major wars of redivision is surely high illustration of the perfect, if frightening, compatibility between charismatic authority and bureaucratic despotism, the stated "opposition" between them being of no apparent avail (both Hitler and Mussolini, obviously, combined charismatic leadership with acute centralization of the state apparati). At any rate, even discounting these empirical instances, there is something rather curious about the uniquely rational being redeemed, for reasons ineffable, by the uniquely "irrational." Finally, and importantly, Weber fails to specify the ever present dialectic of rule and resistance, so obvious in any societal formation, in his analysis of the politics of the "iron cage"—thereby quite deliberately deriving the logic of bureaucracy from purely functional and technological imperatives alone.

In contrast to this, anesthetised, transhistorical theorizing, Marx's ideas on bureaucracy are far more intricate, being historically specific (in keeping with his methodological prepossessions). Against Hegel's insistence that bureaucracy is the universal class, Marx chose to proclaim its more mundane particularism vis à vis the class structure, and hence to its specificity.[4] In some social formations, such as the absolute monarchy of Friedrich Wilhelm III, the bureaucracy is seen to function, by itself, as a ruling class;[5] and, somewhat similarly, in the régime of Louis Bonaparte in France, when the balance between contending classes was one of relative equipoise, the state bureaucracy achieved a comparative, but nevertheless real autonomy, obviating subordination to any specific class constellations. However, in bourgeois societies, the "normal" situation of bureaucracy is theorized as one of being at the receiving end of class dictates (Marxists argue the case for the unique relative autonomy of the capitalist state because of the formal separation of the "political" and the "economic" moments—i.e. state and civil society—in capitalism). Still, in none of these many forms is it to be considered a class-neutral agency, for it securely bears a class denomination throughout; i.e. the state apparatus is intimately situated within the logic of societal conflict over power and possession.

Formal analysis of the bureaucracy in and of itself yields little dividend unless it is further situated within the larger coordinates of class and state power. In all class societies, the state is specified as the instrument of the ruling class, combining the disparate function of class *domination* with that of class *mediation*. The state is the guarantor of the property structure, the defender of class appropriations, and the enforcer of its incumbent juridical relations. Unlike Weber, who defines the state exclusively in terms of the unique *means* employed by it, i.e. its monopoly or quasimonopoly over the means of coercion (thereby smoothly avoiding the issue of its class provenance), Marx defines the state nontrivially, in terms of its general obligations with respect to the reproduction of the system—i.e. in its defense of the original and enduring distribution of property ownership, which constitutes the fundamental set of social relations, the relations of production. Lest this be seen as a Marxist curiosum, it needs be remembered that even Adam Smith (the proclaimed—but quite unlikely—hero of the capitalist millennium) was to put it, as was his wont, more vulgarly, if in a more forthright fashion: the state is constituted, Smith wrote, simply to "defend the rich from the poor" (Smith, 1976, p. 715).

The struggle against exploitation and domination (i.e. against capitalism) is, within Marxism, necessarily inclusive of the struggle against the state, including its various organs, instruments, and apparati. This struggle, to be successful, must aim not at subordinating the bureaucracy, yet again, to a new class-based master, as was virtually the case in Stalin's Russia, but rather at assuring its total destruction—a notion that appears to be drawn by Marx from his study of the class struggles of France of 1848-51, and, perhaps more importantly, from the history of the Paris Commune of 1871. This very idea was to be touted, faithfully, by Lenin in his polemic, *State and Revolution*. In his analysis,[6] the bureaucracy and the standing army appear as the two principal organs of reactionary state power—and the revolution was exhorted to "smash," and demobilize, both. Indeed, Lenin went a bit further, identifying the bureaucracy as the *preferred* form of class rule under capitalism, as the chosen instrument in the strategy of circumventing popular control of parliaments—in favor of the direct executive dictatorship of the bourgeoisie (upon which the bureaucracy was premised to be both functionally and socially dependent, and with which it was at least partially integrated).

The elisions in the Marxian critique lie not so much in its internal theoretical structure, or in its plausibility for a powerful indictment of capitalism, as on a different plane, in the sphere of concrete *praxis*. The history of the still dissolving socialist societies illustrates only too obviously the empirical compatibility of bureaucratic forms of domination with putatively postcapitalist societies (even when allowed to have moved nominally in a Marxist trajectory, as in East Europe), a phenomenon that appeared, in the eyes of critics, far too entrenched and endemic to be theorized as merely "transitional" and temporary. Indeed, the Stalin era undoubtedly consolidated and perfected the existing imperial bureaucracy beyond even czarist imagination; and, until recently and dramatically, the Soviet state showed very few signs of any readiness to dissolve itself, and even fewer signs of preparedness to replace the administration of *people* with, as in the classical Marxian vision, the administration of *things*. Endlessly sophisticated arguments can, of course, be supplied to explain why existing, and dissolving, socialist practice, though a perversion of the original Marxian intent, is still historically understandable if not exactly justifiable. However, none of them can gainsay the obvious lesson of experience: that there is a resounding weakness in Marxian political theory which is apparently unable to visualize the reality of power struggles both *outside of class bounds* (for Marxian political theory, the very definition of "politics" is relations between classes; the circularity of defining class in terms of power, and vice versa, escapes someone like Poulantzas, but argument by definition, of course, carries the risk of rebuttal in like manner) *and inside of postcapitalist societies*, areas in which anarchist and elitist political theory are certainly more suggestive, and possibly even stronger, despite their admittedly cynical prognostications.

In the Weberian scheme, on the other hand, given the immanence of rationalization, capitalism is the highest, perchance even the last, stage of bureaucratization. The capitalist Leviathan is unlikely to be successfully resisted unless some special crisis, given exogenously, precipitates a collapse of the legal order, rendering the state impotent and unable to govern. With Reason thus run aground, the irrational explodes in the (hydra-headed) form of a great *Charismatic Interruption*, a discontinuity that, in time, becomes routinized—for prophets are forever doomed to be followed by a priesthood. Within this analysis, bureaucracies, unless carefully supervised by strong political authority and leadership (whence, apparently, they then function with a "neutral" rationality, carrying on their appointed, routine, and normal functions: of domination!), are susceptible to high corruption; as being, usually, violative of democratic principles; and, occasionally, as being the tools of possible capitalist class domination. That is to say, Weber was fully aware of the potential for "substantive irrationality" in the functioning of the bureaucratic apparatus (although choosing, quite intentionally, to stress its functional "virtues").

Modern pluralist writers find these candid admissions of Weber distasteful. They prefer, instead, to read between the lines where, clearly enough, Weber's more congenial intent is exposed: to show that bureaucracy, while basically functional for capitalism, carries the potential of becoming dysfunctional only in the absence of proper (rational) safeguards. At any rate, pluralist models have now given way to "corporatist" ones, with any lingering, old-fashioned "democratic" ideology almost on the verge of extinction in capitalist political theorizing.

In contradistinction, for Marx, bureaucracy is unabashedly an agent of class rule, a vital part of the system of exploitation and repression, evolved in its modern form from fairly recent Absolutist times. With capitalism characterized as being fundamentally irrational, despite, or even because of, the rational calculus of profit-making, bureaucracy only mirrors the appearance of an ordered isle of rationality though within an irredeemable sea of market anarchy. The internal structurings of bureaucracy (its secrecy, hierarchy, and subordination) appear now entirely consistent with its true social role and political function: to project the semblance of impartiality and objectivity while discharging the basic class dictates of the system in reality. At the limit of popular discontent, only the organized might of the oppressed classes is capable of overthrowing it; for it is people who make and unmake their own history (there being no metahistorical agents) when they, periodically, take matters into their own hands. The age of bureaucracy, far from being an enduring one, then, has objective, dialectical limits set by the maturity of social forces, both technical and political, as reflected ultimately in class struggle and class overthrow.

The two perspectives, of Marx and Weber, could hardly be set further apart. For Weber, bureaucratization is, lapses from the norm apart, a socially rational process—even if this be only formal rationality. For Marx, on the other hand, this rationality is a class-bounded rationality that is, socially speaking, substantively irrational. For Weber, the limits or negations of bureaucracy are external and adventitious; for Marx, the limits are historical, structural, and unavoidable. For Weber, domination is an ineluctable fact of social life, perhaps even inevitably so; for Marx, it is altogether revocable, albeit at specific historical conjunctures not open to any mechanical predictions.

The contrast between the two views is just as vital as we shift to the province of the state. The state, for Marx, is an agency of class domination, no matter what its ancillary functions. It has both a specific origin (when the process of class division is complete and class differences have become irreconcilable), and a specific eclipse (when class society is itself abolished). The state is therefore a dependent variable, an epiphenomenon, the creature of definite forms of economic organization, rather than a necessary, universal fact of life: there have been societies in the past without state organization, and there may indeed be, speaking hypothetically, societies without it in the future. In Weber, however, the causal links are radically different; the state is a political association which enjoys a monopoly over the means of violence, considered legitimate by a majority of those whom it dominates (the methods of this legitimization being more suspect than is apparent in the analysis). But this domination is not necessarily class domination, for the class, status, and power hierarchies do not always coincide. Political power may be quite independent of economic power—the classic statement of pluralism, wherein the economic and the political hierarchies are linked arbitrarily, with no systematic ordering of relationships. In fact, Marxism and Weberian pluralism, at the extreme, provide the competing orthodoxies in modes of social explanation in almost the entire range of modern social theory. But the two perspectives do not, in and of themselves, exhaust the social spectrum. There are other coordinates as well, the most significant being the so-called elitist theory of the distribution of power.

The historical basis for the inspiration of elitist theory is, of course, well documented: the long transition from the *ancien régime* in Europe pitted the democratic aspirations of classes that stood to gain from political democracy (aspirations expressed, mainly, in the form of liberal and socialist movements) against the combined political will of the aristocracy and its allies. Elitist ideology was far from being the first intellectual barricade erected against the tide of democratic thought at a time when socialism and democracy were considered to be fairly synonymous terms;[7] it was in fact a part of the continuing Thermidor set off in the Romantic-Conservative reaction to the rational-critical excesses of the French Revolution. As an ideology it was eclectic, for it continued to straddle the two epochs (feudal conservative and bourgeois liberal) that were drawing apart at the time, the bourgeoisie being in effective economic power, but without yet having acquired the necessary political and ideological hegemony. It is thus not surprising that the principal elitist theorists hailed from areas of Europe where late feudalism was still in its death throes. Nor is it surprising that in the twentieth century this school was to again rear its head in an even more invidious and dangerous form in precisely the laggard capitalist nations of Europe. It is, of course, the dominant variant of elitist theory, as exemplified in Mosca and Pareto, that took its cues from its reactional political philosophy; however, a second variant, marked by the disillusionment of radical aspirations, with Michels and (later) Djilas as its most notable exponents, was called into existence by quite a different set of circumstances: the lived experience of functioning "socialist" institutions. Thus, even while the dominant variant attacked liberal democracy, the other was to target bureaucratic socialism.

Despite its original reactionary political inspiration, the principal impulse of elitist theory identified the problem of state power, clearly enough, in its centralized organization. Cleared of its primal intent, the concept of elites may well be utilized as a useful supplement to Marxian class analysis, e.g., within a class reference, elites may be seen as representing both *interclass* and *intraclass* conflict. Also, elites may be specified in any number of dimensions, intellectual, political, etc., while always being susceptible to a class translation where necessary. That is to say, even if one accepts the class structure as the organizing matrix of power, one can nevertheless still yield to elites as the manifest bearers of this *class instrumentality*. The utility of this concept in description of power relations within postcapitalist societies in the East is especially significant. In fact, speaking more abstractly, elitist theory is likely to be particularly useful in specifying power relations even in societies where the social condition is homogeneous *vis à vis* relations of production—i.e. in the so-called classless societies, past or futuristic. Being fundamentally ahistorical in the explanation of social domination, its elasticity is actually greater than that of class; thus, methodological vices, sometimes, can redound to advantage.

Turning to the main current in elitist theory, it was Gaetano Mosca (Mosca, 1939) who postulated, in a rigorous restatement of the truism that in all societies there is a minority that rules and a majority that is ruled, what is now accepted as the "sociological" distinction between the elite and the masses. He argued that the minority rules by virtue of its superior *organization*: being a compact group, it is better structured to obey a single impulse and to act in concert against a diffuse, divided majority. Of course, it is not organization alone that confers power for Mosca; for the ruling class is also possessed, happily, of a stock of superior qualities, intellectual, moral, and material, which are inherited from similarly endowed ancestors. However, ultimately, a judicious mix of force and fraud in fact maintain it in power, constituting a given *political formula*. Even so, a failure to exercise the subtlety that such a situation demands may render the ruling class unfit to rule, thereby making for its eventual overthrow, in periods of renovation, by others more suitably endowed.

At another remove, it is to Michels (Michels, 1958), representing the "radical" strain in elitist ideology, as much as to variants of anarchist theory, that we owe the rather prophetic insight (when viewed in retrospect) that there is no contradiction between the Marxian class struggle view of history and the idea that the struggle may culminate only in the "creation of new oligarchies which undergo diffusion with the old." Every system of political leadership is, in the Michelsian system, incompatible with democracy, for organization *is* the basis for oligarchy. This is so even when the leadership in question is ostensibly socialist; for, without fail, the (conservative) rationale of perpetuation of the party organization soon triumphs over all other professed (radical) political aims. This oligarchical tendency, however, is, in the main, reinforced not by corruption and deceit (as in Mosca), but rather by dint of an undeniable quotient of skill: the really superior competence of the leadership *vis à vis* the rank and file. Skills not being diffused evenly, a small stratum, structurally isolated from the majority, eventually begins to exercise control over the larger mass, marking a near permanent gulf between leadership and the ranks. Michels's frustration was near total: with the leadership for betraying ideals, with the masses for their mindless idolatry, and with organization itself for begetting oligarchy. If, for Mosca, ruling classes simply replaced each other periodically, history being the "*graveyard of aristocracies*," in Michels, the outcome is ultimately not dissimilar, despite the fundamental differences between them in both political and personal idealism. Significantly, nevertheless, both the Machiavellian cynic (Mosca) and the radical critic of socialist utopia (Michels) understood organization to be the decisive key to domination.

The notion of state and bureaucracy as the critical props in the organization of societal oppression was, as might be expected, most fully elaborated in the writings of classical anarchism.[8] The work of Bakunin, Proudhon, and Kropotkin inveighed passionately against what Proudhon felt to be the disease of the age—*fonctionnairism*, or the absorption of all of civil society into a hypertrophic administrative machinery. Rejecting both bourgeois liberalism and communism alike (i.e. both private property and state direction), anarchism embraced the idea of a federation of decentralized, self-managing communes based on spontaneity and self-determination, where collectivism is possible without authority, administration without bureaucracy, and order without government. Calling for the establishment of a cooperative commonwealth which would coordinate social life without coercion, anarchist theory passionately urged inveterate struggle against the state, identifying state organization, even more compellingly than elitist theory, as embodying a terrifying threat to human emancipation. As the anarchists saw it (quite prophetically it would appear), only by rejecting any and all notions of dictatorship could socialism be made consistent with liberty.

Bureaucracy, Power, and Domination: A Commentary

Many trivial and signal differences apart, Marxist, elitist, and anarchist theory come together in believing modern bureaucracies to be agencies of class rule, elite domination, and societal repression. Aside from these classical theories of power, there is also modern pluralist political theory, a sort of hybrid of Weber and standard elitist theory. Unlike the latter's insistence on a cohesive political elite, modern pluralism speaks of competing plural elites operating on the alleged basis of a democratic access to power. Expressed in the early post-war tradition of Dahl, Lipset, Kornhauser, etc. (and including Dahrendorf, with his curious amalgam of elitist, Weberian, and Marxian ideas), in the full flush of cold war ideology, power is seen as democratically diffused within multiple groupings by a sort of situational determinism that keeps them in a state of permanent flux around spontaneously arising "issue-areas" leading, usually, to the conclusion that either *nobody rules, or else everybody rules;* or, rather, that anybody who is interested has a chance to rule, in some, or other, sphere of authority. A tempered version of classical elitist theory is smuggled in via the insistence that political elites both exist and are, in fact, functionally necessary; but they are a curiously apolitical political elite, content usually with the legally specified constitutional power granted them by an abysmally uninterested, apathetic majority—*the mass society.* Somewhat incongruously, equal access to power is secured unequally by competing interest groups and lobbies. And even discounting the apology for bourgeois democracy, which is the rather obvious intent of this theory, it is clear that the ideal conjunction for democracy is seen as the circumstance of the effective nonparticipation by the masses, whose apathetic slumber is rated rationally functional for a healthy political system. In this sense, the larger issue of domination raised by Marx, Weber, and Mosca is quite foreign to its problematic, its refusal to probe beneath formal structures for historical and structural continuities in fact rendering it a profoundly conservative, and shallow, defense of the status quo. Far from providing the tools for a critical counteraction of social domination, mainstream political pluralism indicates only its own cooptation within that logic itself. The analysis is not "wrong"—but it is superficial, for being formal.[9]

All this aside, it remains to be explained why bureaucracy, as a particular form of administrative power, is so ubiquitous in modern societies. It is tempting to use its apparent ubiquity in modern societies as a justification for coinage of the term "bureaucratic society," similar to the term "industrial society," to cover the social forms of both the (crumbling) East and West, at least as a descriptive category. Analytically, however, this concept must remain deficient for reifying one aspect of a larger political economy; a convergence of bureaucratic forms being quite compatible with entirely different economic bases, i.e. property relations and modes of economic organization.

Structurally speaking, answers can take either of two basic forms, corresponding largely to the views of Marx and Weber, respectively. In Marx, to characterize one mode of explanation, bureaucracy is essentially the creature of a class rationality (not, therefore, of a substantive rationality), so that its peculiar form is fundamentally contingent upon its political content. Carefully cloaking the myth of objectivity and impersonality within the ideology of expertise, bureaucracy is able to insulate its true class intent from the democratic scrutiny of the subordinated mass, its privilege being conditioned upon the ignorance and incompetence of the lay man and woman, and preserved by a duly instituted elitist self-selection process. In Weber's view, at the other pole, the rationality of bureaucracy is something real (and this despite his recognition of the ample potential for class corruption within such an institution), stemming from the given necessity for technological advance which renders, in the context of capitalism, the complex organization, as an archetypical mode, functionally inevitable. One of the progenitors of the idea of technological determinism in social life, Weber essentially collapsed two distinct functions[10]—the *administrative and the technological*—into one; whereas, as has been pointed out, the administrative "expertise" claimed by bureaucracy, unlike genuine technical knowledge, consists merely in an illiterate mastery of a routine of its own invention. The appeal to technological factors, in Weber, may then be seen as a device to rationalize the more prosaic functions of the self-expansion of the state apparati and their increasing social reach in the name of a necessarily specialized, esoteric knowledge.

That we owe bureaucracy to technical determinations is necessarily a gross simplification; the very expertise claimed by bureaucracies is a function of their own monopoly of routine, which in turn stokes their power over the governed. *That the masses are unfit to govern themselves is the first axiom of domination*, not the "fact" imposed by the esoterics of technology. If the people are divested of the skills of governance due to a design of socio-economic deprivations in the first place, it follows that the rationality of the rule of expertise then appears virtually axiomatic (for a stirring critique of "expertocracy," see Feyerabend, 1978). Interestingly, Weber recruits *technological fetishism*,[11] the distinctively reified mystique (or ideology) of capitalist societies, as an auxiliary serving to account for bureaucratic domination.

The two perspectives could hardly be further apart; in one, the logic of domination prevails over the logic of function—while in the other, it is exactly the other way around. Indeed, the contrasting accounts help, quite usefully, to separate those who would seek to *transform* bureaucracy from those who would seek to *consecrate* it. Analytically, though, a purely structural (Weberian) derivation of the necessity of bureaucracy, divorced from a more concrete study of the historical factors making for its ascendancy—which might actually account for its unique configuration—becomes rather an idealist exercise, conducted *in vacuo*, in keeping with the general sterility of functionalist elucidations of social phenomena.

At any rate, whatever their nominal designation in bourgeois theory, the characteristic pillars of the modern state—the common run of standing armies and equally upright bureaucracies—have a fairly specific history in the evolution of European society, stemming from the institutional response of the beleagured nobility to the fourteenth-century general crisis of late feudal society, racked by famine, plague, wars—and mounting insurrection as the peasantry rose in repeated revolts against the repressive renewal of feudal restrictions. The modern absolutist state, deriving from the late fifteenth-century resolution of this crisis, represented the determined effort of a unified aristocracy to centralize the means of administration and coercion with a view to presenting a formidable check to both peasant and mercantile challenges to its hegemony.[12] This centralization, unprecedented in western Europe since the decline of the Roman empire, went, in truth, markedly against the grain of classical western feudalism, a historically given blend of Germanic and Latin institutions, with its characteristic dispersion of sovereignty and parcelization of political and economic jurisdictions. Built for war, administered for the extraction of revenue, and breathing the fire of predatory mercantilism, absolutism (consolidated more or less concurrently in France, Spain, Austria, and England) may be said to have inaugurated the modern era of nationalism. The various bourgeois revolutions, which ultimately superseded aristocratic domination, succeeded only in refining and perpetuating this formidable apparatus, aside from making it more "rational"—i.e. more responsive to the needs of capital accumulation. The bourgeois nation-state, successor to the absolutist state—for all its fraudulent ideology of laissez-faire—was to leave intact the twin pillars of its despotism, the centralized bureaucracy, and the centralized army, in effect preserving the absolutist legacy as a permanent institution, despite vesting "sovereignty," nominally, in "parliaments" and other popular bodies.

To attribute, à la Weber, the evolution of bureaucracy to a steadily accelerating trend of technological correlates (in contrast to the critical social *discontinuity* and schism that it actually represented at the time of its original eruption into European history), without seeing this "technology" as the instrument of a very specific form of social domination, is to violate historical facts, substituting an internal, "functional" micrologic for the essentially external macrorationale. Quite simply, bureaucracy and bureaucratization derive not from any "complexity" of administration (for democratic, bottom-up administration is entirely conceivable, without bureaucracy, if only in a society other than that constituted on the basis of "imperative" coordination from above) rendered necessary by the esoterics of modern technology, but relate rather to a more exoteric, historically derived, political motive: *the concentration and centralization of executive power.*

Who says bureaucracy, therefore, speaking historically, says not merely power and domination in the abstract, but speaks also of the specific context of a centralized nation-state. In this regard, the persistence of bureaucracy in socialist societies, far from being vestigial or adventitious, may be seen to lie in their embrace of the nation-state-centralization dyad, itself the consequence of fairly unique historical conjunctures. The hegemony of "nationalism," the composite ideology of the bureaucracy, the ruling class, and the nation-state, may not be annulled, however, without weakening the critical institutional supports of the centralized state; and it is in this respect that the Marxian and the anarchist call for the dismantlement of the state—in structure and function—carries a special import. In fact, bureaucratic permanence, and thus the immutability of class domination, is predicated grimly, one might conjecture, upon the nonoccurrence of this instance.

As is apparent, then, the poser of bureaucracy, strictly speaking, then devolves into the problem of the centralized exercise of state power (state power is either centralized or it is nonexistent—there are, apparently, no intermediate forms) by those classes and elites that are capable of subordinating political power to their own diverse ends. The resistance to bureaucracy—if it is to be successful, if it is not to remain formalist and/or simply reformist (i.e. impotent)—needs take the form of resistance to the social structure of the distribution of power—i.e. to the social division of property, and to the precise elite and class location within the reproduction of such material relations: absolute power may only be resisted absolutely, that is by going to the root, generative causes of social iniquity.

Of course, the mere dismemberment of state structures, while necessary, is far from sufficient. Rearranging the polity is meaningless without reordering the political economy, meaning property and production relations. It is these relations which need to be reconstituted, to be rid of their hierarchical, unequal, and alienating character—for the logic of administration only reproduces the logic of social relations. The principal axes of an agenda for emancipation would have to couple both the abrogation of the state and the elimination of alienated private property in the means of social subsistence, an agenda common, historically, to both classical socialism and classical anarchism; but, being only prerequisites, these actions far from guarantee a social paradise free from conflict and contest (as in some unrestrained Marxist flights of fancy on the subject of "communism"), as the warnings of elitist theory amply, and accurately, indicate. At any rate, the projected neutralization of economic struggle and coercive state power, arguably, would go far toward making the enduring contest of wills—and surely they must endure!—less destructive of social cohesion and individual freedom; certainly much less so than is apparent, presently, in either contempory capitalist or socialist societies.

The methodological superiority of the Marxian vision is often credited—even if only by Marxists themselves—to its identification of "objective" social processes leading, almost inevitably, to social change, unlike a voluntarist, "utopian," plan to achieve a social paradise. The doubt, among sympathetic critics, is not in the fact that capitalism can be overthrown, but, whether this process necessarily leads to a society where democracy and liberty will, even ultimately, prevail. That private production and appropriation can, and indeed will, be replaced by social production and appropriation is clear enough; but there is no objective determination in any political theory—Marxist or not—*that this is necessarily consistent with democracy and freedom*. Indeed—and the truth must be told—a good bit of Marxian prognostications of socialism seem, and are, just as utopian as any "voluntarist" dreams of a social nirvana. In fact, as an alternative, elitist theory offers a determinism that guarantees such a happy conjunction impossible. Vis à vis Marxian ideas, however, its weakness consists in its ahistorical pronouncements, its antidemocratic normative orientations, and its psychological reductionism. On the empirical plane, of course, its insights, like Michels's, for instance, are far from being negligible—that is, the residue of "truth" in elitist theory survives its faulty methodology and its reactionary politics.

All agendas, Marxist or not, by their very nature, are voluntaristic and idealist, for they prescribe far ahead of concrete experience; but when they capture the imagination of the people, ideas can become the ontologically appropriate driving "material" forces of change. At this moment, such imagination would not seem to be found wanting, with humanism in revolt against arbitrary authority in both east and west: whether nominally socialist, anarchist, or, more simply, "rejectionist" and autonomist. The significance of the various gathering (and "green") oppositions, in the form of the peace movement, the antinuclear movement, the women's movement, etc., consists in their insistence on the right of *democratic self-control*—i.e. on *self-determination*—over their eco-political, social, and ecological destinies; in their affirmation that institutional choices, right or wrong, progressive or regressive, must rest directly with the people, *whose apathy and ignorance—not to mention impotence—can no longer be taken for granted as the rationale for despotism.* For, in one way or another, given the proliferation of autonomous struggles for human dignities worldwide, the masses seem ready to make their own history today as never before, despite the hoary opposition of entrenched vested interests, power elites, and ruling classes. However, energy and enthusiasm notwithstanding, their toils will remain akin to the labors of Sisyphus unless some form of self-provisioning and decentralization—a systematic "delinking" from the structures of power and wealth—remain the active principles of the counteroffensive against nationalism and the state. If not, the promise of a post-bureaucratic society in a system of nonantagonistic social relations will remain conspicuous only by its increasingly tragic absence. It is but a promise, of course; and there is nothing inevitable in the struggle taking this satisfactory form. In fact, the history of many such movements—even revolutions—reinforces only care and caution with respect to the persistence of domination, even tyranny, courtesy of state power. Identifying solutions is always easier, in societal matters, than implementing them.

Notes

1. Max Weber, *The Theory of Social and Economic Organization*, 1947, p. 337.
2. Ibid. p. 338.
3. This overriding theme in Weber's writings is encapsulated accurately in Herber Marcuse's essay "Max Weber," *New Left Review*, 30, 1965.
4. For a contemporary study of Marx's writings on bureaucracy, see Hal Draper, *Karl Marx's Theory of Revolution*, 1977.
5. The many traditions within Marxism are far from being in agreement with this representation of absolutism, where Marx apparently violates the Marxist dicta. See N. Poulantzas, *Political Power and Social Classes*, 1975; and P. Anderson, *Lineages of the Absolutist State*, 1979.
6. It may seem odd to be comparing Weber and Lenin on bureaucracy, or anything else for that matter, but Wright actually pulls off the unlikely comparison to advantage. For an excellent essay, see Wright, 1979.
7. For more in this vein, see Irving Zeitlin, 1968; see also T. B. Bottomore, 1966.
8. The intellectual tradition of anarchism is documented in Guerin, 1970; see also Joll, 1964.
9. The progenitors of this literature hearken back to the late fifties and sixties; see Lipset, 1963; Kornhauser, 1959; Dahl, 1961; and Dahrendorf, 1959.
10. For more in this genre, see Wright, op. cit., 1979.
11. A sophisticated critique of this fetishism is to be found in Trent Schroyer, 1973; also, Bruce Brown, 1973. The Frankfurt School, and Herbert Marcuse particularly, have produced a trenchant critique of the "one-dimensionality" of modern domination, but the overwhelming emphasis on ideology is quite often at the cost of the far more prosaic analytics of political economy. It is instructive to note, however, *contra* to

the *oeuvre* of these traditions, that *social systems cannot, effectively, be identified—or distinguished—by ideology alone*.
12. For a scintillating exposition, see P. Anderson, op. cit., 1979.

TWO

~

Marx and Political Theory: Theories of State, Class, and Power

> ...Once the state has become an independent power in regard to society, it produces forthwith a further ideology. It is indeed only among professional politicians, theorists of constitutional law and jurists of private law, that the connection with economic facts gets completely lost. Since in each particular case the economic facts must assume the form of juristic motives in order to receive legal sanction; and since, in so doing, consideration of course has to be paid to the whole legal system already in operation, the consequence is that the juristic form is made everything and the economic content nothing.
> —F. Engels, *Ludwig Feuerbach*

4
~
The Iron Law of Oligarchy: A Critique of Michels

> *There is no essential contradiction between the doctrine that history is the record of a continued series of class struggles and the doctrine that class struggles inevitably culminate in the creation of new oligarchies which undergo fusion with the old. The existence of a political class does not conflict with the essential content of Marxism, considered not as an economic dogma, but as a philosophy of history...*[1]

And, so saying (and these are prophetic words indeed, given some of the recent revealments in Eastern Europe), Michels went on to develop a theory that, in objective consequence, if not in subjective intention, attacked the theoretical premises of social democracy, and socialism, broadly, in line with what has since come to be known as "elitist" theory. Elitist theory itself was the ideological response of conservative political interests to the practical challenge posed by democratic theory led, in the main, by Marxist and other affiliated currents in nineteenth-century Europe (unlike its appropriation by capitalist interests in the twentieth century). The French Revolution of a century earlier had alerted the traditional ruling classes of Europe to the threat to established authority presented by the negative critical spirit of the Enlightenment. The ruling ideology had long since been geared to the suppression of social criticism—with the Romantic-Conservative reaction emphasizing, rather, the values of stability and integration, and invoking the sanctity of tradition and order (hearkening back to pre-Revolutionary times) as a sanction for social peace.

It was principally the challenge of Marxism (alongside both anarchist and independent working-class movements) which restored the legacy of the Enlightenment, thereby once again raising the spectre of mass revolt, and the possibility of the violent entry of the masses into political life (from which they had been suitably insulated). Accordingly, much ideological energy was expended to stem the drift into "chaos" by calling attention to the proverbial incompetence, ignorance, and stupidity of the ordinary people as against the superior traits of the ruling classes which, therefore, could claim a deserved right to control and exercise political power. The theories of Pareto and Mosca went to great lengths in expounding the suggested inevitability of elite domination in societies where ruling class virtues were hypothesized as being less than widespread. The notion of a "circulation of elites" was advanced as a rebuttal of theories of class conflict, and the historical inevitability of minority rule promoted as a negation of the utopia of a classless society.

Upon reflection, it is no surprise to note that the critics of democracy and socialism, whether Mosca and Pareto (Italy), or Michels and Weber (Germany), hailed from those regions in Europe which were, as yet, the weakest links in the emerging capitalist chain—where the late feudal superstructures were still extant and the political influence of the aristocracy (a measure of the former) still significant. The bourgeoisie in Europe, of course, had already conquered economic dominance, although it had not yet acquired complete political and ideological hegemony. Nor is it entirely surprising that elitist ideas reared their ugly head in even more vicious form in precisely the same areas of Europe even later into the twentieth century.

In spite of the ultimately elitist implications of Michels's ideas, he nevertheless deserves, perhaps, to be distinguished from the more vulgar champions of aristocratic privilege. It is important to note that Michels's frustration with democracy is more directly empirical, reflecting a very personal experience; the pains of being a German Social Democrat were borne twice over by Michels: once in his frustration with the party itself, and a second time when his academic career was blocked in Germany because of his politics. This personal more than ideological revulsion, accordingly, stemmed more from a frustrated democratic idealism than

The Iron Law of Oligarchy: A Critique of Michels

from a narrow, calculating political cynicism. That qualification is not necessarily intended to underrate the quite serious theoretical problems that beset, and weaken, his sociological testimony. It is raised only to suggest that his fellow travelership in the elitist club was conceived—at least originally, and despite a later degeneration—of somewhat nobler egalitarian motives than the others.

The so-called Iron Law of Oligarchy stemmed from Michels's guiding belief—nurtured through a singular personal experience—that every system of leadership is necessarily incompatible with the major postulates of a purist notion of democracy. Since political parties ostensibly required leadership in some form or other, it followed, for Michels, that all party structures were essentially (fundamentally) undemocratic in their internal functioning. The basic needs of party organization, the tactical need for self-preservation, and the technical necessity for expert leadership forced not only the frequent violations of professed principles, but also the domination of an indispensable governing stratum over an increasingly dispensable rank-and-file. This oligarchical tendency is said to set the rather mundane goal of perpetuation of the organization over the professed political aims of the party and professional politicians; that is, to gain control over the party machine by virtue of their "superior" skills.

It is interesting to note that the notion of the essential competence of the leader which is said to divide him/her from the incompetent rank-and-file is perhaps too easily accepted by Michels (a reflection, perhaps, of the standards of political culture extant within the German SPD at the time). The leader does not attain that position by virtue of any other less estimable traits, such as, for instance, corruption or deceit. Since the professional skills required in political decision-making are said to be lacking in the majority of the party membership, a small stratum quite "normally" becomes structurally and functionally isolated from the latter, increasingly exercising control over party affairs. The majority slowly yield their political rights to this small stratum over a period of evolution. The fact of eventual oligarchic domination is said to be further consolidated in the psychological sphere by the slow psychic transformation of the personalities of leaders into domineering characters, alongside the growing isolation of the majority from the decision-making process both leading to, and deriving from, the apathy and ignorance of the latter. As a consequence of this ineffable tendency, democracy comes to be denied within the very agency that is pledged to fight for it. Given such ineluctable characteristics, Michels suggests that, even if such a party were to be successful in ushering in an external democracy without, it would only mean that:

> ...the majority of human beings, in a condition of eternal tutelage, are predestined by tragic necessity to submit to the dominion of a small minority, and must be content to constitute the pedestal of an oligarchy.[2]

Michels's frustration was total: with leadership for their selfish betrayal of party ideals; with the masses for their stupid idolatry; and with the organization itself for producing the tendency of oligarchy. The trace of anarchist complaint is quite unmistakable as he in despair quotes Proudhon[3] to the effect that "The human species wants to be governed; it will be. I am ashamed of my kind. "

In many places in his writing, it is difficult to understand why Michels seemingly abandons sociological analysis to sweeping psychologisms on human nature, the latter not always measuring up to the promises and maturity of his own social insights. A sense of bitter personal frustration, out of which his book, *Political Parties*, was obviously written, perhaps explains some of the theoretical eccentricity that shades his work—which remains significant not because of it, but in spite of it. Perhaps, in analogy to Marx (where competition produces monopoly, of itself), Michels wished to show that democracy, too, of its own, produced its antithesis: oligarchy.

~

It is instructive, at any rate, to glance at Michels's professed aims in writing his book. In his own words:

> We had to inquire whether, and within what limits, democracy must remain purely ideal, possessing no other value than that of a moral criterion which renders it possible to appreciate the varying degrees of that oligarchy which is immanent in every social regime. In other words, we had to inquire if, and in what degree, democracy is an ideal which we can never hope to realise in practice. A further aim of this work was a demolition of some of the facile and superficial democratic illusions which trouble science and lead the masses astray. Finally the author desired to throw light upon certain sociological tendencies which oppose

The Iron Law of Oligarchy: A Critique of Michels

the reign of democracy, and to a still greater extent oppose the reign of socialism.[4]

Michels thus attempted, it would seem, a sociological demonstration of the inevitability of oligarchy by means of a simple, but dramatic, empirical investigation. If he could demonstrate that the largest socialist party in Europe, a front-rank fighter for democracy, was itself organized oligarchically—in spite of its pledged democratic aspirations—then the assertion could be established, beyond doubt, that "...every party organization represents an oligarchical power grounded upon a democratic basis."[5]

Even more so, it would prove—or so Michels thought—that a party which could not democratize its own internal structure would hardly be the proper agency to effect the democratization of society as a whole. (Some would anticipate an early warning here of the later phenomenon of Stalinism.) The argument is ingenious, if not wholly effective: for, firstly, there is no necessary structural identity, sociologically speaking, between the internal practices of a party and its external aims and goals, so that the one need not deny, or affirm, the other; secondly, party structure and practice may vary, quite appropriately, as a tactical matter, with its own perception of the overall political frame within which it is operating, to say nothing of its internal policy being constrained, without the benefit of an option, by external realities. For instance, a party organized for electoral battle might well have organizational considerations that differ from a party intent on conducting guerrilla warfare; and again, party structures battling in the context of dictatorship without are likely to differ from those operating in a plural arena. Finally, internal purity itself is no guarantee of external success in aims; for internal democracy may be a necessary, but not a sufficient, condition for assuring success in the struggle. Achieving success in specific aims, though, would be a function of sociological (among other) realities outside the control of the party apparatus.

Of course, none of this is to suggest that Michels's critique of democracy, in some of its well-known forms, is ill-conceived. In fact, quite the contrary: long before Michels, Marxist and anarchist writers have pointed to the illusions of political democracy in the face of unyielding economic oligarchies, and the fact that disparities of wealth and power negate the mechanical—almost impotent—equalities of the political franchise. However, the Marxist critique does not imply that it is simply "organization" that is at fault (unlike anarchist theory, which indeed does): similarly organized political structures have served effectively quite diverse political purposes in history. Rather, organizations need to be understood, historically, in the context of the political economy of the social formations in question—which would imply an investigation of social relations, structures of political consciousness, and the degree of hegemony of the ruling ideology. Curiously, Michels ignores the potential interdependence of social structures—the political vis `a vis the economic and so on—all the more surprising from one who took such great pains to emphasize his continuity with Marx. If organization were the (only) determinant of oligarchical power (instead of being an instrument of it), then indeed there would be no hope for democracy; unfortunately—or perhaps fortunately—political equations are not resolved quite so easily. The dialectic of social processes intercedes to make the problem of causation far more complex—as Michels, the professed student of historical materialism, might have known.

The Iron Law of Oligarchy not only demonstrated the impossibility of democracy, for Michels, but also the naiveté of socialist theory—the Marxist faith in the proletariat as the emancipatory class ridiculed as yet another instance of the (misplaced) radical humanist faith in the masses:

> The great error of socialists, an error committed in consequence of their lack of adequate psychological knowledge, is to be found in their combination of pessimism regarding the present, with rosy optimism and immeasurable confidence regarding the future. A realistic view of the mental condition of the masses shows beyond question that even if we admit the possibility of moral improvement in mankind, the human materials with whose use politicians and philosophers cannot dispense in their plans of social reconstruction are not of a character to justify excessive optimism.[6]

Again, it is the stasis of "human nature" that is called upon to defy any and all schemes of social progress, and human emancipation, without any real discussion as to how or whether this apparently congealed transhistorical residuum is subject to any form of transition whatsoever, along with altering the social and institutional arrangements. Indeed, the question might well be asked of Michels: how is it possible for such apparently unchanging human traits to have accommodated the various transitions in the state of servitude of the laboring half of humanity (men and women) all the way from slavery to the relative legal freedoms of today, to take the history of Europe alone? Obviously, social institutions do not, in any simple sense, reflect "human nature," but, rather, the contest of social wills between the rulers and the ruled, a contest mediated by cultural, ideological, and technical transformations.

Elsewhere, Michels warns against an uncritical acceptance of socialist leadership (and what could be more prophetic than this?) and the ever present danger of successful revolutions giving way to revisionism and/or restoration. These are warnings that it would be dangerous, not merely foolhardy, to ignore today, given the spectacle of the self-annihilation of the actually existing "socialisms" of Eastern Europe. Indeed, there is much to be said for interpretations of these crumbling socialist regimes, as Michelsian instances of oligarchy and minority appropriation, although it is equally clear that such a simple explanation would possibly not do justice to the overall political complexities involved in their decline. Perhaps what Michels perceived as the strength of his argument might actually be its enduring weakness: that the peculiar elasticity of his iron laws cover all manner of regimes only because any form of indirect representation, and all forms of delegation of authority, are conceived as oligarchical forms of government, simply by definition. Wherever leadership exists, oligarchy is not far behind; if so, most of human history and most of the human race in most of the world appears foredoomed, with political struggles taking on the aspect of the labors of Sisyphus. And yet history itself is a forceful reminder that considerable political gains have been won by working people, despite Michelsian obstacles. Perhaps the Michelsian argument boils down only to suggesting that more might have been accomplished faster if mass struggles did away with bureaucratized parties and cults of leadership.

If Michels was pessimistic about the nature of democracy and socialism, he nonetheless did see an escape from the seemingly intractable problem: the ideal government, he wrote, would doubtless be that of an aristocracy gifted both with technical competence and moral rectitude. Similar to Max Weber, Michels pinned his political hopes not on ordinary movements or organizations, but on:

> ...persons endowed with extraordinarily congenital qualities, sometimes held to be justly supernatural and in every way far superior to the general level. By virtue of these qualities such persons are deemed capable (and often they are) of accomplishing great things, and even miraculous things.[7]

And thus, the radical democrat, the fierce critic of the perils of leadership, turned, ultimately, almost irrationally, to the charismatic leader for the political salvation of humankind. Regrettably, not long after his writing, the country of his own empirical studies (Germany)—not to mention the country of his chosen citizenship (Italy)—would offer up such an individual, much to the everlasting disgrace of European civilization. It does little to restore our faith in Michels's personal integrity when we realize that he was to go on to be a court favorite of Mussolini, aside from holding a professorship in the rabidly fascist University of Perugia.

In conclusion, given Marx's own astonishing elision on political issues in postcapitalist society, even Michels's analytic weaknesses show up as strengths, as courageous and animating attempts to come to terms with the issue of political power, an issue on which traditional Marxists have been, unconscionably, either reductive or elliptical. Despite his many shaky presumptions and doubtful generalizations, Michels's work is a stern reminder that eternal vigilance is the price of any kind of freedom from despotism. In more concrete terms, it is a warning to all movements for emancipation—democratic, socialist, or otherwise—that power surrendered is power lost, a warning that anarchist political thought has tried to emphasize—to its credit—from at least Bakunin on, in the European tradition. While Michels is quite innovative in focusing on the problem of bureaucratization, much like Max Weber, his argument would have been considerably strengthened had he couched it in terms of the preexistence of centralized state power—the most potent tool of class or elite domination (an issue on which his work is remarkably silent)—rather than on the nature of internal organization of political parties. The weakness is one of a strong micro analysis that is never placed in the context of a macro theory of politics.

Notes

1. Robert Michels, *Political Parties*, 1959, p. 354.
2. Ibid.
3. Ibid. p. 367.
4. Ibid. p. 368.
5. Ibid. p. 365.
6. Ibid. p. 366.
7. Robert Michels, *First Lessons in Political Sociology*, 1965, p. 122.

5

~

The Ruling Class: A Critique of Mosca

To place a discussion of elitist theory in perspective, it is vital to understand the historical context in which it arose, since that forms the real basis of its sociological inspiration. Methodologically, this is justly antipodal to the orthodoxy that holds with the so-called "genetic fallacy," where origins are deemed to be irrelevant to functioning—a reactionary elision aimed at disguising the real roots of social theorizing. The nineteenth century was the scene of dramatic intellectual debates, ideological struggles, and political conflict between the votaries of the new political order that was still being constituted and the old that, though clearly on its way out, was still strong enough in intellectual academies, and social philosophy in a more populist sense, to exercise a dominant sway among the ruling interests of Europe. On the one side were the democratic aspirations of the classes that stood to gain from political democracy, struggling as they were to overthrow a repugnant political order and led primarily by liberal and socialist thinkers of various ilks. On the other were the combined political will of the aristocracy and its feudal-commercial allies seeking to resist this challenge.

In the eyes of regimes that were still shaking from the tremors of the French Revolution of a century earlier, the greatest challenge to established ways of political thinking was raised by Marxism, and the threat of mass revolt that it represented. Elitist ideology was far from being the first intellectual barricade thrown up against the tide of democratic thought: it was only part of the continuing Thermidor set off by the Romantic-Conservative reaction against the critical spirit of the Enlightenment. As an ideology, it was eclectic, for its apologists were really straddling two separate epochs, with eyes and heart set on the system which was disintegrating before them.

The bourgeoisie was in effective economic power in Europe—it had, however (though not for want of trying) not yet assumed political or ideological hegemony. It is not at all surprising that the principal elitist thinkers were the products of those areas of Europe that were still bastions of a late feudalism characterized, relatively speaking, by a lower level of capitalist development than their eighteenth-century forerunners, Italy and Germany. Nor is it surprising that such thinking was to magnify into even more dangerous and invidious forms once again, later, in the twentieth century, in precisely the same regions.

~

The term "elite" gained much currency via the social and political writings of Vilfredo Pareto, during the last quarter of the nineteenth century, in which he advanced the notion of the "circulation of elites" as the driving motor of political development. It was Gaetano Mosca, however, who presented what is now regarded as the "sociological" distinction between the elite and the masses which, after much elaboration and amendment, remains a term still in use in political sociology through the pioneering interpretations of Schumpeter and Lipset. To quote Mosca:

> Among the constant facts and tendencies that are to be found in all political organisms, one is so obvious that it is apparent to the most casual eye. In all societies—from societies which are very meagrely developed and have barely attained the dawnings of civilisation, down to the most advanced and powerful societies—two classes of people appear—a class that rules and a class that is ruled. The first class, always the less numerous, performs all political functions, monopolises power and enjoys the advantages power brings, whereas the second, the more numerous class, is directed and controlled by the first, in a manner that is more or less legal, now more or less arbitrary and violent.[1]

The Ruling Class: A Critique of Mosca

Mosca tried to elaborate a sociological justification of what, at first sight, appeared to be a commonplace truism—that in all societies are to be found a minority that rules and a majority that is ruled. The minority rules, according to Mosca, by virtue of its superior organization; being a compact group, it is better structured to obey a single impulse and act in concert against the diffuse, divided majority. As he put it:

> A hundred men acting in concert, with a common understanding, will triumph over a thousand men who are not in accord, and can therefore be dealt with one by one.[2]

Although organization implies power, for Mosca, it is not sufficient to constitute a ruling class, since the members of the ruling class are not only organized, they are also possessed of superior qualities—material, intellectual, and moral—which are inherited from similarly situated ancestors. But the first or primal step taken toward the constitution of the ruling class is not, significantly, made clear: whether they seize power because of superior organization or superior qualities is left an open question. In any case, real historical sequences are rarely elaborated by Mosca—a clue to this mode of theorizing—nor indeed are they necessary to his scheme of things. Once established and in power, of course, the ruling class maintains its domination by an astute combination of force and fraud (reminiscent, of course, of Machiavelli). The rulers must always be ready and prepared to use ruthless force to keep the masses in subjection, for those who seek to dominate cannot afford to be soft-bellied or squeamish about the use of violence—a ruling stratum that loses such "vigor" becomes unfit to rule, and is soon overthrown by new groups that display these virtues more successfully. Aside from this willingness to resort to military means of suppression, the other tactic of the ruling class is to employ what Mosca terms the "political formula"—hardly an original idea, but rather a clever, catchy restatement of what earlier thinkers had called ideology, or the process of legitimation and value-consensus typical, in some measure, of all stable, long-surviving regimes. One is reminded, in this context, of the host of political analysts in the tradition of Machiavelli (European or otherwise; witness the writings of the Indian philosopher Kautilya, in this regard, for just one nonEuropean view) who have advocated the use of subterfuge and subtlety in securing the loyalty and support of the ruled.

MARX AND POLITICAL THEORY: THEORIES OF STATE, CLASS, AND POWER

However, in spite of the intelligence and cunningness of the organized minority of "superior" individuals who constitute the rulers, challenges to authority do arise, particularly with the emergence of new social energies and social groups which demand recognition from the powers that be, and which cannot be—apparently—suppressed indefinitely. There is, therefore, in Mosca's conception, an oblique reference to the apparently dim processes of structural evolution, all the more difficult to deny or ignore since they were actually concurrent with Mosca's own writings. During such periods of "renovation," as he called them, the ruling class may either be vanquished, or it may open its doors, selectively, depending on its capacity to absorb—or co-opt—the new social forces. The main dynamic of history is located precisely in these struggles between the rulers and the ruled, a struggle mediated in modern times by the new middle classes created by the new forces of science and technology. But, no matter which side is triumphant, the net result is always the same old division into a ruling minority and a ruled majority—the inevitable equation of power in human society.

Mosca's conceptualizations are a queer, syncretic mixture of random sociological, psychological, and philosophical speculations on the nature of society. However, compared with Pareto's fancies, they still retain a measure of sociological insight and political understanding. For in Mosca, at least, there are no fables of foxes and lions, nor the suggestion that we live in an irrational world where sentiments are the only driving forces, nor a series of dubious psychologisms on whose flimsy structure a political theory of the elite is built. Mosca's elite is constructed out of an accurate perception of political realities (i.e the realities of power) albeit drawn out of a limited range of historical fact; and, in spite of its psychological stilts, it still walks with political and military legs on solidly institutional ground. The elite has discernable sociological facets—power, wealth, education—quite sufficient, in Mosca's characterization, to enable it to rule, unmindful of the distraction of either character or virtue. The quite unnecessary psychological residues are introduced by Mosca only to serve quite a different function than a mere description or definition of the elite: they are ushered in to justify—not explain—the rule of the elite. The ruling class rules not only because it is powerful, but because it is ideally fitted to rule. It becomes clear, then, that Mosca is not merely a student of political elites: he is, in fact, their champion!

The Ruling Class: A Critique of Mosca

In spite of the rather stark outlines of his presentation, there is still controversy over the precise demarcation of the ruling class. There is a suggestion, in Mosca, that, aside from the elite and mass, there may yet be another category—the subelite Pareto's "nongoverning elite" comes to mind), a large group of the middle classes which serves as a buffer between the rulers and the ruled, thereby preventing an unhealthy polarization between the two extremes. The subelite is, however, not only a base for potential membership in the ruling class; it is also, in a fashion, an extension of government (there are, probably inaccurate, but nevertheless suggestive parallels between this subelite, Saint-Simone's "Council of Newton," and Mannheim's "intellectual stratum"). This amendment probably suggested itself after Mosca's own brief experience with twentieth century European democracies. At any rate, there is sufficient evidence to show that the political class is neither a homogeneous entity nor a monolithic organization. He concedes that it represents (or is forced to represent) diverse social groups and interests, a compromise that has to be made if the united front against the masses is to be preserved. It is, of course, not quite clear how the elite withstands all the variety of meanings ascribed to it by Mosca—its internal composition being dubious in the extreme—but, vis à vis Mosca's presentation of the masses, it does come across rather vividly. Nonetheless, at least one scholar confesses to being baffled:

> ...political class is a puzzle. One does not exactly understand what Mosca means, so fluctuating and elastic is the notion. Sometimes he seems to think of the middle class, sometimes of men of property in general, and then again of those who call themselves "the educated." But on other occasions Mosca has in mind the "political personnel"...Mosca's political class is nothing but the intellectual section of the ruling group. Mosca's term approximates Pareto's elite concept—another attempt to interpret the historical phenomenon of the intelligentsia and its function in political and social life.[3]

~

Mosca's concepts (and Pareto's, for that matter) were not merely academic, scholarly contributions to a new social science they claimed to be founding; they also represented—by their own admission—deliberate intellectual efforts undertaken consciously to debunk socialist theory (well before any serious socialist experiments had gotten under way), the theory of elites being, in their opinion, the necessary armory for rebuttal of the theory of class conflict advanced by Marxist scholarship. To quote:

> In the world in which we are living, socialism will be arrested only if a realistic political science succeeds in demolishing the metaphysical and optimistic methods that prevail at present in social studies.[4]

The rejection of socialist assumptions is not merely empirical: it is philosophical and ideological as well, a blanket critique of the entire humanistic tradition of the Enlightenment thinkers which culminates, at least in one pole, in the revolutionary doctrines of socialism. Mosca's revulsion for socialism takes on almost pathological forms—indeed, he views the latter almost as a disease afflicting the lower orders which must be eradicated before a veritable holocaust overtakes the world, and all that is virtuous is forever lost:

> Socialist doctrines offer the lower passions too vast and fertile a field in which to multiply and spread in a rank growth.[5]

This revulsion, of course, sprang from fear—a dread of the masses gaining control of political power through the pernicious mechanism of popular suffrage; hence, the frontal attack on democracy, as well:

> ...the democratic doctrine is altogether spurious and aprioristic—political power never has been, and never will be founded upon the explicit consent of the majority.[6]

Mosca's conception of the ruling class, not unintentionally, runs counter to socialist and democratic theory on all scores. In its very initial definition, it denies the socialist goal of a classless society, and then defends minority rule by suggesting that the ruling class in effect deserves to rule because of the (alleged) superiority of its individual members. There is little awareness of political economy in Mosca, and an even more meagre understanding of the forces making for social development. His typology is descriptive and ahistorical, making the common error (not excusable for being common!) of treating a specific historical datum as universal and immutable. His assumptions about human nature and human psychology (both class divided between elite and mass) are both questionable and pernicious, apart from being rooted in a very narrowly limited area of historical experience, albeit presented as eternal truths.

More fundamentally, Mosca's philosophical premises do not allow for the consideration of the possibility of human perfectibility via the medium of an alteration of institutional arrangements that bind people to society; it is a restrictive and cynical conception of the human genius, and one that is totally ignorant of the changing dialectic between material necessities and human possibilities. At best, it is an arrogant and uncritical defense of aristocratic power and privilege; at worst, a narrowly conceived ideological polemic, ignorant in the extreme of both social structure and social process.

~

Employed more judiciously, and less tendentiously, of course, Mosca's concept of the ruling class can have some interesting applications. For one thing, it can be turned against western-style *bourgeois* democracies where capitalism is succored through the mechanism of a definite political formula (i.e. nominal political democracy and plurality of "interests"), while force is readily employed when the formula breaks down (as in Chile, Grenada, Northern Ireland, Panama, and the many ghettoes of urban America). In fact, Schumpeter adapts the concept, positively, to fit western democracies, where elites compete for the support of the masses in order to gain the right to govern them. In such a conception, which certainly descriptively fits the functioning of liberal democracy, elites are made quite compatible with democracy, and are the very mainstay of democratic regimes: the exclusion of the masses is as likely justified as not (although with a definite paranoia of mass participation and mass movements à la Ortega y Gasset), for example in the early work of Robert Dahl (also Nelson Polsby) and his interesting paradigm in *Who Governs?*, of "homo civicus" and "homopoliticus," with the happy assumption that membership of the elite is "open," at least in principle.

In this modern version of elitist theory, the ever expanding middle classes are the new insulating cement of the system, the subelite of Mosca, the new base for social recruitment upward, the ideological guardians of the capitalist order. Only one proposition of Mosca is conveniently ignored by these present-day elitist theorists of democracy (the contradiction involved is almost missed by this genre!): that the political struggle is a struggle between the rulers and the ruled! Democratic ideology does not permit such radical interpretations of reality; indeed, political conflict is now termed "competition between elites," a horizontal—fraternal?—struggle between more or less equal groups (in the original Dahl, for instance, there are different "issue-areas" that generate different elite/mass dichotomies in a plural political world). The theory of revolution, also implicitly present in Mosca's work, is too unpalatable for the weak stomachs of modern-day liberal democrats, only too happy to rest content with mass apathy, the condition, apparently, for comfortable class domination, with liberty, property, and Bentham, especially if one is white, male, and Tory.

Above all, therefore, both elitist theory and Mosca's propositions about the ruling class are ideologically loaded notions aimed at the mystification of social reality. Far less are they the simple subject matter of an unbiased social investigation, careless as to where theory might lead: their invention and propagation was, historically speaking, for definite, polemical purposes. To employ them as descriptive constructs, innocent of their real roots, may be an interesting exercise, though fraught with the risk of a high political fall out. As Bottomore points out, more generally, with respect to the origins of elitist discourse:

> The concept refers to an observable social phenomenon and takes its place in theories which seek to explain social happenings, especially political changes. At the same time the concept makes its appearance in social thought at time and in circumstances which at once give it an ideological significance in the contest between economic liberalism and socialism. Even later, in our allegedly post-ideological age, the concept cannot be regarded as a purely scientific construct: for every sociological concept and theory has an ideological force by reason of its influence upon the thoughts and actions of men in their everyday life. It may have this influence either because it is impregnated with a social doctrine, or because, while it excludes any immediate doctrinal influences, it nevertheless draws attention to and emphasizes certain features of social life and neglects others, and thus persuades men to conceive of their position and their possible future in one set of terms rather than another.

The Ruling Class: A Critique of Mosca

To criticize a conceptual scheme or a theory in its ideological aspect is not, therefore, simply to show its connection with a broader doctrine of man and society and to oppose doctrine to it: it is also, mainly, to show the scientific limitations of the concepts and theories.[7]

Modern elitist theory, therefore, is (unabashedly) in the lineage of Mosca and Pareto, impassioned with a similar political agenda: to limit the activities of the masses within the confines of existing power and property equations. In Mosca's time, it was felt that the best means to do this was to exclude the propertyless from the political order; today this is done by their inclusion in the system so long as their demands remain reconcilable with the economic and political requirements of the ruling class. To employ Mosca's language, the political formula has changed, though the fact and intent of class domination has not. How long the current formulas will endure is, of course, the question that challenges radical democrats today.

Notes

1. Gaetano Mosca, *The Ruling Class*, 1965, p. 50.
2. Ibid. p. 53.
3. Antonio Gramsci, quoted in T.B. Bottomore, *Elites in Society*, 1966, pp. 11-12.
4. G. Mosca, op cit.
5. Ibid.
6. Ibid.
7. T.B. Bottomore, *Elites in Society*, 1964, p. 20.

6
~
Classical Marxism, NeoMarxism, and the State: A Retrospective

It has lately been quite customary, if not exactly fashionable, among contemporary practitioners of social science—Marxian and otherwise—to lament, and laboriously at that, the alleged absence of a theory of the state in the framework of Marx's writings, a tendency that came to a peak in the seventies and eighties. It is relatively easy to dismiss such talk when the source is one of the many variants of bourgeois ideology, despite the latter's intellectual sophistry (or perhaps because of it !) and academic guile. It is quite another matter, however, when such ideas are echoed in the works of what might be termed, for want of a better phrase, the committed intelligentsia working in a general Marxian frame of analysis. Marx provided—but within a Marxian frame, of course—as complete a theory of the state as consistent with the practical goals of classical Marxism—so that, if contemporary academic Marxian scholars detect elisions and empty spaces, it is possibly because they have, in very separate and individual ways, moved away from those classical objectives. This is not at all to pass judgment on the value of those objectives themselves, whether in affirmation by classical Marxism or in their apparent denial by neoMarxians; I am only pointing out that the rationale of the depiction of the state in classical Marxism cannot be found outside of the latter's self-imposed agenda of emancipation. The various attempts to "update" Marx in the post-war efflorescence of neoMarxian writings have not amounted to very much, either intellectually or politically.

This century and this age originally held promise to be an age of revolution, where many fond Marxian hopes seemed to be on the verge of realization (the Bolshevik Revolution and the Great Depression being cases in point). As it is, however, it has turned out to be, at least in the European segment of the world (east or west), the era of the near total triumph of bourgeois ideology, if not exactly capitalist social relations; far from being a Marxian epoch, it has now proved a Weberian one, after the intellectual genius who captured the spirit of capitalism as no other since. It is only entirely appropriate that Max Weber—unlike his current epigones amongst the mainstream—saw the Marxian system as an opulent gold mine from which virtually all of social science could be (in a double sense) extracted, so long as it could then be transformed into a weapon against Marxian attributions, Weber being critically aware (more than the latter-day Marxians sometimes) of the class content and class basis of concepts.

Few in our own day—especially among the ilk of those who are still trying to formulate a theory of the state—either remember or realize that Marx virtually founded, arguably, the very discipline of political sociology—not merely a "theory" of the "state"—and that all of official social science since Max Weber has struggled (successfully, apparently) to soften and subdue its radical implications. In other words, the vanguard ideologists of capitalism saw, read, and understood the Marxian theory of politics long before contemporary pedagogy initiated discussions, totally permeated with what Marx might have called the "illusions of the epoch," on such subjects. It is bad enough to fight ideological battles on the home terrain of the bourgeoisie, but the cause is surely lost a dozen times over when we are compelled to forge our weapons—analytical concepts—from the very armory of the latter.

Today, faith in Marx, of course, is to be found flagging, at least in the European tradition of Marxism, but in a rather singular sense: it is the revolutionary Marx who has disappeared from the lexicon, while all the other Marxes are invited to sit in on academic debates, where splendid contests are held in sublime theoretical virtuosity. But classical Marxism was, above all things, revolutionary. This is not to praise or condemn it—merely to state that it is only in the agenda of emancipation that the raison d'être of classical Marxian "analysis" can be found. Of course, it aspired to be a science—but not at all in a positivist sense: it was both more and less, it was a science of revolution. In a classical Marxian sense, the theory of the state or any other social structure can only be located, thereby, in the context of a theory of radical transformation. And, in the run of western academic Marxism, the grand failure of all theorists of the state, in the seventies and eighties, to offer any advance over classical insights stems precisely from the divorce of their agenda of analysis from the agenda of transformation. In this sense, the failure to locate and "construct" a theory of the state is linked up with the dramatic failure of western Marxism in a purely political sense, with splendid theoreticians totally isolated from—and quite often in contempt of—anything passing for a mass movement, eager instead to jump on the bandwagon of the latest in bourgeois ideology (functionalism, systems analysis, structuralism, poststructuralism, postmodernism, etc.), which has remained a rich lode of creativity—sad to say—in comparison to its neoMarxian "critics."

Given this preamble, perhaps appropriately, we might wish to start with Lenin—who, it might be agreed, was better placed than most to "study" this esoteric institution, in the tradition of classical revolutionary Marxism, having indeed overthrown one and led another (tainted only, one might say, with the disrepute of practice!), all within a rather short life span. Many western Marxists would disregard, even disparage, Lenin. Poulantzas,[1] for instance, dismisses Lenin's writings on the grounds that they were too "polemical" (on that score one could equally disregard Marx, Engels, Gramsci, Mao, in short, virtually all of revolutionary Marxism!); of course, Poulantzas makes the charge in a diatribe against Miliband, but let us not quibble over this little matter of consistency. It illustrates, tellingly, if sadly, the triumph of the bourgeois idiom in western Marxism, where a depoliticized (nonpolemical) search for academic "truths" might make for a secure professional career, but only at the price of jettisoning vital Marxian luggage. The odd thing is that while Marxian academics flaunt such ragged trousered philanthropy, the mainstream, for its part, is quite aware of the connections between science, ideology, and the class struggle (banning Marxists, for one thing, from academe wherever possible, with a commendable astuteness). It is the Marxians who have become bourgeois, one might say to their detriment, and the bourgeois who have remained, cynically, "Marxian" in their appreciation for Marxist truths about politics, to their enduring benefit.

At any rate, to turn to Lenin speaking of the Marxian approach to social institutions in a lecture on the state delivered to Sverdlov University in 1919:

> The most reliable thing in a question of social science, and one that is most necessary in order really to acquire the habit of approaching this question correctly and not allowing oneself to get lost in the mass of detail or in the immense variety of conflicting opinions—the most important thing in order to approach this question scientifically is not to forget the underlying historical connection, to examine every question from the standpoint of how the given phenomenon arose in history and what principal stages this phenomenon passes through in its development, and, from the standpoint of its development, to examine what the given thing has become today.[2]

All of which, it will be clear, is a simple but accurate paraphrase of the host of Marx-Engels writings on method, which should, by now, belong to any primer on historical materialism. Lenin never claimed any profundity other than that derived from the founders of socialism. And, by way of cross checking, if we turn to Engel's treatise on the origin of private property and the state, we find an original and systematical elaboration, if schematically presented, of the historical development of the state apparatus, its "functions," economic, political, ideological, etc—all this in a true sense being just an elaboration; for the ideas underlying the analysis had already been treated explicitly, and in detail, in earlier joint efforts, e.g., *The German Ideology* (1846), the *Communist Manifesto* (1848), and in many individual works of Marx, such as *The 18th Brumaire* (1852) and *Critique of the Gotha Programme* (1875); and, again, in joint efforts such as the writings on the *Paris Commune* (1870-71). The schematism was inevi-table for another important reason: Engels wrote political documents, not doctoral dissertations. The sophisticated armchair Marxists who sneer at the schematism might well ponder this Engelsian handicap.

Throughout these writings, a single theme recurs almost *ad nauseam*: that the state is located in the arena of class relations, in the conflict between class interests—i.e. it is a dynamic notion with little of the institutional rigidity that has been associated with the later "structuralist" interpretations that so dominated the discourse of the seventies. Even that most autonomous of states, the Bonapartist state, does not escape this class determination of the nature of this intervention in the life of the collectivity:

> And yet the State power is not suspended in midair. Bonaparte represents a class, and the most numerous class of French Society at that, the small-holding (Parzellen) peasants.[3]

Political relations are class relations, class relations are property relations, property relations are production relations; and when the last mentioned undergo transformation (given the fundamental antagonism within the mode of production between forces and relations), a ripple effect, mediated finally by the nature of class conflict, persuades changes in the "functions" of the state—all of which points to a study of historical development, and the articulation of modes of production extant in a given social formation.

It is singular that almost all neoMarxian attempts at delineating a theory of the state flounder on a lack of historical perspective, even if lip service is paid to the notion of "history." Instead, history is surmounted by a crude structure-functionalism, as in this not unrepresentative work,[4] which starts with the "question" of the state, beginning with the observation that "the state in capitalist society broadly serves the interests of the capitalist class," and arguing this to be a "premise"' to be found in the Manifesto in its "classic" form. In the very next line, this "premise" suddenly becomes an "axiom"; and then comes the question: why does the state serve the interests of the capitalist class? Although sounding innocuous enough, such treatments follow the route of functionalism, which similarly starts with premises, axioms, and so on, and then on to dangerously similar—facile—"questions." The hazard of the previous question is not that it is asked at all, but that the answer is sought, quite invariably in a descriptive sense, nonhistorically. Even more hazardous, such structuralist arguments ignore the vital theoretical connections between the concepts of state and class, and pose the relationship as if it were an empirical proposition to be demonstrated with reference to some readily ascertainable "facts."

Small wonder, then, that, in trying to establish this "connection"—superfluously—a whole range of bourgeois concepts are borrowed, whether from the Mosca-Pareto school of elites (as in Miliband) or from Max Weber's "Institutionalization and Legitimation" (as in Habermas), or "Structure-Functions" à la Easton-Parsons (as in Poulantzas and Offe).[5] In all this confusion, no substantive advance is made over the traditional Marx-Engels-Lenin view of the matter. Even Skocpol's work (later in time than Poulantzas, Offe, and Wolfe) stressing the autonomy of the state similarly breaks no new ground whatsoever, for the "task" itself is antithetical to the Marxist impulse: to study the state for the sake of drawing out abstract impulses can only lead to a morass of partial, empirical insights that may never recur again. The Marxian exhortation is to engage the state, not to study it as if it were some laboratory animal. Indeed, it is challenging state power that best "answers" to a specific state's hidden and revealed capacities, so in a sense even the "understanding" aspect, so dear to neoMarxism, is best served through a critical engagement (though that is not quite the sort of learning that the average neoMarxian academic has in mind). Max Weber understood matters better than much of neoMarxism when he wrote that the state is best understood not in terms of its "ends," which are dynamic and open, but rather its means: the monopoly—or near monopoly—of the means of violence.

By way of illustration, here is a conclusion from one late seventies attempt to formulate a Marxian theory of the state:

> The particular shape of the capitalist state has been the result of class struggle, and struggle can continue to affect that shape. Thus, Wolfe argues, the state should be seen as an appropriate arena for class struggle. As Wolfe reminds us, the ultimate purpose of constructing a Marxist theory of the capitalist state is not just to study the state, but to transform it.[6]

If this is advancement, we are advancing only in the direction of Marx and Lenin (if only at a rather crippling pace): no further.

Let alone any theoretical advance in this academic fabrication of a theory of the state, the record, on occasion, seems to lean almost toward retrogressions; here is one such instance drawn from the work of Claus Offe—as his reviewers put it:

> Offe's analysis of the contradiction between the State's role in the accumulation process and the selective mechanisms which determine its

class-character suggests that the state may also become relatively autonomous from the logic of accumulation itself.[7]

What has really happened, perhaps, is not that the state has become relatively autonomous from the logic of accumulation—a truly preposterous notion to uphold in light of even bourgeois Keynesian wisdom on the issue!—but that Mr. Offe's analysis has become absolutely autonomous from the realities of the social world. So much for neoHegelianism and neoWeberianism, both of which make a happy liaison in Offe (aside from his seventies persona, which showed ample promise of such things, his later efforts such as *Disorganized Capitalism* [1985] continue to carry the same idiosyncratic mix of Weber, Hegel, and Marx, usually to the detriment of the last mentioned). Relative to Claus Offe, of course, his reviewers are even yet further autonomous from Marxian theory as they seize upon "evidence" backing this newly "liberated" state:

> Responding to the economic dislocation caused by the Vietnam war these writers argued that American Imperialism is more in the interest of the state than in the interests of capitalism.[8]

Ideology, apparently, scores again. What then, one might ask, is Imperialism (good-bye, Lenin), what then is the State (good-bye, Engels), and what, if at all, is Capitalism (good-bye, Marx)? It is not that one should be reluctant to dispense with Messrs. Marx, Engels, and Lenin—for that would be altogether too doctrinaire!—nor that a competing theory of the state could not exist: but why, in the name of Marx, should one be constrained to call such modes of random theorizing "Marxian" at all? Yet again, the message is brought home, via Lenin's exhortation quoted earlier: to refuse to delineate a phenomenon historically, and only to ask questions of structure and function, is to thwart understanding altogether. In the case in question, it is the self-motivated state of Hegel, transformed by mainstream political sociology into a class-neutral, integrated state, that is now reintroduced into Marxian analysis as the new "free" state. "It is a line of thought which we feel is worth pursuing," say the reviewers: into some harmless academic retreat, is all one can hope! Sartre was genuinely prophetic when he wrote that all pretensions aiming at overcoming Marxism—at least within a capitalist context—end up as essentially preMarxist ideas, only refurbished.

MARX AND POLITICAL THEORY: THEORIES OF STATE, CLASS, AND POWER

In a sense, it would seem that the real object of inquiry might, rather, be a Marxian theory of politics that both encompasses, and finally prevails over (in practice), the notion of the state. A separate or logically distinct theory of the state would seem, in this light, a secondary (if not actually a redundant) idea. Marxian political theory has, of course, contributed most of the elements of contemporary capitalist ideology, in terms of concepts that have now quietly passed into the official lingo of capitalist social science: class, class interest, class conflict, ideology, consciousness, bureaucracy, revolution, alienation, exploitation, crisis, etc.—which is only to be expected, considering that all social science after Marx was simply, as Zeitlin put it, a debate with Marx's ghost, bearing the imprint of the original impulse it struggled against; as even a critic of Marxism has it:

> That Marx ranks among the major political theorists is a widely accepted opinion in our time. The histories of political thought commonly accord him a chapter or two, and the great age of political theory in the modern West is often viewed as running from Machiavelli to Marx.[9]

The idea of the state being a guarantor of property relations, so repugnant to bourgeois political sociology today, was commonplace in the thinking of the eighteenth and early nineteenth centuries, and was by no means a discovery of Marxism. A long tradition of political theory from Aristotle through Machiavelli to Locke (even wise old Adam Smith) recognized it as perfectly in the normal order of things. Even the class struggle, Marx claimed, was not his specific discovery:

> And now as to myself, no credit is due to me for discovering the existence of classes in modern society, nor yet the struggle between them. Long before me bourgeois historians had described the historical development of this class struggle and bourgeois economists the economic anatomy of the classes. What I did new was to prove:
> 1. that the existence of classes is only bound up with particular, historic phases in the development of production.
> 2. that the class struggle necessarily leads to the dictatorship of the proletariat.
> 3. that this dictatorship itself only constitutes the transition to the abolition of all classes and to a classless society.[10]

Classical Marxism, NeoMarxism, and the State: A Retrospective

Of course, it needs to be clarified that while bourgeois theory in its radical phase well acknowledged the class struggle (and indeed promoted it in its own struggle against the feudal aristocracy), the apologetics that set in after Marx, and after the bourgeois had won political power, refused to take cognizance of any such social disturbance in the essential harmony of the capitalist social order.

On the other hand, the notion of a class determination of class consciousness and ideology (the "sociology of knowledge," in official parlance), and hence their specific political content, sketched, for instance, in *The German Ideology*, are specifically Marxian contributions later to be developed by Gramsci (quite unaware of the existence of this Marxian work!) in his concept of "hegemony"; but classical Marxism does not offer a structural-functional view of either society or politics, nor a sociology of institutions with the state, bureaucracy, army, etc., playing out neatly apportioned roles to fulfill some teleologically given "necessary" functions. Such a view is better sought in the Weberian writings of Messrs. Gabriel Almond, James Coleman, Lucian Pye, Sidney Verba, etc. All this, by way of illustration of a single point: unless a theory of the state is expressly subsumed under a wider theory of politics, the results can only tend toward a structural empiricism, seeking lodgings securely in the domain of capitalist ideology. As Poulantzas argues:

> For concepts and notions are never innocent, and by employing the notions of the adversary to reply to him, one legitimizes them and permits their persistence...In the extreme case, one can be unconsciously and surreptitiously contaminated by the very epistemological principles of the adversary, that is to say the problematic that founds the concepts which have not been theoretically criticized, believing them simply refuted by the facts.[11]

This is Poulantzas at his best: and yet he falls prey to precisely the tendency he deplores. The system of the state, he tells us, is a combination of repressive apparatuses and ideological apparatuses (to repeat a ghastly word!), so that the state ends up comprising the church, the schools, the mass media, and even the family. All of society, then, it would appear, ends up being consumed by this all-devouring Leviathan: the state itself (Hegel rides again). Now, it is true that there is a passage in *The German Ideology* which says:

MARX AND POLITICAL THEORY: THEORIES OF STATE, CLASS, AND POWER

> Since the State is the form in which the individuals of a ruling class assert their interests, and in which the whole of civil society of an epoch is epitomised, it follows that the State mediates in the formation of all common institutions and that the institutions receive a political form. Hence the illusion that law is based on the will, and indeed on the will divorced from its real basis—on free will...[12]

Civil society, here stated, is politicized by the fact of class-determined state activity: the state mediates, yes, but it does not, emphatically, expropriate society! Capitalism is a long way from that early societal stage where, in a certain sense, the family is coterminous with the production unit and exercises political functions; and even in that remote context, it is society that swallows the state, and not *vice versa*. Again, the failure to distinguish between politics, as such, and the state leads to bizarre formulations. Culture and ideology are not state determined: their political content is given by their class content, itself based on the specific moment they straddle within the social relations of production.

A refusal to look up the basic tenets of historical materialism for serious theoretical clarification, part of the curiously Oedipal effort to go beyond Marx, has been a characteristic tendency of western academic Marxism responsible for a flood of pseudo literature on pseudo problems; the relative autonomy jinx is one such, leading only to an elaborate typology of states (as though a taxonomy amounted to a theory), without ever being able to answer the question of autonomy itself. Posed in this manner, of course, there can be no theoretical answer, for the universe of the empirical is infinite, while a theory can only suggest overdetermined tendencies operating between variables. The so-called "superstructures" in Marxian analysis are all considered to be relatively autonomous from actual production relations, or rather from the mode of production, understood as an articulated combination of a specific mode of appropriation of the product, and a specific mode of appropriation of nature, with the state being only one of the elements in the superstructural domain. The contradictions of class interest, which historically necessitate the state, and which, when subjectively perceived, translate—potentially—as class conflict, are the final determinants of this autonomy, which therefore can only be historically variable.

The state guarantees production relations (property relations) and their reproduction; how smoothly or how successfully it does this is a

Classical Marxism, NeoMarxism, and the State: A Retrospective

function of the actual economic power of the ruling classes, and the extent of their hegemony over society, not to mention the degree of subservience of the subaltern classes (which depends on the class apprehension of the subalterns of their class situation). Politics, as a process, is the effort to subjugate, manipulate, and control all institutions and classes in line with the requirements of the ruling class, and concomitantly it includes the efforts of the subaltern classes to resist this domination: if repression, including both physical and ideological coercion, is the ongoing means of ruling class control, revolution is the ultimate means of resistance of the oppressed. It is this is the Marxian "theory" of politics that is never referred to in neoMarxian writings: the bane of structuralist influence being quite self-evident in the impotence with respect to "processes" as opposed to "structures." At any rate, a study in the concrete of the state (for example, *The 18th Brumaire*) is always necessary: but this empirical research, the *sine qua non* of political action, by no means leads to a new or improved theory of the state. In a historical materialist understanding, there *is* a Marxist theory of the state and politics (otherwise, the Bolshevik and Maoist revolutions would have been quite impossible and the theory and practice of Lenin and Mao quite unintelligible), and it is only because of the existence of such a theory that empirical research becomes possible at all, in a meaningful way. Positivism mingles very poorly, it would seem, with the spirit of Marxism.

One other point. Most of the researchers in the field of the state seem overly intrigued at discovering that the state performs economic functions (yet, again, the concepts of the state and the economy are drawn from bourgeois discourse, serving only to confuse analysis). A case in point is provided by reviewers of James O'Connors's famous *Fiscal Crisis of the State* (1973) when they argue that:

> One of the main results of this analysis is that the state loses much of its superstructural character. The state is increasingly involved in accumulation, as earlier Marxist thinking emphasized, but to participate actively in creating those conditions. Although the state is not rigidly...circumscribed by accumulation, there is a strong dialectical link.[13]

Analysis couldn't possibly degenerate further; the only dialectical link to speak of is the rather weak one between these writers and classical

MARX AND POLITICAL THEORY: THEORIES OF STATE, CLASS, AND POWER

Marxism. Here is the obverse of the earlier case discussed: either the state balloons and flies away, as with Offe, or civil society—as the reviewers imply—simply digests the state, as in their claim. Of course, either way, the crucifixion of the original Marx is accomplished quite effortlessly. By way of correction, we might turn to Sweezy:

> The fact that the first concern of the state is to protect the continued existence and stability of a given form of society does not mean that it performs no other functions of economic importance. On the contrary...[14]

Or, better still, to Engels:

> The reaction of the state power upon economic development can be one of three kinds: it can run in the same direction, and then development is more rapid; it can oppose the line of development...or it can cut off economic development from certain paths, and impose on it certain others...[15]

The state, however, thereby does not cease to be "superstructural," i.e. it is preeminently a political institution, regardless of its other interventions discharged from time to time, though obviously not in any mechanistic way that separates economics from politics.

The concrete political analysis of a given state, at a given conjuncture of class conflict, is hardly an academic question tied to the pursuit of knowledge for its own sake (for the latter is a quintessentially bourgeois task far less innocent than our contemporary tide of progressive scholars, seeking to fill formal textbooks with positivist renderings of classical Marxism). Classical Marxism might well be completely mistaken in its epistemology and ontology (I make no transfactual claims for its validity), to say nothing of its brand of politics; be that as it may, however, within it, the search for a theory of the state outside of a theory of revolution is default, in the first instance, or else the *XIth Thesis on Feuerbach* simply would have been written in vain.

The strange thing about these impotent attempts to reformulate a Marxian theory of the state is that they are entirely oblivious to the truly glaring weaknesses in Marx's theory of politics in postcapitalist societies (weaknesses exposed dramatically by recent events in east Europe but always latent as problems in Marxist discourse applied to the issue of power under socialism), an area where "research" has always seemed more warranted, and potentially invested with payoffs. But utopian notions of the withering away of the state have rarely been questioned by the same strand of theorizing that is otherwise so eloquent in laying threadbare the lineament of Marx's conceptualizations of the state; again, the delinquency stems from the original political default already identified. Since radical change was never on the agenda, the issue of the withering away of the state required no comment. After all, they never expected the capitalist state to even alter, let alone wither away, anymore than they expected capitalism to dissolve. Not only has neoMarxism always sought a niche within capitalism—albeit a critical niche—but also structure-functionalism conceives of social phenomena in stasis; how else could these positivists have "studied" their object unless it, in complement to their effort, obliged them by standing still? And so they continued to knock on an open door, in all its utter, ultimate futility. It is this brand of Marxism that has all but ensured the eclipse of Marxism as a serious political entity in western capitalism, despite a certain glorified ghettoization in the seventies and eighties. Today, it is becoming clear that even this ghetto status might be nearing an end. The choice therefore stands rubric on the walls: either neoMarxism has to finally dissolve itself in bourgeois ideology altogether, or it has to rediscover its classical parentage. The way things are going, the former option appears to be the more likely one.

Notes

1. Nicos Poulantzas, "The Problem of the Capitalist State," in Robin Blackburn, ed., *Ideology in Social Science*, 1972, p. 239.
2. V. I. Lenin, *The State*, 1965, pp. 4-5.
3. Karl Marx, *The 18th Brumaire of Louis Bonaparte*, 1972, p. 105.
4. David Gold, Y. H. Lo, and E. O. Wright, "Recent Developments in Marxist Theories of the Capitalist State," *Monthly Review*, 5, Oct. 1975, pp. 29-43.
5. Offe's writings, as referred to here, are drawn from *Kapitalistate*, 1972 through 1974.
6. D. Gold, Y. H. Lo, and E. O. Wright, *Monthly Review*, 6, Nov. 1975, p. 45.
7. Ibid. p. 48.

8. Ibid.
9. Robert C. Tucker, in "Marx as a Political Theorist," in Shlomo Avineri, *Marx's Socialism*, 1973, p. 126.
10. Karl Marx, "Letter to Weydemeyer," London, 5th March, 1852, from Karl Marx and Friederich Engels: Letters in *Marx and Engels, Collected Works*, 1983, pp. 62-65.
11. Nicos Poulantzas, in Blackburn, op. cit., p. 241.
12. Karl Marx and Frederich Engels, *The German Ideology*, 1974, p. 80.
13. Gold, Lo, and Wright, op. cit., Nov. 1975, p. 42.
14. Paul Sweezy, *Theory of Capitalist Development*, 1970, p. 244.
15. Frederich Engels to Conrad Schmidt, London, 27th Oct., 1890, in *Karl Marx and Friederich Engels: Selected Correspondence, 1846-1895*.

THREE

~

POLITICAL ECONOMY AND POLICY: THE FOUNDATIONS OF CLASSICISM

...Ricardo's ruthlessness was not only *scientifically honest* but also scientific *necessity* from his point of view. But because of this it is also quite immaterial to him whether the advance of the productive forces slays landed property or workers. If this progress devalues the capital of the industrial bourgeoisie it is equally welcome to him. If the development of the productive power of labor halves the value of the existing fixed capital, what does it matter, says Ricardo. The productivity of human labor is doubled. Thus here is *scientific honesty*. Ricardo's conception is, on the whole, in the interests of the *industrial bourgeoisie*, only *because*, and *in so far as*, their interests coincide with those of production or the productive development of human labor. Where the bourgeoisie comes into conflict with this, he is just as *ruthless* toward it as he is at other times toward the proletariat and the aristocracy.
—K. Marx, *Theories of Surplus Value*, Part 2

7

The Riddle of Laissez-Faire: Tales of Ricardo

It is almost trite in the history of economics to maintain that the great policy legacy of the Ricardian period, if not all of classical economics, is the policy imperative of laissez-faire.[1] Indeed, this was the solid view of the period until twentieth-century revisionism, in the form of Robbins, Coats et al.,[2] argued the case for the classicals as what might be termed "enlightened interventionists"—thereby converting those nineteenth-century zealots into a variant of latter-day liberals. It turns out, however, that this latter view is itself quite unsustainable for ignoring the repeated references to the idea of laissez-faire in the works of the Ricardian period. Prima facie, then, it would appear that there is room for either a contradiction in Ricardian writings, or simply for sheer confusion propounded either by Ricardo or the latterday reviewers. Actually, the fundamental Ricardian point vis à vis laissez-faire has been missed by generations of writers on Ricardo for lack of a materialist, or rather a realist[3], understanding of what Ricardo was up to in that very turbulent period of English history between Waterloo and the repeal of the Corn Laws in 1846.

POLITICAL ECONOMY AND POLICY: THE FOUNDATIONS OF CLASSICISM

It has been quite customary, for instance, to maintain that no specific policy mission occupied the Ricardians such that one could systematically relate theoretical pronouncements to policy imperatives. This view was argued with a persistence, for instance, in Schumpeter,[4] that itself suggests an attempt to rewrite history. However, Ricardian political economy is almost the first textbook instance of a school of science explicitly rationalizing class politics. It is, of course, quite understandable that the mainstream critics are unlikely to admit the case for Ricardo as the champion of the industrial bourgeoisie, for, in one form or another, all of mainstream economics rationalizes the interests of industrial capitalism. While this is a trivial point made unnecessarily important by the persistent denial of it by the mainstream matters are rather curious when one realizes that even Marx held off, frequently, on this rather obvious charge of class partisanship. The reason for this is also quite simple: Marx saw himself as the heir—as the ultimate heir—of the classical tradition, such that Ricardo could then be regarded as a lumbering proto-Marxian.[5] This requirement was satisfied by two aspects of Ricardo's work: his adherence to some form of a "labor theory" of value, and his alleged insistence on the necessity of class conflict in capitalist society. Actually, Marx misread Ricardo—perhaps even deliberately—on both these scores. For Ricardo came to a theory of value (and not specifically the labor theory, to which he came later) by pure chance in trying to justify his so-called theory of distribution,[6] set up so as to blame landlords for all the ills of English capitalism. The struggle was between rents and profits, and Ricardo was anxious to obtain priority for the latter social income and the social order that lived off it. Even then, it was not the labor theory of value so much as a labor standard or measure that Ricardo was after, useful in comparing changes between agricultural and industrial values over time. The labor theory of value was embraced as part of his larger search for an "invariable standard," which alone could help him prove that the Corn Laws were actually depressing the general rate of profit, i.e. that the agricultural rate of profit helped pull down the general rate, such that landlords could be shown up as dastardly villains holding back the general progress (identified merrily with a rising profit share!) of society as a whole. This kind of instrumental use is of quite a different order, as Marx might have realized, than his own very different preoccupation connected with his toils in developing a theory of surplus value.

The Riddle of Laissez-Faire: Tales of Ricardo

On the other hand, the class conflict apparently embraced by Ricardo is also quite spurious. Ricardo repeatedly declared that, were the Corn Laws to be removed (and landlords put in their place), the rate of profit would be perpetually buoyant, leaving little scope for any conflict of interest between the various social orders. Thus, the admission of class conflict or, less grandiosely, the sectarian struggle between two factions of the ruling partnership (commercial and industrial) can hardly be taken to mean that Ricardo countenanced society as class divided, as in the Marxian sense. In fact, despite trying to beguile workers into the general agitation against landlords, Ricardo always counseled caution not to press matters too far; for, ultimately, the threat from below was seen as a greater threat than the struggle between the other two orders, based as they were on property ownership—albeit over differing means of production. The truth is rather simple, if surprising to some: Marx mistakenly credited Ricardo with achievements that he believed paralleled his own (but always, of course, in a lesser key!), so as to be the one who bettered the greatest (for so he was thought) of the classicals. Historically, this is a misjudgment; for much of the vaunted genius of Ricardo actually came as a reluctant response to the brilliantly incisive probings of Malthus,[7] that otherwise insufferably retrograde apologist for the landed interest. And, in this regard, Malthus, sad to say, has still not received his intellectual due for having been the great stimulator of the Ricardian intellectual enterprise.

~

At any rate, Ricardo simply cannot be understood until the Ricardian policy mission is charted in its entirety. While the real history of this policy crusade is intricate, the overall agenda can nonetheless be summarized here in a paragraph.[8] After Waterloo, with Napoleon safely placed on an indefinite sabbatical, the agrarian and industrial orders withdrew their self-imposed curbs imposed by virtue of the impending threat from France, and battled it out in as many forums as were to be found available. This incidentally accounts for the 1815 timing of Ricardo's *Essay on Profits*. From the manufacturers' point of view, there were now but three issues that stood in the way of England becoming the workshop and foundry of the world: the Poor Laws,[9] for having impaired capitalist work incentives in the rural countryside, thereupon affecting both the mobility and availability of "hands"; the Corn Laws,[10] for preventing import of cheap corn—thereby raising domestic wages (or so it was believed by industrial employers)—and for serving as a prime obstacle against the emergence of a foreign market for domestically manufactured industrial goods; and, lastly, the Reform question, for the denial of franchise to major manufacturing towns and the manufacturing interest, generally, on account of the stranglehold over both houses of Parliament exercised by the landed aristocracy, which thereby prevented the shaping of economic policy in accord with industrial interests.

All of these three major issues engaged the Ricardians to the hilt. The entire Ricardian model was constructed—artificially—to build an ironclad case against the Corn Laws (as Winch[11] puts it succinctly with respect to the *Principles* of 1817, it was "an ingenious attack on the Corn Laws writ large"), such that all of Ricardian theory was directed to achieve this simple policy end. On the other hand, all of Ricardian political attentions were concentrated on achieving reform of the franchise—for which purpose Ricardo actually purchased a seat in the Commons. Even given the rather pragmatic history of the economics profession, it is still altogether rare to see a policy compulsion so totally enveloping a theoretical project as in Ricardo's case. It forms, accordingly, almost the textbook case of theory as a simple restatememt of policy. But the price of this kind of practical theory—eminently successful in its time—could only be a sudden historical irrelevance once the policy crusades had been won. Accordingly, Ricardian "economics" died a rapid and inglorious death once the Reform Act had been passed in 1832, with repeals of the Corn and Poor Laws following, as correctly anticipated by Ricardo.

There should no longer be any mystery, therefore, as to the rationale for the sudden extinction of the Ricardian model: it was slain by its own practical success. Having been constructed piece by piece to serve a limited purpose, it became gloriously useless once the purpose had been consummated. Practical success, in economics—as with the instructive case of Keynes—is no guarantee of lasting theoretical endurance. In this respect, both the mainstream account of the displacement of Ricardian economics and the Marxian version are misleading and false. Schumpeter,[12] for instance, argued that Ricardo had been replaced because true theory, i.e. marginal utility theory, supplanted the false Ricardian labor theory. This would imply that the truth always wins out against falsity, a rather naive view of paradigm change in the social sciences where historical appropriateness to a given task as defined by a given rank within a given social order—rather than any abstract truth value—is the ultimate warrant of sufferance, shortlived as that might yet be.

The Marxians,[13] on the other hand, have argued as if a class-conscious conspiracy on the part of the bourgeoisie suppressed Ricardo for being too radical by far in his alleged embrace of class conflict and the labor theory. This vulgar explanation fails because it smacks of pure voluntarism, such that a self-conscious attempt on the part of a sectarian group to reorient science actually wins out. Historical materialism, in fact, suggests otherwise: paradigms rise and fall because they are generated by material conditions, changing when those material conditions themselves change.

The historical irrelevance of Ricardo after 1846 (when the Corn Laws were repealed) is, therefore, more consistent with the original Marxian inspiration than the pseudoMarxian explanation that has reigned in the works of Meek and Dobb, et al., albeit inspired by Marx himself in a prefatorial statement made in 1873 in an Afterword to the second German edition of *Capital*,[14] suggesting that, with the maturation of the class struggle after 1830, "genuine scientific research" was replaced by the "evil intent" of apologetic, vulgar economy. The implicit suggestion in this account that admittedly bourgeois "science" (i.e. the phase of Ricardian political economy) could, nonetheless, be devoid of any "apologetic" or nonscientific intent is problematic in the extreme, given Marx's own development of a general theory of ideology. What then is the possible meaning of attaching the term "bourgeois" to writers like Ricardo, in Marx's own usage, if not to mark it out as something less than ideal with respect to a notion of proper science? To state the matter bluntly, Marx did not always function as a "Marxist" (and, indeed, this is true by his own rather famous, if not always respected, admission). At any rate, however this issue might be resolved, the far simpler hypothesis remains: that Ricardo's interest in "science" was limited entirely to his antipathy to the Corn Laws, and to his strong interest in sustained capital accumulation. Very specific policy concerns predetermined his scientific inquiries and ultimately constrained his "findings," or the consequences of the research program. If this be not "apologetics," then neither is it "science" in any acceptable sense of the term.

POLITICAL ECONOMY AND POLICY: THE FOUNDATIONS OF CLASSICISM

What, then, are we to make of laissez-faire? Once the policy parameters are scaled in, in the manner suggested, the unravelment is fairly painless. Ricardo found himself pitted against a paternalist, protectionist state in the clutches of a late aristocracy, commercially minded but jealous of its role as custodian of all orders of society. Both the Poor Laws and the Corn Laws were examples, it will be noted, of forms of protectionism albeit considered perverse forms of the same by the industrial middle orders. Bear in mind, however, that the Poor Laws and the Corn Laws "protected" wages and rents, respectively—what the industrial bourgeois were demanding was a similar protection, but for profits: laissez-faire objectively, therefore, is simply the withdrawal of support for all incomes other than profits, of all obstacles to capital accumulation. After all, the state as constituted was the preserve of landlords who looked askance at the growing power of industrial wealth unconnected to traditional landed property and to any traditional notions of a social compact.

Of course, the industrial middle classes had no use for a state hostile to their interests: in this sense, laissez-faire was a defensive slogan protecting the manufacturers from interference by a landlord state (not a principle, then, but a practical necessity). But there was more subtlety to this. Both the Poor Laws and the Corn Laws were being viewed as examples of protectionism (we have already seen how these laws were thought to be affecting industrial capital): what could be better than the slogan of laissez-faire, by which token the Poor Laws and the Corn Laws could each be delegitimized as representing violations of an abstract principle, rather than as affecting negatively the selfish class interest of the manufacturers?! So, laissez-faire was the rapier used to slay the "perverse" protection offered the poor and the landlords by a state beholden to the latter. The point could not be simpler: Ricardo could have no qualms about a state that could be expected to assist in capital accumulation via the primacy of profits, but he could not tolerate intervention from a state resting in the wrong hands: hence, he both meant and did not mean laissez-faire![15] If laissez-faire is understood in terms of the policies outlined above, it will become clear how unerringly right Professor Letwin[16] was when he wrote that the Ricardians were prone to "view economic theory as a particularly elegant way of demonstrating the merits of laissez-faire" and that, in effect, is all that Ricardian theory amounts to. It was not a guileless, innocent theory that then, of a sudden, pointed to a policy directive seized upon by the less scrupulous, as some would have us think (see, for instance, the work of Grampp, 1960, 1965 in this regard); it was that a prior, preconceived policy bias dictated the shape and direction of theory construction. Grasping this simple insight is fundamental to stripping the many veils shrouding Ricardian discourse.

This point is extremely instructive, and not just in terms of an understanding of Ricardo. Economics has always been a material, practical science of social engineering, not an abstract science inquiring dispassionately into the eternal verities of the economic order. And yet, its practical agenda has always been cloaked in a mantle of generalities in order to better achieve its hegemony over interests opposed to its policy goals. Thus, Ricardian economics triumphed over landlord-based political economy (Malthus) and the "political economy of the poor"[17] (as Senior contemptuously called the work of Hodgskin and Thompson), even while pretending to high, nonsectarian principles. It is the function of critical political economy to take the emperor's abstract theoretical garments off to reveal the very practical corpus within. And so it is with Ricardo. Ricardian laissez-faire was: (a) a hands-off call to an enemy state; but, more positively, (b) it was a positive call to the correctly organized bourgeois state to do its utmost to assure both capital accumulation and the welfare of the capitalists. Ricardo did not live to oversee item (b) on the agenda but, with Keynes, we should now understand fully well that true laissez-faire encompasses all manner of remedial interventions. The bourgeois, as Marx once wrote, have no principles—save that of deriding all principles. The fact that today Eastern bloc Marxists have been revealed, regrettably, to be not at all dissimilar does not by even a whit alter that judgment.

Notes

1. It is this popular perception that is repeated by J. M. Keynes in *Essays in Persuasion*, 1972, pp. 274-275.
2. L. Robbins, *The Theory of Economic Policy*, 1953; A. W. Coats, ed., *The Classical Economists and Economic Policy*, 1971.
3. Realism is a developing new philosophy for the human sciences which, in many respects, transcends a simple Marxian perspective. See, for instance, the work of R. Bhaskar, *Reclaiming Reality*, 1989.

4. J. A. Schumpeter, *History of Economic Analysis*, 1954.

5. Marx tended to write the history of economic thought in such a way as to make his own work the culmination—in the theory of surplus value—of centuries of previous scholarship; in so doing, attention has been drawn away, in an ahistorical fashion, from the independent preoccupations—given by time and place—of Smith, Ricardo, and others.

6. It should be noted the Ricardo had worked out, to his own satisfaction, a theory of distribution prior to any thinking about a theory of value; for a lucid account of the early Ricardo, see T. Peach, "David Ricardo's Early Treatment of Profitability: A New Interpretation," *Economic Journal*, 94, 1984, pp. 733-751.

7. Malthus's contributions to Ricardian political economy have constituted the unwritten chapter in all accounts of the classical period. Keynes did recognize Malthus's insights, but for quite the wrong reasons. A brilliant account of Malthusian criticisms of Ricardo is to be found in the yet unpublished work of Terry Peach, especially a paper entitled "Ricardo and the Invariable Standard," presented to the English History of Economics Conference, Manchester, Sept. 1987.

8. For detail, see R. K. Kanth, *Political Economy and Laissez Faire*, 1986; also R. Kanth, "The Decline of Ricardian Politics" *European Journal of Political Economy*, 1/2, 1985, pp. 157-187. On the Social Foundations of Ricardianism, see R. K. Kanth, "The Material Foundations of Political Economy" in Kanth and Hunt, eds., *Explorations in Political Economy*, 1990.

9. For an account of the involvement of political economy in the anti-Poor Law agitation, see R. G. Cowherd, *Political Economists and the English Poor Laws*, 1978.

10. The classic story of the English anti-Corn Law movement is to be found in D. G. Barnes, *A History of the English Corn Laws, 1660-1846*, 1961.

11. D. Winch, "Introduction," in Ricardo, *On the Principles of Political Economy and Taxation*, 1974, p. vii.

12. Schumpeter, op cit., 1954.

13. See R. L. Meek, "The Decline of Ricardian Economics in England," *Economica*, n.s., 17, 1950, pp. 43-62; and M. Dobb, *Theories of Value and Distribution Since Adam Smith*, 1973.

14. K. Marx, *Capital*, Vol. I, 1967, pp. 24-25.

15. It is this historical duality that has been completely misread by almost all standard accounts of the issue.

16. W. Letwin, *The Origins of Scientific Economics*, 1964, p. v.

17. T. Hodgskin, *Labor Defended Against the Claims of Capital*, 1964; W. Thompson, *Inquiring Into the Principles of the Distribution of Wealth*, 1963.

8

The Demise of Ricardianism: Some Theses on Ricardo

After Kuhn,[1] a pseudo-sociology of knowledge approach has gained ground in mainstream discussions within the area of what has come to be termed "paradigm-shift" in the sciences. In point of fact, of course, the "sociology" is completely subjectivist, individualist, and rationalist, suggesting that there is, in the social sciences, clearly demarcable "progress" between paradigms, measurable analytically, although for diverse "sociological" (this being, in fact, social psychology rather than sociology) reasons various individual scientists either withhold or proffer their support, depending on circumstances, for the nouvelle critique. This is a tidy little hermeneutic[2] tale; but one that offers only a descriptive videotape of the rites of passage in ideational systems, without any analytical supports purporting to explain the transitions involved. The failure is one of deftly divaricating science from its real social basis, of stripping the politics from class society and presenting scientific models as though they bore total autonomy from social struggles. This, of course, represents an idealist deviation from reality; in fine complement, there is a materialist variant of this position as well, with Althusser, where science is similarly sanitized, freed from praxis.

At any rate, the reality of class struggles in class society upsets this fairy tale quite dramatically. Indeed there is no single grand tradition of economic theorizing, only different schools preoccupied with different issues studied from different (class) points of view. The rise and fall is

POLITICAL ECONOMY AND POLICY: THE FOUNDATIONS OF CLASSICISM

not, primarily, one of theory, but rather one of issues, modes of production, and classes: e.g., Malthusian ideas "failed" in the struggle with Ricardo not because they were "wrong" (indeed, it was Malthus's acutely perceptive critique of Ricardo that pushed the latter to yet further complex heights of theory construction), but because the landlords failed as a class to win victory over manufacturers. Thus, the Kuhnian model is dead wrong if applied uncritically to the social sciences: schools are not replaced by others by virtue of superior explanatory frameworks, but by altered material conditions. Analytical "progress," accordingly, may only be measured unequivocally within schools, but not between them, since both objects of analysis and perceiving subjects are likely to be different. A careful reading of the real Ricardian agenda, in this context, places an interpretation on the issues of political economy as a science, and the ultimate eclipse of Ricardo, for instance, that differs not only from a Kuhnian reconstruction but also from a conventional Marxian analysis. Let us consider, by way of illustration, the following arguments drawn from my own study[3] of the fall of the House of Ricardo.

Contrary to traditional "Marxist" accounts, I have argued that Ricardian economics was not "dumped" for its radical overtones (as in the Dobb and Meek reading) by class-conscious neoclassicals, but because it became practically irrelevant after the success of the Ricardian cause. The Ricardian model, bereft of the Corn Laws, is no model at all. As Ricardo himself makes clear, the removal of the Laws, coupled with free importation, makes for uninterrupted accumulation with no necessary conflict of interest between different classes; the rate of profit is, henceforth, perpetually buoyant: that is to say, the Ricardian model became politically obsolete and expired, one might say, quite naturally. To believe that Ricardian theory was set aside for ideological reasons by scheming economists is to subscribe involuntarily to both idealism and voluntarism, where social ideologies are the product of conspiracies that can succeed regardless of material conditions. Rather, ideology is the product of material conditions and cannot, for long, outlast changes therein. Ricardian theory was not the inspired conspiracy of some loosely organized social platform; it expressed concretely the struggle of industrial capitalism against the last vestiges of the political economy of the landlords—and therein lay its historically limited relevance.

To dispose of another enduring myth, Ricardo was not more scientific, in some rarefied sense, than the so-called apologists that followed, as

Marx upon occasion hinted. His rigor, while admirable, was ultimately *spurious*, and the mere adoption of the labor theory of value should not be grounds enough to constitute the difference between scientists and apologists (Marxian enthusiasm for the theory of surplus value notwithstanding), there being a lot more to classical political economy than merely a theory of value.

It is, similarly, *not true* that political economy is a science only so long as the class struggle is latent, as Marx apparently thought, in what might well have been a throwaway remark: the neutrality of science and even its correctness was as doubtful in the case of Ricardo as later, when the class struggle is allegedly considered to have become more manifest. Indeed, the historical fact that Luddites were active even before Ricardo set off on his theoretical quests gives the lie to the idea of the *latency* of the class struggle in early nineteenth century England. Of course, the Ricardian period was of tremendous significance in the social history of England, being the decisive stage in the struggle to establish the supremacy of industrial capital; and the Ricardian school—vastly more so than Smithian economics[4]—was directly involved in the transformation of England in an industrial capitalist direction, constituting, in fact, the principal intellectual vanguard of that class.[5] To see Ricardo as suffering from any class innocence, in this regard, therefore, is patent nonsense.

It is quite revealing, to turn to another dimension, to see how the different mainstream traditions in economics, all the way from their Smithian inception, investigate essentially different objects of analysis as given by evolving capitalist reality: Ricardo-distribution, Jevons-allocation, Keynes-employment, and so on, but all from a common class point of view of the custodians of capitalist society. So neoclassical economic theory—at best—is neither more apologetic nor even less "correct" than Ricardo's speculations: they *all bring a similar intent, but applied to a distinctly different problem*. Being axiomatic systems, in the main, their "truth" is contained in their fundamental premises, which reflect, as they must, the vantage point of the ruling class. As Marx once wrote, the ruling ideology is the ideology of the ruling class; and the "science" of economics fits well within that general cast. Indeed, it would be surprising if it did not. Ultimately—although this may not be of intrinsic interest—this "reading" vindicates the broader Marxian method of historical materialism, no matter how much it may be at odds with putatively "Marxian" theories, and some statements of Marx himself.

Ricardo's example is also instructive as to the uses (and abuses) of the so-called hypothetico-deductive method that has, for the longest time, dominated the discipline. The premises of Ricardo so thoroughly overdetermined his theoretical conclusions that to place assumptions above reproach, as with Friedman,[6] is to rationalize, uncritically, at the very doorstep of science, a priori politics: a methodological predilection that, at the very ground floor, reneges on scientific responsibility. Assumptions are the keys to the scientific kingdom in the social sciences. Their realism (or lack of it) is too important an issue to be simply sidestepped in favor of some predictive or other instrumental capability that a model may be shown to have, *despite counterfactual tendencies known to be contained at the very inception of the analysis*. The economists' strength, as someone pointed out with reference to the Ricardians, lay directly proportionate to their distance from the facts. The tendentious nature of the Ricardian enterprise possibly demanded a certain skepticism toward contradictory evidence. But the Ricardian evasion was not a virtue then; and it must not be allowed such a status now.

Although as clever a political economist as any before or since, this reading of Ricardo does soften some of the more exaggerated compliments often paid to the high "science" of Ricardo, usually, but not exclusively, in the Marxian tradition. In fact, it is quite astonishing how influenced even mainstream history of thought traditions are by the original Marxian essays in *The Theories of Surplus Value*. Aside from the obvious logical rigor (although equally matched by an awesome obtuseness, not usually commented upon, as represented in his tortuous exercises over the "invariable" standard) and the general aura of *scienticity* enveloping Ricardo's work, it is his embrace of the labor theory, and his apparent attachment to the notion of class conflict, that endears him to Marx. However, Marx both overestimated and misread Ricardo's attachments to these ideas: the ultimate Ricardian vision of capitalism is *not* one of a society rent hopelessly by class conflict, but quite a harmonious utopia. As Ricardo put it, economic progress is checked only by "the scarcity and consequent high value of food and other raw produce," with free trade, i.e. cheap imports of corn, "...it is difficult to know where the limit is at which you would cease to accumulate wealth" (Ricardo, 1951-73, 4, p. 179; see also Blaug, 1958, p. 33), so long as workers submitted to Malthusian laws of nature and both workers and landlords submitted, equally mildly, to the laws authored by a manufacturer-led

The Demise of Ricardianism: Some Theses on Ricardo

Parliament. Moreover, the antithesis between science and ideology, usually sustained in the Marxian tradition, falters if applied to the Ricardian case. Taking Ricardo as the scientist and Ms. Martineau as the vulgar ideologue, for instance—not far from how history has perceived them, it would appear that, in this case, science and ideology were quite complementary, differing only in their being addressed as a discourse to different audiences, to the literati, in the first instance, and to the masses in the other. Both of them, however, shared identical premises and support similar policies, *differing only in how they move from premise to policy, i.e. in the mode of argument*. Neither, it will be remembered, would brook any refutation, either on theoretical or empirical grounds. So, in this case, it would appear that science was merely formalized ideology, whereas ideology was simply popularized science. Two different languages, but, nevertheless, delivering the same message.

Interestingly, the ordinary interpretation of the famous addition to the chapter "On Machinery," as representative only of Ricardian candor and intellectual honesty, might have a far simpler explanation (one that nonetheless does not detract from the common insinuation of the incorruptible integrity of Ricardo) than is normally advanced. Now both mainstream and Marxist scholarship are convinced of the intellectual integrity of Ricardo, in admitting that the introduction of machinery is detrimental to the interests of the working class. For instance, Pasinetti[7] believes that, "...the chapter 'On Machinery' appears...an honest acknowledgment by Ricardo of the limitations of this theory"; in a similar vein, Rubin[8] holds that "with his great, and characteristic honesty and scientific candor...he acknowledged that...machinery is often injurious to the interests of the class of laborers.

In so focusing on the science of Ricardo, *perhaps they fail to appreciate the political significance of the chapter "On Machinery"*: consider that it is this chapter which finally clinched the Ricardian argument that the interest of landlords is opposed to all other interests. To explain: the declining net product spells declining rates of profit even as rents rise, so the issue of the diametrically opposed interests of the landlords and manufacturing capitalists was, plain to see, the consequence of restriction of importation of foodstuffs compelling recourse to marginal lands. However, why did the Corn Laws necessarily disadvantage the *working class*—aside from the threat of the stationary state, which would put an end to all accumulation, presumably a long-run eventuality in the model since constant real wages leave workers materially unaffected in the Corn Model, with or without the Laws? It is the chapter "On Machinery" that securely links the Corn Laws with the *short run*—i.e. the *immediate*—unemployment and dis-tress of the working class, suggesting that it was the high price of food that (through its stimulus to wages) *was making inevitable the greater substitution of fixed for circulating capital.* (So the Luddites, in reality, were not merely the victims of the normal progress of a mechanized, capitalized society, but the special victims of an *abnormal* speed-up of mechanization engineered by the existence of the Corn Laws.) Ricardo is quick to point out that he is not objecting to technical progress as such—for he could hardly be unaware that this process would survive unchanged after the repeal of the Laws—but merely to the forced pace owing to abnormal conditions, *conditions which could, at least, be temporarily avoided if the price of food were to sink lower than it was.*

So the irresistible implication was that the landlords, in the very short run, distress both workers and capitalists through their insistence on the Laws. The integrity of Ricardo went well beyond the personal—the holy book was to leave no exit possible for the defenders of the English *ancien régime*: the chapter "On Machinery" closed a gap through which the workers might, otherwise, easily have slipped out of the ranks of the general mobilization.

This kind of practical understanding of the design of a model prevents the expression of naive deductions from apparently abstract models by those who fail to understand (knowingly or otherwise) their real purpose. A scheme instrumental to one purpose is then taken out of context, whether to defend or to attack the model, the entire exercise being one of splendid irrelevance. Just one instance in this comment, by Pasinetti:

> At the beginning of the ninteenth century, the Ricardian theory...was a remarkable step forward in the evolution of economic thought. When reconsidered more than a century and a half later, it obviously reveals many shortcomings and deficiencies...Many of Ricardo's pessimistic conclusions have not been borne out by the economic history of the industrial countries.[9]

Obviously, Professor Pasinetti has not understood the purposive pessimism of Ricardo, and sees it as a model applicable, in general, to "the economic history of the industrial countries"; not seeing the

The Demise of Ricardianism: Some Theses on Ricardo

specificity, the model is universalized and then, obviously, faulted. Now, the relevance of Ricardo to the present stage of capitalism is a problematic issue. In a simple sense, his model, constructed on faulty premises, has *no application whatsoever*—no more in our period than in his own. However, in many third world contexts, where agrarian capital is pitted against industrial capital, replicating the English experience of the early nineteenth century, his struggles will be well understood, and perhaps his false theorems might even be invoked. Marx, of course, understood the Ricardian problematic well when he wrote that, under certain conditions, private property in land is an obstacle to economic growth and, in particular, to industrialization. Certainly, the struggle in postrevolutionary Russia between the Kulaks and the state's repressive resolve for accelerated industrialization was, strikingly, a repetition of the Ricardian struggle. At issue then, as in Ricardian times, was the relative prices of agricultural and manufactured goods (corn versus cotton, in the Ricardian period). Partisans of industrialization—Ricardo as much as Trotsky—were out to subordinate agriculture to industry in order to provide cheap raw materials for industry. However, the issue must be treated with care, for it cannot simply be assumed, a priori, that high agricultural prices, i.e. agrarian prosperity, is inimical to either economic growth or industrialization. It is all a matter of context, and the time frame. Perhaps it might be said that, in the very short run, high farm prices might inhibit infant industrialization efforts, but in the longer run it might provide both the surpluses and the demand for industry. So the paths chosen by Ricardo and Stalin need not be thought of as the *only* ones. *Private property in land, contra Marx, need not be an obstacle to industrialization.*

Returning to Ricardian prognostications, the stationary state, as Professor Blaug has wisely reminded the student of Ricardo, was only a "methodological fiction to scare the friends of protection"; it is not a pessimistic anticipation of the course of an ideal capitalism. Indeed, the opposite is true, for the stationary state, as we know, is brought on by the Corn Laws, and in fact turns progressive with free importation. The dangers of generalizing other Ricardian theorems run similarly, and consequently the effort ought to be abandoned. The neoRicardian fashion of demonstrating the truth of the proposition that the profit rate is, in general, dependent upon the conditions of production of wage goods is pure makeshift, for it rests upon assumptions as dubious as those assumed by Ricardo himself. Similarly, the Sraffian distinction between basic and nonbasic goods is purely a definitional issue bearing no obvious connection with reality. Sraffian model-building—the so-called neoRicardianism—in this respect is, practically speaking, as superbly irrelevant as neoclassical architectonics.

Ricardo had the good sense to write theory in service of a cause that excited him; we might do well to emulate his high sense of purpose! The consistency between paradigm and policy is too obvious to be credibly denied in the case of Ricardo, but more importantly his theory was an elaborate rationalization for policy, i.e. it was policy objectives that prompted the theoretical construction. Still the *Kontrartheorie* would speak otherwise, as in the opinion of Tribe (1978, p. 146), who argues that "It would be quite erroneous...to conceive this remobilization of theoretical statements into political argument as the causal (sic) *raison d'être* of these statements." At least as applied to Ricardo, however, the thesis of the independence of theory from policy is pure delusion.

In conclusion, I wish to quote Toynbee,[10] who, marveling at Ricardo's finesse in logic, philosophized that "...systems are strong not in proportion to the accuracy of their premises, but to the perfection of their reasoning," even while wondering at the "curious" contrast in Ricardo between the "looseness and unreality of the premises...and the closeness and vigor of the argument." Actually, both these facets indicate something quite contrary to Toynbee's observation: that systems are strong not in relation to either the accuracy of their premises or the perfection of their reasoning, but in relation to their ability to answer to the practical needs of the time. Both the success and the failure of Ricardo hinged upon this rather trivial, but sometimes forgotten, fact. For social science, arguably, is generated by social purpose and mediated by social interests; its findings, usually, are axiomatically true, i.e. true by definition, assuming away the existence of internal inconsistency. Most of the time, however, we, as part of the scientific establishment, are occupied in tracing aspects internal to paradigms,[11] either to improve or to prove them defective. Occasionally, it is enlightening to glance at the social purposes being rationalized by these elegant edifices, for this illuminates a different kind of raison d'etre, one existing in a dimension external to theory. The strength of a paradigm may then be seen to derive not merely from its correspondence with reality, but by its consonance, also, with practical, social necessity.

The Demise of Ricardianism: Some Theses on Ricardo

It is this instrumental nature of social science which renders it a social project, to be judged as critically as any—and all—social institutions. The a priori halo of purity often surrounding "science"—usually the construct of the beneficiaries themselves, i.e. the scientists, something that peaked in England during the Ricardian era—needs to be dimmed with far more skepticism than we commonly allow. For social science shifts gears and paradigms change as social struggles and social relations restructure themselves. Ultimately, all theory—like the Ricardian—bears the patent of transience as new problems render the old archaic. Any notion of scientific continuity, thereby, in the evolution of the many schools of economic policy and theory, is possibly both chimerical and delusive. The insights of previous scholarship, engaged in problems and policies past, are then, in ridiculous teleology, seen as fumbling, incomplete anticipations of today's conventional wisdoms. In the social sciences, the last marginal increment of knowledge does not represent the pinnacle of an absolutely given truth, but only an intuition relative to our own preoccupations. The truth is that, from Smith to Keynes, economics has always been a series of rather submissive offerings to the jealous god of practical relevance.

Notes

1. T. S. Kuhn, 1962.
2. As Bhaskar writes, "...Kuhn...[cannot] explain how there can be a clash between incommensurable descriptions, or say over what such descriptions clash" (1986, p. 2).
3. See Kanth, 1986.
4. Smith's straightforward disparagement of merchants and manufacturers might be taken as a simple repudiation of his allegiance to industrial capital in any direct sense; however, it remains true that his insistence on laissez-faire, by delegitimizing landlord and merchant control over the state, indirectly—*with the help of Ricardian interpretations of the idea*—paved the way for the triumph of industrial capital.
5. To treat the Ricardian system as the ideology of manufacturers would seem trivially obvious, until one confronts the fact that this connection is always disguised in mainstream theorizing—as, for instance, in Grampp (1960). A far more sophisticated veil of discretion is

drawn over the subject by M. Blaug, (1958a), in a work which remains one of the clearest treatments of the entire Ricardian oeuvre.

6. M. Friedman, 1953.
7. L. Pasinetti, 1977, p. 21.
8. I. Rubin, 1978, p. 239.
9. L Pasinetti, op. cit., p. 17.
10. A. Toynbee, 1920.
11. Traditionally, commentators—Marxist or mainstream—on the Ricardo question have taken what I term the "internal" view of the paradigm; the work of Dobb, Sraffa, and, more recently, Bharadwaj (1983) are cases in point—their work, among other things, points to the "surplus" emphasis in Ricardo (Ricardo being seen as the most important forerunner of Marx). While this approach has its merits, it usually fails to grasp the larger connections between theory and society.

9
~
Political Economy and Policy:
The Malthus-Ricardo Embroilment

The extraordinary neglect of Malthus in histories of political economy, outside of discussions pertaining to demography and ecology, is a significant indicator of the intrusion of ideological considerations in most economic narratives which, routinely, can only pretend to pedestrian renderings of a rather straightforward, if somewhat antiquated, divide in the history of the discipline. Both Marxist and mainstream primers in the history of economic thought—unfailingly reliable indicators of prevailing academic orthodoxy—routinely omit a chapter on Malthus; see, by way of confirmation, the texts of Dobb, Ekelund, Blaug, and Rubin, about as wide a spectrum of opinion as can be imagined. The prevalence of grid readings and teleological accounts which, anachronistically, view the past history of the subject through the newest lens discovered—as though the marginal increment of knowledge were indeed the most significant one!—have all but guaranteed a certain *rigor mortis* to the discipline, beset as it is with the deep running fault of pro and contra capitalist debate. It is this, largely undeclared, war of perspectives that has doomed Malthus to either share the allotted lot of a grand satan whose writings constitute a "libel on the human race," as Marx had it, or to be quietly ignored, disparaged by neglect, on matters considered central to political economy proper. There has been, of course, a third categorization, far more favorable to Malthus if foredoomed to remain a minority view, in which he is asked to don unexpected robes as the true fountainhead of a "correct" political economy—if only tradition had heeded the truth—as Keynes was to eulogize him decades later: "If only Malthus, instead of

POLITICAL ECONOMY AND POLICY: THE FOUNDATIONS OF CLASSICISM

Ricardo, had been the parent stem from which...economics proceeded, what a much wiser and richer place the world would be today!" (Keynes, 1972, pp. 100-101.)

In either case, the real, historical Malthus has been shoved aside, unrecognized and unknown for the real part he played in the development of Ricardian political economy, which took its lead from Malthus almost as much as opposing him in the grand political struggle between the aristocracies of land and capital that was the key setting for the period (and ideas) of both Malthus and Ricardo. This paper is addressed to the issue of this alarming historical indiscretion, not with a view to encapsulating the overall genius of Malthus in his many capacities as theorist, polemicist, and apologist for special interests (attributes that Ricardo shared, it is not always recognized, in equivalent measure), but only to commence the effort of a necessary rethinking of these matters, an effort freed from the constricting grids emanating from either of the two grand traditions represented by Marx and Ricardo, and their several epigones, respectively.

~

As argued earlier, practical policy objectives inspired the principal "theoretical" pronouncements of classical economics in the Ricardian period, with theory serving merely as a formal restatement of prior policy initiatives. As Letwin put it succinctly, the Ricardians were prone to "view economic theory as a particularly elegant way of demonstrating the merits of laissez-faire" (Letwin, 1964, p. v). In this dubious struggle, with politics masquerading as science, it was Malthus who, in his 1798 *Essay on Population*,[1] written as a fierce rejoinder to the 1795 Declaration of the magistracy of Berkshire (called the "Speenhamland Amendment" to the Elizabethan Poor Laws) and its follow-through, Pitt's Poor Law Reform Bill of 1796, initiated the intellectual battle—and hence the era—that was subsequently to be taken up by the Ricardian enthusiasts. In histories of thought, Malthus's *Essay on Population* is usually presented as an attack on the radical egalitarianism of William Godwin, although the truth—while certainly inclusive of that assertion—is a trifle more complex). Actually (and this is a matter little known), however, the 1798 diatribe was preceded by a pamphlet—which Malthus was not, eventually, to publish—entitled *The Crisis* and penned in 1797 (see the anonymous memoir of Malthus in Malthus's *Principles*,[2] 1836, p. xxxv), directed exclusively against the measures of William Pitt, particularly as these pertained to poor relief. Thus, the *Essay* itself may be viewed as merely the ultimate extension, more fully specified, of Malthus's earlier polemic, one in which the opposition to public relief—welfare—is extended dramatically to encompass a fierce rejection of any and all alternatives to a class-dominated, hierarchical society (read this to mean, of course, England). In Malthus's own words, "...the principal argument of this *Essay* only goes to prove the necessity of a class of proprietors and a class of laborers..." (*1798 Essay*, p. 177).

The issue, broached by Speenhamland, was simplicity itself. The rural squirearchy, enlightened by the dreaded example of the French Revolution, had decided that they were not willing to risk anarchy and revolt in their constituencies, facing famine, dearth, and commercial crises, as they did with increasing severity in the latter quarter of the eighteenth century. Setting aside the justly termed "Laws Against the Poor," they recognized the right of the poor to public relief, with the extent of relief tied to the price of corn. It was this act of enlightened statesmanship (to be derided as "paternalism" by hostile critics with axes of their own to grind) that was seen as an abomination by manufacturers and their intellectual allies, the political economists, for killing the "incentive" to labor—i.e. for blunting the cutting edge of starvation, and for raising the tax burden on profits. As Ricardo was to write in his *Principles*,[3] the poor rates are a "tax which falls with peculiar weight on the profits of the farmer...it will be a general tax on the profits of stock..." (Ricardo: *Works*, vol. I, p. 257) from which, it was assumed, all taxes were ultimately paid. Less public spirited—and more bourgeois minded—landlords, no doubt, similarly felt that the cost of the poor rates exceeded their social benefit.

Evangelical humanitarians, and people of goodwill nationwide, supported this sanction of charity (see Cowherd, 1956, 1978, for more on this), and for a while their christian and moral arguments carried public sentiment with them. A pastor himself, Malthus well understood the power of these sentiments. They could only be checked by appeal to sterner imperatives than the dictates of conscience: the laws of nature ("These laws...appear to have been fixed laws of our nature..." *1798 Essay*, p. 70; and further, "I see no way by which man can escape from the weight of this law..." *1798 Essay*, p. 72)—which of course, as he would go on to preach, were the laws of God ("...we turn our eyes to the book of

POLITICAL ECONOMY AND POLICY: THE FOUNDATIONS OF CLASSICISM

nature, where alone we can read God as he is..." *1798 Essay*, p. 201. Malthus's reading, of course, confirmed readily that "the Being...arranged the system of the universe...according to fixed laws," 1798 *Essay*, pp. 70-71. The *Essay* was ostensibly written to "vindicate the ways of God to man" (p. 200). Malthus was, of course, quite certain that he had accomplished this task. As he writes, "...the principle of population, instead of being inconsistent with (divine) revelation, must be considered as affording strong additional proofs of its truth" (1830 *Summary View of the Principle of Population*, reprinted in Malthus, 1970, p. 272).

Malthus's position as christian minister was, in fact, of critical significance in the public image, for "Parson Malthus" could not, accordingly, be viewed as "unchristian," despite his invocation of the laws of the jungle in the treatment of human—i.e. social—adversity. "The sorrows and distresses of life," he was to write, blithely, "...soften and humanize the heart...[and] generate all the christian virtues..." (1798 *Essay*, p. 209). And his appeal to science suited the fashion of the times, an age (still) of Newton (the specific adulation of the grand and consistent theory of Newton may be found on pages 126 and 163 of the 1798 *Essay*), Hume, and positivism ("...experience, the true source and foundation of all knowledge," *1798 Essay*, p. 72; and this prepossession was not abandoned even later: "...we wish, with M. Say, to make political economy a positive science, founded on experience..." Malthus, *Principles*, p. 33). Malthus's claims for his science were inexorable indeed: they were, no less, "incontrovertible truths" (*1798 Essay*, p. 80). It is small wonder, then, as to the centrality of "mathematical propositions" (those daunting, but dubious, ratios!; see the *Essay*, pp. 74-76) in the spurious, if powerfully suggestive, argument made in the *Essay*, to the effect that the power of propagation must exceed—except for intervening catastrophe—productivity in agriculture (and this in a country the envy of Europe, one that had come through a successful agricultural revolution in both the social and technical senses!).

Ignoring the specious logic (confusing fecundity with fertility, to name merely one issue)—and never mind that Keynes was to offer praise in this regard to Malthus's finesse for what he would call, thereby raising an obvious error to the status of a methodological precept!, "inductive verification"—the wild extrapolations (the doubling of population every twenty-five years and so on), the policy message, at least, was irresistibly clear: any welfare provided the poor would only increase their numbers, and hence the overall magnitude of wretchedness. Instead, it was more humanitarian (christian?) to simply let nature take its course, thereby adjusting optimal numbers to available capacity. Malthus had provided a scientific case against the Speenhamland reform and, more generally, against relief to the poor. The less enlightened had not yet learned to fight the bogey of diminishing returns implicitly raised in the analysis by virtue of its reference to the fixed supply of land; economics has since learnt to "assume" increasing or diminishing returns at will, depending upon the proposition to be proved! The first Ricardian lesson had just been taught, and a grand tradition initiated—still extant to our day—of using the formalism of science as an instrument to serve more murky social designs.

Science as a cloak for private purposes had been invented for economics, and Ricardo (and his present-day progeny) would carry the idea to still greater lengths in his own work. As Ricardo agitated against the Poor Laws in Parliament, he would invoke Malthusian science as his main prop: "The pernicious tendency of these laws is no longer a mystery," he was to say, "since it has been fully developed by the able hand of Mr. Malthus; Ricardo, *Principles*, p. 106). Indeed, in his own early model of the economy (his 1815 *Essay on Profits*, christened the "corn-model" by Sraffians for highly debatable reasons)—penned in haste as he sharpened tools with which to deal with his pet policy problem, the Corn Laws—it is Malthusian population dynamics that form, along with the notion of diminishing returns, an implacable scaffolding. (Ricardo, like Malthus, would rule out technical progress, at least to the point of seeing it as ultimately unable to thwart the ineffable workings of that irresistible tendency toward abating returns; again, mind you, in English agriculture, easily the most technically advanced agriculture of the time!) And, in fact, consideration would show that the Ricardian so-called Corn Model is quite inconceivable without Malthusian equipment: the perfectly elastic supply curve of labor at the subsistence wage (to employ an obviously nonRicardian terminology), a necessary assumption, is drawn from—and in fact based upon—Malthusian population mechanisms. Likewise, agrarian diminishing returns, again a necessary assumption, is an idea touted originally by Malthus in conjunction with his theory of rent—an idea which Ricardo would absorb into own his rival system, albeit with modification. "Mr. Malthus," he would write, "...has satisfactorily explained the principles of rent." Ricardo, *Principles*, in *Works*, vol.

I, p. 398). Both of these axial supports of the Ricardian model are fundamentally Malthusian in inspiration, and reflect, even at this early stage, the enormous Ricardian debt to Malthusian ideas.

~

Malthus's contribution to the Ricardian crusade—via his diatribe against the Poor Laws expressed in his pseudopopulation theory—would have been quite enough to secure him the role of an original inspirer of the Ricardian project. In fact, Schumpeter's assignation of the "Ricardian Vice"—arguing from assumed strong cases—needs correction: it was a *Malthusian* corruption to begin with! But in reality, Malthus was to serve Ricardo even more and better, for it is in his role as defender of the political economy of landlords, against Ricardo's unrelenting antipathy toward the latter, that Malthus distinguished himself as, ultimately, the most profound critic of Ricardian theory in Ricardo's own time. Patiently and persistently, Malthus exposed the specious nature of Ricardian assumptions and the egregious errors in his reasoning, all the way from the problems with the original 1815 *Essay on Profits* to the last gasp of the "invariable standard" in the continually amended—under pressure of Malthusian criticism—versions of the *Principles*. If anyone impressed upon Ricardo the ultimate futility of his search for the "invariable measure," it was Malthus—not out of ignorance as to the meaning of Ricardo's quest, as with many (including Ricardo's own loyal following, such as McCulloch, for instance), but secured with a full knowledge of Ricardo's logical and political concerns. In the reshaping of the notion of the invariable measure of value, if not all of the *Principles*, Malthus was the greatest single influence on Ricardo of all economists past or contemporaneous, in spite of—or perhaps because of—the enormous differences between their ideas and interests. And yet both the logical force and the powerful impact of Malthus's criticisms of Ricardo have been consistently overlooked in most contemporary discussions of the period.[4]

But whence Ricardo's project? In much the same way as Malthus's 1978 *Essay on Population* was the definitive scientific attack on the Poor Laws, Ricardo's 1815 *Essay on Profits* was intended as an irrefutable cannonade directed against the Corn Laws. It was subsequently to be rewritten with more care, despite its enduring inadequacies, as the famous *Principles* of 1817—a work which Winch correctly characterizes as an "ingenious attack on the Corn Laws writ large" in (D. Winch, *Introduction to Ricardo's Principles*, 1974, p. vii); it is instructive to note, however, that Ricardo intended his work to be a rejoinder to Malthus's 1815 *Inquiry into the Nature of Progress of Rent*, and 1815 *Grounds of an Opinion* (both following upon the heels of Malthus's 1814 *Observations on the Effects of the Corn Laws*), published earlier, such that even the struggle over the Corn Laws—as with the Poor Laws—was essentially inaugurated by prior Malthusian initiatives. The gap between the two separate Malthusian diatribes, which in fact might not have existed other-wise, was most likely due to the Napoleonic threat, which imposed a tactical unity on the warring classes until the resolution of Waterloo. However, the latter event opened up the floodgates of debate and strug-gle, initiating a battle finally to be won by the industrial legions, massed under the determined, even inveterate, leadership of Ricardo.

As viewed by manufacturers and their allies, the political economists, the case against the Corn Laws was, in truth, simple enough: that the forcible restriction on importation of corn was compelling recourse to poorer domestic lands, thereby raising costs—via the corn wage—and depressing (ultimately) nonagrarian rates of profit. Additionally, and for good measure, the Corn Laws were said to have prevented a foreign market for manufactured English goods that could be—in a classical, colonial sense—exchanged profitably for cheaper, foreign food. The Portuguese-wine-for-English-cloth idea, presented by Ricardo and touted *ad nauseam* in textbooks ever since as a "theory" of international trade, thus neatly captured, as in metaphor, how emergent industrial Britain (the scourge of the nonEuropean world for at least a century) was, for quite some time to come, to view the rest of the world—as its subordinate colony.

The matter, of course, was—at least in principle—open to a determinate, empirical test. But it is an index of the political economy of the time—and the weak, almost nonexistent notion of validation within that tradition—that few such attempts were made with any seriousness. More characteristically, the problem was simply "assumed" to exist, and a theoretical model, itself built upon untested "assumptions," was erected to "prove" (with or without the benefit of any corroborative evidence) that the problem indeed must exist and would, by implication, continue to exist until either the Corn Laws were repealed, or the entire "neat produce" (sic) of the nation were paid off in the form of rent to the class of landlords—a class whose interest was said to be implacably contrary to the entire national interest.

Ricardo's 1815 *Essay on Profits*, accordingly, had a simple problematic; to connect—or to show—the rise in corn wages (as leading) to a fall in the general profit rate. By extending this farm model to cover the overall economy, Ricardo felt that he had fully demonstrated his proposition that the rate of profit varied with the intensity of the force compelling diminishing returns. (Ricardo had quickly predigested the Malthusian theory of rent, published only weeks earlier, seeing its tremendous value for his own ideas on distribution.) But Malthus had no difficulty exploding the pretensions of the *Essay*. (In fact, Malthus had ruled out the Ricardian idea that it is the "profits of the farmer which regulates the profits of all other trades," Ricardo: *Works*, Vol. VI, pp. 103-104. As he put it, "...I have always maintained that when corn rises, though other commodities would rise they would not rise in proportion..." (Malthus, in Ricardo: *Works*, Vol. VI, p. 222). Likewise, he debunked the notion that there could be a "material rate of produce" as early as 1814: "In no case of production, is the produce exactly of the same nature as the capital advanced. Consequently we can never properly refer to a material rate of produce..." (in Ricardo: *Works*, Vol. VI, p. 117)—thereby rejecting as improbable the alleged product-capital homogeneity that Ricardo is said to have worked with in the *Essay*,[5] even before the latter had been published. That the discussion could not be conducted outside of a value reckoning in simple physical terms ("exchange value is not...always proportioned to its quantity," Malthus, in Ricardo: *Works* Vol. VI, pp. 140-141) was, further, made categorically explicit. The Ricardian farm model would not do when reality was otherwise—with dualism, at least as far as capital structures went, requiring, therefore, an articulated theory of value to explain changes in the terms of trade between agricultural and manufactured goods; this connected with the "diminishing returns in agriculture" argument that buttressed the entire Ricardian analysis.

Ricardo's abandonment of Smith's value theory, and his "competition of capitals" view of decline of profitability (still implicitly, if recedingly, assumed by Ricardo in his *Essay*), had to do, ultimately, with the force of Malthus's criticism; that is to say, the search for a labor standard of value was set off by Ricardo's understanding that his case could not be proved within Smithian value and distributive parameters, a concession forced upon him by the penetration of Malthus's observations regarding the inadequacy of the original *Essay on Profits* model of the economy. But Ricardo, in his writing of the *Principles*, where, initially at least (in the first and second editions) a simple labor theory was thought sufficient to establish his critical relationship—such that labor time itself could suffice as an invariable standard—continued in his slumbering ignorance—or avoidance!—of the real issues. Malthus's rejection of the pure labor theory idea was straightforward: "There are...causes practically in operation which prevent the exchangeable value of commodities from being proportioned to the quantity of labor employed upon them...It is scarcely possible, indeed, to take up two commodities of different kinds, which will be found to exchange with each other in proportion to the quantity of labor worked up in each..." (Malthus, 1836 *Principles*, p. 91). In the first and second editions of his *Principles*, the invariable standard was simply assumed: "If we had then an invariable standard..." (Ricardo, *Principles*, 1st ed., in Ricardo: *Works*, vol. I, p. 56). Again, it took a Malthusian chastisement to rouse Ricardo, grudgingly, from his dogmatic slumbers. This underscores, incidentally, the driving practical necessity, epitomized in the Ricardian endeavor, arbitrarily to "prove"—regardless of the logical demands involved—a case that was already, a priori, considered to be true; i.e. when the agenda is not one of science, as normally understood, but of simple political expediency. Regrettably, Ricardian findings uniformly preceded Ricardian investigations.

In fact, Malthus had little difficulty showing that, once divergent capital structures were admitted, price changes could not simply be linked solely to alterations in labor expenditures ("We can infer nothing respecting the rate of profits from a rise of money wages, if commodities, instead of remaining of the same price, are variously affected, some rising, some falling, and a very small number indeed remaining stationary," Malthus, in Ricardo: *Works*, vol. II, p. 286). Such a perfect measure simply could not exist. Bit by bit, then, in successive editions of the *Principles*, Ricardo was forced to yield the issue, at least on the limited, and yet vital, question of a measure invariant both to distribution and technical change. The extraordinary success of Malthusian probings may be gauged by the abject, if long-drawn, Ricardian surrender when the vaunted "invariable standard" boiled down, in the last edition, to fixing on gold(!) as the least objectionable standard in question—and this from a scholar who had castigated Smith for "confusion" in value matters. It was Smith, it will be recalled, who had originally shown the unreliability of precious metals as measures of value. As Malthus was to say, in this context: "He is of course compelled to acknowledge in the outset, that a measure so constituted, would be a perfect measure of value for all things produced under the same circumstances precisely as itself, but for no others." But what a prodigious concession this is! What a full and entire acknowledgment is it at once that the measure can be of no use" (Malthus, *Principles*, pp. 124-125).

The characteristically Ricardian response to the destruction of his model, and hence of his "ironclad" case against the Corn Laws, is also instructive: Ricardo continued to believe, to the end, in the correctness of his cause. So much so that, even having conceded logical defeat ("Of such a measure, it is impossible to be possessed..." Ricardo: *Works*, Vol. I, p. 43), he went on to suggest that the real, empirical significance of Malthusian modifications could not be more than a few percentage points ("The greatest effects...could not exceed 6 or 7 percent." Ricardo: *Works*, Vol. I, p. 36—whence, of course, the Stiglerian 93 percent theory of value idea), thereby shifting terms, suddenly, onto a very different terrain altogether. Indeed, manufacturers and their political allies, blissfully ignorant of the holes in Ricardo's models, continued to quote him for their cause, as if an oracle were being consulted and held to witness. And they were to win their struggle handsomely, regardless of the correctness of his ideas, even as Malthus would receive short shrift at the hands of the Ricardians. (Malthus was to write to Sismondi, "The Edinburgh Review has so entirely adopted Mr. Ricardo's system of Political Economy it is probable neither you nor I shall be mentioned in it..." Ricardo: *Works*, Vol. VIII, pp. 376-377.)

Poor Malthus, railing impotently against the Ricardians, had to drink the bitter cup to the dregs, for the phantom of spurious science that he himself had unleashed in his 1798 *Essay on Population* (based as it was on tendentious reasoning and motives political) had now come back to haunt him in the form of Ricardianism—which would now effectively dispossess Malthus's cause (defending the landed interest) just as efficiently as his own arguments had disarmed the friends of Speenhamland. Diminishing returns, which were rallied against the amended Poor Laws, were now effectively being roused against the Corn Laws by his personal friend and political adversary. Ironically, Malthus was to find himself, discreetly, questioning in Ricardo the very assumption that he had made in his own *1798 Essay* as to the pace and effectiveness of technical change in agriculture ("...But unless it could be shown that no improvements were to ever take place either in agriculture or in manufactures...the [Ricardian] doctrine is evidently not correct in practice," Malthus, in Ricardo, *Works*, vol. VI, pp. 139-140)! The bogey of diminishing returns, raised by Malthus in favor of landlords, was now effectively used against that same group by Ricardo, who argued that their effect was merely to depress profits and raise rents—such that rents could be construed a pure and simple (and unjustified) transfer income to landlords. (As Cannan wrote: "...the agriculturists imagined they were strengthening their case for protection by insisting on the greater cost of growing wheat on the additional land which had recently been turned to that purpose," Cannan, 1964, p. 231). Malthus could only protest this in vain: "When a given value of capital yields smaller returns, whether on new land or old, the loss is generally divided between the laborers and capitalists, and wages and profits fall at the same time. This is quite contrary to Mr. Ricardo's language" (Malthus, *Principles*, p. 152). Even more pointedly, "Mr. Ricardo has supposed a case...of a diminution of fertility...and he thinks it would increase rents by pushing capital upon less fertile land. I think, on the contrary, that in any well cultivated country it could not fail to lower rents, by occasioning the withdrawal of capital from the poorest soils..." (Malthus, *Principles*, p. 144). So did the biter get bit, on this piece of intellectual sophistry, as unsupported by any decisive evidence in what it denied as in what it sought to affirm (quite in consonance with the doubtful validity of the Ricardian assertion it sought to refute).

~

Nor was the Malthusian contribution only with respect to criticism of Ricardo's faulty value theory. In fact, via Keynes, Malthus is best remembered—or should be—as an early critic of capitalist complacency about the self-regulating nature of their favorite system. By exploding the myth of Say's Law against the grain of the Ricardian tradition ("It has been thought by some...writers, that although there may...be a glut of particular commodities, there cannot possibly be a glut of commodities in general...This doctrine...appears to me to be utterly unfounded and completely to contradict the great principles which regulate supply and demand," Malthus, *Principles*, p. 315), by pointing to structural weaknesses inherent in a system where the link between production and consumption is both weak and indirect (earning for Malthus the obloquy, from the Marxists, of being an "underconsumptionist," while receiving praise from Keynes for the same), by thereby showing the limits to laissez-faire ("It is obviously impossible, therefore, for a government strictly to let things take their natural course..." *Principles*, p. 16) in favor of legitimate intervention, by calling for public works ("It is also of importance to know that, in our endeavors to assist the working classes in a period like the present, it is desirable to employ them in those kinds of labor...such as roads and public works..." *Principles*, p. 429), by drawing attention to the problem of "hoarding" as against saving ("No political economist of the present day can by saving mean mere hoarding," *Principles*, p. 38), and by drawing attention to the dangers of both ("...the principle of saving, pushed to excess, would destroy the motive to production..." *Principles*, p. 7), by indicating the fiscal aspects of the national debt ("By greatly reducing the national debt...we may place ourselves perhaps in a more safe position...but grievously will those be disappointed who think that, either by greatly reducing or at once destroying it, we can enrich ourselves..." *Principles*, p. 427), Malthus inaugurated a cautionary, *regulative* vision of capitalism that was, in fact, to become the mainstay of the Keynesian mainstream in our own century. He pointed to the demand side weaknesses of classical economics ("...the conversion of revenue into capital pushed beyond a certain point must by diminishing the effectual demand for produce throw the laboring classes out of employment...accompanied by distressing effects...and by a marked depression of wealth..." *Principles*, p. 326). He further alluded to the importance of unproductive consumption ("...it is necessary that a country with great powers of production should possess a body of consumers...not themselves engaged in production," *Principles*, p. 398; and, again, "...the greatest powers of production are rendered comparatively useless without effectual consumption..." p. 411) in a system where realization is at least as important as production. Malthus was, therefore, perhaps (within the classical tradition) the greatest forerunner, other than Senior, of the postclassical "exchange"-based economics that was to supplant the Ricardian school in the late seventies of the century. And with the exception of the later generation of Senior, no classical economist came closer to the "three factors of production" vision of the neoclassical tradition, as well as the latter-day insistence on not making invidious distinction between "productive" and "unproductive" activities. "Almost every person indeed, must occasionally do some productive labor..." (Malthus, *Principles*, p. 48), at least to the extent of not seeing "unproductive" activities as somehow prejudicial to the societal interest. ("It should also be constantly borne in mind, that Adam Smith fully allows the vast importance of many sorts of labor, which he calls 'unproductive,' Malthus, *Principles*, p. 48.) In fact, the neglect of Malthus possibly has provenance in this paradox that, in himself, Malthus contained the major ideas of both Keynesian and neoclassical theories aeons ahead of either tradition—all the more extraordinary when it is remembered that he came to maturity in the age of Smith (last quarter of the eighteenth century), rather than that of Ricardo.

Additionally, of course, part of the disrepute that still attaches to Malthus is based upon his championship of agrarian and landed interests in an age that, both in its capitalist and socialist variants, holds up industrialization as the touchstone of progress. This makes him out as something of a romantic reactionary, rather than the truth, which is that Malthus was a cautious progressive seeking a compromised capitalist development. He was attempting to reconcile order with change without the necessity for a destructive, internecine struggle between the two coevals within the same emergent ruling class—the oligarchs of land and the captains of industry, respectively. (In this he more closely approximates the later Bukharin in the Soviet industrialization effort.) And lastly, the spurious *1798 Essay* now has become—deservedly—the relatively permanent millstone around the memory of Malthus. It tragically, but inevitably, recalls to the average student the howlers from an ill-conceived propaganda piece, as against the inspired brilliance of his easy disposition of Ricardo's clumsy analytical blunders, or his surprisingly modernist presentation of political economy in his own *Principles*, penned in 1820 as a riposte to the Ricardian work. Although Malthusian ideas are, in content, complementary to—and consistent with—the neoclassical world view, with respect to the form assumed by the latter in our own century, Malthus would have had some misgivings. "...The science of political economy bears a nearer resemblance to the science of morals and politics than to that of mathematics..." he wrote (*Principles*, p. 1), underscoring his appreciation of economics as a *social* science, in spite of its axiomatic and deductive nature, as presented, in fact—with a hint of contradiction—in his own account. In his own words, in economics we are dealing with "so variable a being as man" (*Principles*, p.1).

It is, however, a statement on the policy relevance of economic science that virtually all of the very contemporary sounding criticisms of Ricardo (on theory, policy, and method) emanating from Malthus were logically necessitated by his own contra policy agenda; the economic importance of landlords ("unproductive consumers"), the challenge to Say's Law, the resistance to laissez-faire, the stress on effective demand, and the plea to make practical correction to all general principles in economics (a wise reminder to our profession given to theoretical recklessness, as it is) were all necessary to obstruct the Ricardian programme, that was itself built upon contrasting positions on these same issues. The fact that he was more correct on these matters than Ricardo—sometimes in logic, sometimes in empirical fact—did little, of course, to establish Malthus's reputation. Social science does not—nor could it—live by its truth content alone.

In fact, Malthus received rough treatment at the hands of the Ricardians, dizzy in their euphoric adulation of the age of industrial capital. What was useful to the Ricardian cause (the principle of population, diminishing returns in agriculture, etc.) was scavenged happily by their ilk. (Ricardo, in all plainness, took essentially Malthusian theories of rents and wages, and added to them only a rather dubious notion of profit decline, under highly controlled conditions. There is no real theory of profit in Ricardo, only a vaguely implied deduction idea; and that sufficed—amazingly—to constitute his much vaunted theory of distribution. As for his theory of value, it has all the unrequited splendor of a simple labor theory, i.e. it was a grand, but quite total, failure). What did not fit into the great Ricardian programme—or was simply embarrassing—was either rejected with contempt, or ignored with a stony silence. Class struggle then, as now, was the ultimate arbiter of the social truth.

What is remarkable about the Ricardo-Malthus encounter is not its secure basis in their diverging support for contrary class interests—which is quite simply irrefutable—but perhaps their rather amicable personal relationship.[6] Of course uninformed, or merely tendentious, scholarship would seize upon the latter to try and gainsay the former. In fact, Malthus would himself argue: "It is somewhat singular that Mr. Ricardo, a considerable receiver of rents, should have so much underrated their national importance while I, who never received, nor expect to receive any, should probably be accused of overrating their importance. Our different opinions, under these circumstances, may serve at least to show our mutual sincerity, and afford a strong presumption, that to whatever bias our minds may be subjected in the doctrines we have laid down, it has not been that, against which perhaps it is most difficult to guard, the insensible bias of situation and interest..." (Malthus, *Principles*, pp. 216-217).

In both what it affirms and denies, this statement is rather dismally shallow political sociology. Firstly, and most importantly, direct class membership is neither a necessary nor a sufficient condition for class affiliation. Secondly, and this is trivial, Ricardo's fortune did derive originally from profits—in the bourse—and only subsequently from rents, quite the usual pattern of transition in the England of the time. Thirdly, the Church of England—an institution which Malthus served formally—derived its revenue primarily from tithes on landed income, so that Malthus's parsonian entitlements were anything but unconnected to landed property, even though he may not have (as he claims) directly received rents. Finally, it needs be remembered that the struggle between corn and cotton was not a do-or-die class struggle between the haves and the have-nots, but rather a squabble between the senior and junior partners of the ruling alliance. Both had stakes in property ownership, political stability, and ultimate stewardship over the laboring classes. In this respect, quite apart from their personal friendship, which need not be doubted, the two orders they defended were not exactly implacable enemies. Profits and rents were at odds only to the extent that the former were attempting to establish suzerainty over the latter, indicating the altered economic and political balance between the two strata. The two ranks, in fact, were to make immediate peace (forming a solid phalanx against workers) once the Reform Act had been passed and the Corn and Poor Laws repealed (and rents were subordinated to profits). Under such circumstances, it is not difficult to appreciate the lack of any bitter blood feud between the two rival champions.

~

The choice between a Malthus and a Ricardo, apologists for landlords and manufacturers respectively, is, accordingly—for one not enamored of either property owning order, in the scheme of capitalism—a futile one. It is easy to see, however, why Ricardo has traditionally come off looking better, because the sympathies of economists—as defenders of the regime of capital—are definitely, now as then, with industrial capital. *Indeed, economics—excepting some marginal schools—itself may be defined as the crown jewel of the latter's hegemonic ideology.* There are other reasons, of course, why even the critics of capitalism, such as the Marxists, have tended to vote along with their class enemies on this issue. Industrial capitalism, through development of productive forces and the objective socialization of labor, lays the groundwork for the construction of socialism, in the orthodox, Marxian account. Hence, any mechanism that stands in the way of capital performing its allotted tasks, social or technical, is seen—almost automatically—as reactionary. Thereby, peasant modes, tribal societies, and/or native traditions that offer resistance to capitalist advance, all come to be seen as reactionary impediments to the march of progress—with progress defined exclusively in terms of the modalities of the capitalist revolution. The logical limits of this perspective are plumbed—in all their craven depths—in Bill Warren's inspired "Marxist" defense[7] of the terrors of colonialism, the slave trade, and imperialism as necessary, civilizing medicine for the historically obsolete peoples of the third world. (Malthus, as well as his favorite social class of paternalist aristocrats, fell afoul of this view—indeed agenda—of progress.) Hence their championship of Ricardo—despite, it needs be remembered, the latter's single-minded opposition to even minimal relief to the working poor in times of penury, dearth, and wretchedness, as sanctioned by the sparse charity of Speenhamland. Even so nominal a political right as suffrage was only to be allowed workers, by Ricardo, on the basis of property ownership and assured loyalty to the capitalist order. As Ricardo wrote to Trower, "In other words...you [wish for]...a good choice of representatives and this is precisely what I want. If I cannot obtain it without limiting the elective franchise to the very narrowest bounds, I would so limit it...but I am persuaded that we should...get our object...by extending the electoral franchise—not indeed universally to all people, but to that part of them which cannot be supposed to have any interest in overturning the right to property..." (Ricardo: *Works* VII, pp. 369-370). (Under this sound bourgeois prescription, a limited set of workers won the right to vote, after bitter struggle, as late as 1867; women, of course, the other subaltern order within

Political Economy and Policy: The Malthus-Ricardo Embroilment

English capitalism, had to wait until 1918 for political membership. Those who automatically see capitalism and democracy as "Siamese twins," to use a phrase of Warren's, need to reflect further. In this apparently "Marxian" account, Ricardo's concrete moves against the working class are either forgotten or rationalized in view of his superior contribution to the maturation of the capitalist revolution in Britain.

Of course, however, that is not the whole story. Giving implicit credence to the general view that Ricardo was the "greatest of the political economists" (or as Rubin, faithful to his master, puts it even more grandiosely, "Ricardo's theoretical constructs, once altered and corrected...are...one of the great monuments of human thought..." I. I. Rubin, 1989, p. 244), Marx insisted upon first inheriting, and then improving upon, the Ricardian patrimony—so much so that Marx could be viewed (presumably to his own satisfaction), as he is often termed, as the "heir" to the classical tradition—the one who had "bettered" the greatest of the economists. The most politically class-conscious of the bourgeois economists of the classical school was, accordingly, to be singled out by Marx for almost unreservedly lavish compliments for the virtue, ostensibly—if amazingly!—of his analytical insights (something even a "retrograde" Malthus had shown to be riddled with holes!). But, of course, the truth is not hard to see: Ricardo had espoused, in Marx's understanding, a "labor theory"; never mind that Marx did not understand the limited heuristic nature of Ricardo's instrumental use of the idea; by no stretch of the imagination could Ricardo be conceived as ever being, or even wanting to be, on the same turnpike as Marx leading to a theory of surplus value. Yet Marxists often argue as if Ricardo were a brilliant, if slightly bumbling, precursor of Marx, coming close, yet missing, the ultimate philosopher's stone. As Rubin writes, "Although Ricardo does not inquire directly...the general direction of his thinking leads him to the concept of surplus value..." (Rubin, 1989, p. 260); also, "...we find in Ricardo the embryonic shoots of a theory...but it was left to Marx to develop the theory..." (Rubin, p. 255). Marx himself, of course, paved the way for such a left-handed appreciation of Ricardo, wherein Ricardo is reproached for not having followed through with the Marxian agenda. "Ricardo's writings should have led him to the distinction between surplus value and profit," he writes, (Marx, *Theories of Surplus Value*, Part 2, p. 427); and again, "Instead of labor, Ricardo should have discussed labor power..." (*Theories of Surplus Value*, Part 2, p. 400). This despite that, at least initially, Ricardo's "labor theory" was no more than a device, more a labor *measure* than a labor theory, used to help compare changes in agrarian and industrial values over time. Amazingly, Marx seems quite unaware of the real reasons for the recourse to a labor valuation in Ricardo; "But at last Ricardo steps in and calls to science: Halt! The basis, the starting point for the physiology of the bourgeois system...is the determination of value by labor time...This then is Ricardo's great historical significance for science..." (*Theories of Surplus Value*, Part 2, p. 166).

Had Marx compared Ricardo's ideas in his *Essay* with the reformulations in the *Principles*, and had he read Malthus's intervening criticisms of the former, he would have had a better appreciation of the Ricardian attachment to the "labor" theory, and a sounder understanding of Ricardo's own programme!

Aside from harboring a labor theory, the appeal of Ricardo for Marx lay in his apparent sanction for some form of "class conflict" in his vision of capitalism. Interestingly, Ricardian ideas were mistrusted by class-conscious neoclassicals for this same reason despite its utter falsity. Ricardo had an essentially harmonious vision of social relations within capitalism, so long as the Corn Laws were repealed and cheap corn could be imported freely. Given that the rate of profit would be perpetually buoyant, the bogey of the "stationary state" was simply, as Blaug wisely notes, a piece of "methodological fiction" to scare the friends of protection. Ricardo's "class conflict" existed principally between landlords against the rest of the "people," and between capitalist and laborer, at least temporarily, owing to the dislocation caused by the hasty introduction of machinery, itself precipitated by the Corn Laws—never mind that this latter was an afterthought, politically conceived, presented in the third edition of the *Principles*. That was enough; Ricardo could now be conceived as a protoMarxian giant! It goes without saying that Marx, untrue to his own materialist method (as in the writing of the more dehistoricized sections of *Capital* itself), missed the real agenda underlying Ricardo's theories by a mile. And Marx's loyal epigones, with neither the courage nor the intelligence—not to speak of originality—apparently, to stir beyond Marx's own pronouncements, have loyally stuck to this version to this day. Proof of this proposition may be found by picking up a copy of any Marxist history of thought text, where Marx's working notes in the *Theories of Surplus Value* are faithfully transcribed or reworded (plagiarized?), usually only to the detriment of the original Marxian passion, originality, and/or insight.

At any rate, Malthus, therefore, has been slain twice: once by the Ricardians, who ensured that his ideas would be ignored by virtue of their near-monopoly of the more popular organs of scholarship in Malthus's own time, and by pro-manufacturers' ideology generally, and a second time, by the Marxian tradition—with its wont of hailing Ricardo as the superior political economist of the classical school (despite, it will be noted, the latter's shaky position on Say's Law, his notion of the "impossibility" of a general glut and the accompanying denial of crises, the tendency toward underconsumption in capitalism, etc., viewed in relation to the strong Malthusian criticism of these ideas). Now, the Marxists can well afford to ignore Malthus, for, at least ultimately, their social vision involves—or should involve—a rejection of both Malthus and Ricardo, as well as their larger social schemes. But for mainstream currents, this neglect is a sorry one, for Malthus was one of their own, a brilliant and original intellect, capable both of science and propaganda (the two requirements characteristic, apparently, of every effective economist!) and wasted only by his arguing in conservative fashion against the stream of gathering capitalist political and social forces. It is only fitting then that, as an enlightened capitalist spokesperson, to employ his own self-description, Keynes would offer public tribute, however opportunistically, to the genius of Malthus for pointing to weaknesses within capitalism—weaknesses that were, apparently, no more admissible in Keynes's time (witness the obduracy of what was to be called the "Treasury View") than they were in Malthus's own period.

To the toiling poor within capitalism, however, either in the metropolis or in the degrading periphery of world capitalism, Malthus must necessarily remain—given the misdeeds still committed against them in his name—the archsatan, whose writings on and about them remain, in Marx's unsurpassably eloquent phrase, a "libel on the human race," all the more vicious for coming from one who occupied the hallowed space of a minister of the anointed church of emergent capitalist, and firmly christian, England of the early nineteenth century. It is quite appropriate, therefore, that as we pay tribute to Malthus's intellectual genius, belatedly, we nonetheless remind ourselves of its regrettable propinquity to what Southey called, in equally categorical prose, "bad arithmetic, bad morals and bad theology."

Notes

1. References to the 1798 *Essay* are drawn from T. R. Malthus, *An Essay on the Principle of Population and a Summary View of The Principle of Population*, 1970.

2. References to Malthus's *Principles* are taken from T. R. Malthus, *Principles of Political Economy Considered with a View to Their Practical Application*, 2nd. ed., 1964.

3. References to Ricardo's *Principles* are drawn from, D. Ricardo, *The Works and Correspondence of David Ricardo*, edited by P. Sraffa with the collaboration of M. H. Dobb, 1951-73.

4. The work of Terry Peach is a salutary exception to the general disregard of Malthus; see Peach 1984, 1987.

5. There is, of course, no explicit evidence of such an assumption in the *Essay*; nor does it appear to be either a necessary or a sufficient one to prove the Ricardian case—but there is no doubt, nonetheless, that Ricardo was working with a notion of the profit share being measured in physical terms, so as to abstract from monetary fluctuations.

6. For a recent comment on this matter, see Robert Dorfman, 1989.

7. Bill Warren, *Imperialism: Pioneer of Capitalism*, 1980.

FOUR

~

ECONOMICS AND EPISTEMOLOGY: TOWARD MATERIALISM

> ...Realism is not a theory of knowledge or truth, but of *being*—although as such it is bound to possess epistemological implications. Accordingly, a realist position in the philosophy of (natural) sciences will consist, first and foremost, of a theory about the nature of being, rather than the knowledge of the objects investigated by the science—to the effect that they endure and operate independently of human activity, and hence of both sense-experience and thought. So Realism is immediately opposed to both empiricism and rationalism, wherein being is defined in terms of the human attributes of experience and reason.
> —R. Bhaskar, *Scientific Realism and Human Emancipation*

10

The Foundations of Economic Analysis: Toward Realism

It is a remarkable index of the existing distance between models in economic theorizing, Marxist or neoclassical, and the social object that they claim to either describe, explain, or predict, that few questions are ever addressed to the realist content of their suppositions.[1] Even when these contending paradigms engage each other, rarely is attention directed to what Max Weber might have called "fundamental assumptions";[2] instead, energy is usually dissipated in struggling over the attendant policy implications or the mechanics of the theoretical apparatus, without an examination of the infrastructure of suppositions upon which the edifice actually rests. Premises being taken as given, the struggle then is joined either over matters of internal consistency or over the policy directions indicated by a model. But models, more likely than not, tend on average to be true to their own presumptions, and thus the data and ideas they generate are similarly constrained by their initial assumptions. Accordingly, debates between paradigms turn out to be quite generally frustrating, with neither side convinced at all of the arguments of the other.[3] Historically, this problem has been raised in the manner of Kuhn[4] as the problem of "incommensurability" between different schools, without, of course, any clue as to how such problems can be adjudicated or surmounted. More than occasionally, this very real problem has been "resolved" in the manner of the postAlthusserians, suggesting that social truths can only be relative, and therefore that science is only a form of social partisanship where one declares at the outset one's article of faith and then joins the fray, presumably against similarly endowed antagonists.[5] In various degrees and in various guises this very Weberian idea has, as well, had the sanction of some mainstream writers, such as Myrdal, Schumpeter, etc.

The alternative to this perceptual relativism has been the positivist[6] tradition, whether amongst the Marxists[7] or the mainstream. In their domain, facts are alleged to speak for themselves without filters or assistance from theory, with the scientist usually defined as a passive sensor objectively recording reality, with little causal interaction between scientist and the object of study. In standard positivist discourse, the neutrality of the scientist and the scientific enterprise is taken as given, with the world conceived as a closed system such that invariant regularities can be both perceived and recorded. The monism and absolutism of positivism, coupled with an ingenuous naiveté about the social nature of science, have turned it usually into an ideology that does not recognize ideology as a thing-in-itself, whether in support of Friedmanite[8] discourse or Stalinist dogmatism. Wedded to a narrow empiricism confined to an examination of surface phenomena (and epiphenomena), positivism has, quite notoriously, denied itself the need for a search for generative mechanisms or even for any desire for providing explanations for social phenomena, with prediction being defined as the more instrumental, and inclusive, function of science.

At one level, therefore, social science seemed caught in a bind, between the Scylla of relativism and the Charybdis of positivism, between a denial of the objectivity of knowledge and the dogmatic assertion (without proof) of the neutrality of science conceived in empiricist fashion. At another level, a very definite polarity reigned between individualism and collectivism as approaches toward the study of social phenomena, this duality referring not so much to matters of epistemology (as in the relativist/absolutist dichotomy), as to ontological issues. Neoclassical theorizing, for example, in almost all its forms, has relied upon the atomized individual as the unit of social action and behavior, in the manner of methodological individualism à la Popper,[9] seeing society as only the plural of the individual, with pre-given motives gratuitously ascribed to homo economicus, conceived as a universal historical subject, regardless of space-time referents. At the opposite end of the pole was Durkheimian[10] sociology reifying the social and imposing collective determinations on individual spheres of social action. Variants of institutionalism and Marxism were prone to use this organicist and positivist model by way of a counterweight against the heroically "free"

The Foundations of Economic Analysis: Toward Realism

individual of neoclassical exaggerations. While the one model denied social agency (or "interdependencies," as they might be called), the other reified it, leaving the human being a passive object of history. The "enlightened" Marxist occasionally tried to reconcile the antinomy between these two opposed views by trying to link them "dialectically"[11]—implying that socially predetermined individuals nonetheless were able to react back and change society—succeeding only in reaping the errors of both models, retaining both voluntarism and reification rather than disposing of these twin errors of social formulation.

Organized social science—economics included—found itself in the prison of these apparently irreconcilable dichotomies with disputes routinely falling into the premeasured no-man's land formed by this implacable rivalry. This is not to gainsay unorthodox efforts to break out of this moribund state by way of imaginative excursions, the work of Bachelard[12] and Feyerabend,[13] for instance, in the direction of science as a matter of psychology and science as a matter of little consequence, respectively. While both these nonconservative departures from mainstream views have had considerable influence on recent discussions, neither perspective has been able to completely dislodge the central divides in science as already identified, for reasons that themselves belong to the area of the philosophy of science. The failure in these corrective visions is perhaps best located in their weak ontological visions of the nature of society, something that *transcendental realism*—as reflected in the work of Roy Bhaskar[14]—seeks to set right. As a vital new paradigm in the human sciences, Bhaskarian realism seeks to resolve the classical antinomies that have divided social science by offering a vantage point from which both individualism and collectivism can be corrected, such that neoclassical theory can be convincingly refuted, while orthodox Marxism and Stalinism can equally be rejected in favor of the original insights in the classical Marx, insights into the real ontology of societies, on whose irreducible basis alone we can hope to construct efficacious categories to explain and understand the dynamics of social existence. In what follows, in stages, the realist vision is described, encapsulating the varied intellectual moments of the oeuvre of Bhaskar.

~

Realism itself, as a recurrent tendency in social philosophy, has had many varied referents. In its simplest form, realism asserts the independence of the objects of scientific discourse from the activity of science and the scientist. In this general sense, any perspective can bear the realist title for simply asserting the independent existence of the disputed entity in question, be that a universal, a material object, a proposition, etc. Consistent with this formulation, scientific realism is validated when we can demonstrate that the terms of the discourse are believed to possess real referents—independently of the theorizing. Actually, however, it is unnecessary to demonstrate that the scientists actually believe in that proposition, so long as it can be shown that their behavior lends credibility to it. This much, of course, did not require a Bhaskarian elucidation, being a readily identifiable position even if its significance has usually been underrated. The specific Bhaskarian supplement to this is in his bold theorizing of a *metaphysical realism*, an elaboration, in his words, of "what the world must be like prior to any empirical investigation of it and for any scientific attitudes or activities to be possible."[15] In this rendering, epistemologies must be both bound to, and referred to, ontology; for realism is seen not as a theory of knowledge or of truth, but of *being*. This is critical, for now both empiricism and rationalism can be rejected for defining being in terms of the very human attributes of experience and reason.

Stated differently, what is being maintained is that every theory of knowledge presupposes a theory of the objects of knowledge, i.e. a theory of what the world must be like for knowledge to be possible at all. This priority of ontology rejects the postHumean idea (which Bhaskar terms the "epistemic fallacy") that ontological issues may always be transposed into an epistemological key. Of course, it is not being asserted that knowledge can be reduced to being, for that would be to subscribe to the "ontic fallacy," something equally to be avoided. Epistemology provides us with the *transitive* dimension in our studies of the world around us. Ontology demands, on the other hand, recognition of the *intransitive* dimension of reality, a reality that predates and preexists this, without need for a human world of perception and experience. The sciences, especially the social ones, have been guilty of the taint of anthropomorphism, centering the universe on human atttributes as if—as in the Christian view—it were all designed so as to be perceived by the sovereign human subject.

Transcendental realism—to use the term favored by Bhaskar—involves a careful recognition of the various parameters of the transitive and the intransitive in the social study of society. It necessarily involves the following predicates: an *ontological realism* implying that society is an intransitive, knowledge-independent, irreducible, real object of scientific knowledge; an *epistemic relativity* in the transitive domain, suggesting that knowledge about the social object cannot be but socio-historically limited and constrained; and the possibility of *judgmental rationality*, implying that, nonetheless, despite epistemic limitations, it is possible to sort the true from the false in the competing claims to knowledge. Additionally, Bhaskar posits a metacritical dimension allowing for a self-reflexive scrutiny of all the philosophical and sociological presuppositions presumed by the discourse, a metacritique being defined as a logical procedure seeking to identify the "presence of causally significant absences in thought," or, in other words, to identify what "cannot be said in a scheme about what is done in the practice into which the scheme is connected."[16]

Bhaskar claims neither uniqueness nor certainty for his approach, but hopes to show, nonetheless, that it is "demonstrably superior" to the various irrealist accounts in fashion today, the proof of the pudding resting entirely in the eating of it.

The central idea behind transcendental realism is the decisive importance of an ontology of the real for the practice of science. But the real is far from being the flat, "empirical" terrain beloved by positivism, for the very first recognition is one of *ontological depth*, a recognition of the multilayered stratification of a highly complex, differentiated reality. It is this ontological reality of a layered universe that demands that knowledge move, necessarily, from manifest phenomena to deeper or anterior levels of phenomena, the search being one of locating generative or causal mechanisms within the triple layering of reality, within the domains of the real, the actual, and the empirical (generally collapsed into one in positivist discourse, or denied independent legitimacy as with the subjective idealists). By way of illustration, the principle of gravity is irreducibly located in the intransitive realm of the real; it is actualized in the falling apple; and then, should a perceiving subject be proximate, becomes part of the empirically constituted experience of the latter. But nature is not, as in the vulgar positivist view, always so transparent (nor is the observer gifted only with a guileless innocence). In fact, contrary to Hume, constant conjunctions are only rarely visible in nature (if nature were easy to "read" there would be little need for a "science" of nature) but need, in fact, to be recreated in the laboratory. The point being made is a powerful one: causal laws (the real) are ontologically distinct from patterns of events; and events (the actual) are similarly distinct from experiences (the empirical). Positivist empirics is therefore guilty of two category mistakes: of reducing causal laws to constant conjunctions of events (confusing powers with their exercise), and the latter to experience, thereby making the real a property of the empirical, rather than the other way around. Gravity, as a property of the real, operated even when its several actualizations remained unperceived or uncomprehended by human subjects; it would, accordingly, remain operational even in a nonhuman world stripped suddenly of all human experience.

Transcendental realism asserts the *non*identity of thought and being, of the objects of the transitive and intransitive dimensions. In so asserting this, the Bhaskarian realist denies empiricism for limiting the concept of the natural order to what is given in human experience; it also denies idealism for seeing it as a human construct. For realism, the cognitive possibility is determined by the nature of the (independent) object (for it is humanity that is the contingent phenomenon in nature, and knowledge a cosmic accident). The "forlornness" of the universe, as Heidegger saw it, acquires in Bhaskar, thereby, an important scientific legitimacy.

~

The implications of transcendental realism for economic theory, although varied and complex, are quite decisive. As mentioned early on, neither neoclassical theorizing nor conventional Marxian economic theorizing can escape unscathed from the implicit critique immanent in the realist framework. It could not be otherwise, considering that realism is a devastating refutation of positivism, and positivism, in various referents, has tended to cut across both of these major schools in political economy. Upon subjection to realist scrutiny it becomes apparent that positivism, while purporting to be a *method* for science, is actually a fairly sophisticated *ideology* for science, wherein Bhaskar conceives of its (historical and functional) necessity—-despite its readily identifiable errors.

Bhaskar argues that, while positivism is a theory of the nature, limits, and unity of knowledge, it, surprisingly, is not a theory of its possibility. This is because positivism sees scientific knowledge, apparently, as quite an unproblematic affair for, within it, there is no serious contemplation

The Foundations of Economic Analysis: Toward Realism

of its own limitations and possibilities. Besides, being a theory of knowledge, it presupposes a very definite ontology of societies, whether or not it is aware of such presuppositions. It is the enduring weakness, if not outright error, in this ontology, that renders positivism defunct and irrelevant as a sane method for science. For the positivist posits, implicitly, an ontology of closed systems and atomistic events coupled with the perception of the scientist as a passive sensor and recorder of pregiven, unmediated facts—derived from constant conjunctions—rendering social knowledge an individual attribute. Positivism entails, as already seen, double reduction: causal laws are reduced to constant conjunctions, and the latter foregrounded in individual experience; reducing causal laws to events and events to experience, positivism fails to locate the independent, intransitive existence of causal laws, while at the same time failing to recognize human experience as a social product and knowledge as a social production (compounding the error in ontology with an error in epistemology). In the words of Bhaskar, positivism "can sustain neither the idea of an independent reality nor the idea of a socially-produced science."[17]

In so doing, positivism gainsays the transience of historical knowledge, the hierarchy and differentiation within reality, and the transformational nature of society. Further, positivism ignores the possibility of causal interdependency between scientific subject and social object—the transitive dimension—aside from overlooking the fact of the openness of social systems where invariant regularities simply need not occur, barring chance. Reifying and naturalizing "facts," positivism effectively dehistoricizes them. Fetishizing science, it fails to see science as a social production. Reducing knowledge to human experience, it humanizes nature while simultaneously—for its monism—naturalizes society. Being at once ahistorical and asocial, it fails to account for both scientific change and any transition in the "facts" that it so very dispassionately brings to light.

This same ontological inadequacy dooms that near kin to positivism, *methodological individualism*, which maintains that facts pertaining to social phenomena are not only reducible to facts about individuals, but are indeed explained by the latter. In this extraordinarily alienated view, army becomes just the plural for soldier, and society the plural of the individual. In his crushing refutation of this mistaken methodology, Bhaskar points out that any advertence to motives or rules for the individual always involves reference to irreducibly social predicates. Thus, writes Bhaskar, "a tribesman implies a tribe, the cashing of a cheque a banking system".[18] Micro statements cannot simply be added up to form coherent macro situations; the logic of the latter cannot be derived from the former. A singularly telling example offered suggests that, in all simplicity, the garbage collector's reason for collecting garbage is not the reason, usually, that society wants garbage collected; similarly, a soldier's motive for joining an army might have little to do with the rationale for the existence of such an institution. The logic of the whole is quite apart from the logic of the parts.[19]

Even more strongly, realism challenges the attribution of rationality and maximizing behavior to the sovereign "free" individuals. As Bhaskar writes, "to say that men are rational does not explain what they do, but only at best...how they do it".[20] So, in trying to explain everything, the assumption of rationality explains nothing, being only an a priori attribution without explanatory content, failing only as grand tautology, casting no light whatsoever on actual empirical behavior.[21] In this light, neoclassical thinking is only a normative theory of efficient action recommending "a set of techniques for achieving given ends," rather than a social science, for it arrives only at a pre-given praxiology under the delusion of generating a (spurious) sociology. In this regard, the grand collation of mistaken agendas consecrating the triple alliance between positivism, methodological individualism, and neoclassical motivational ascriptions could only constitute a blueprint for a colossal default in the search for a science of economics, a default guaranteed almost a priori by this straightforward denial of the real ontology of societies in general, and capitalism in particular. The articles of doom are underwritten by the double error in neoclassical theorising, the disastrous coupling of an empiricist epistemology with an individualist ontology of society.

Within a realist matrix, revealing the ontological inadequacy of the triad formed by positivism, methodological individualism, and neoclassical "assumptions" about homo economicus is indeed simple enough. But the power of the realist critique goes even further, for it is not content simply with demonstrating inadequacy. A true critique, as per Bhaskar, needs to go beyond falsification and demonstrate the conditions for the necessity for the persistence of the false paradigm, i.e. to reveal the ideological intent or content of the intellectual system in question. To designate a system of ideas as "ideological" requires us, in terms of our alternate theory, to: (a) explain most or all of the phenomena covered by it; and (b) to explain additionally significant phenomena not covered by it; then (c) to account for its historical genesis; next (d) to indicate the conditions for its reproduction and their limits; and finally (e) to locate its present function.

The social function of positivism, then, in the words of Bhaskar, is to "conceal the historically specific structures and relations constituting sense-experience in science".[22] By naturalizing facts—converting social objects into things—positivism effectively dehistoricizes them. First atomizing and then reifying social "facts," the positive account induces, aside from its monism, a fusion of the world with experience (in its empirical realism), and the reduction of knowledge to experience.

Infusing certainty into scientific knowledge imparts a legitimacy to the scientific *status quo*, while reducing it to common empirical apprehension lends validation to the postulates of "common sense." The unmistakable presentiment sanctioned by the positivism is that things are as they appear, as they seem (Bhaskar sees in this concession to common sense the possibility inherent in positivism of justifying the status quo, regardless of "whatever and wherever that is"). In this regard, the very denial of the notion of a possible disjuncture between appearance and reality—i.e the absence of a theory of ideology—makes the enterprise itself profoundly ideological. Positivism, in its denial of the transfactual, independent existence of the scientific object, in its denial of science as a social production, in its limitation of the world to the range of human sense-perception, in its denial of the validity of the cognitive claims of other social practices besides itself, functions as the "limit form of empiricism"—as an ideology for science.

Similarly, neoclassical assumptions universalize for all times one possible set of behavioral characteristics, arguing, à la Hume, that "mankind is much the same in all times and all places," a comment that flies in the face of the most trivial discoveries of modern social anthropology; the real irony in this antihistorical stance is that positivism, originally with Comte, purported to be a theory of history. The conceptual world of positivism is flat for the lack of differentiation in reality. The real world is stripped of all its concealed or opaque mechanisms, of its ontological subtlety, of deceptive appearances, of powers and potentialities of which we might be unaware, consisting only of "the passing flux of experience, as described by common sense," a closed system ruled by constant conjunctions—its shallowness matched only by its everyday accessibility. Auguste Comte, of course, had been quite forthright about the political intent of positivism (which he considered a deterrent to the negative—meaning critical—philosophy of the Enlightenment). In his words,"...the positive spirit tends to consolidate order, by the rational development of a wise resignation to incurable political evils...A true resignation—that is, a permanent disposition to endure steadily, and without hope of compensation, all inevitable evils..."[23]

~

Transcendental realism offers a penetrating critique not merely of neoclassical pretensions, but also of vulgar Marxism and some aspects of Marx's own intellectual predilections, for the critique of positivism is not a chariot that may be arrested at will. The critique of Marxism, similarly, takes the form of pointing to enduring ontological inadequacies in the Marxian schema which render some of its suppositions invalid. Central to a critique of Marx is a rejection of the "material base/ideational superstructure" metaphor, an important element of both Stalinist and nonStalinist discourse, the main difficulty here traditionally being the unsuccessful effort to reconcile the thesis of the relative autonomy of the superstructures with the idea of their determination—in the last instance—by the base. The metaphor itself provides the inspiration for the two common errors plaguing Marxian discourse, these being: (a) super idealism, where the superstructure is completely emancipated from the base (as in Althusser,[24] where science is totally autonomous) and (b) reductionism, where the superstructure is simply an epiphenomenon of the base (as with Lukacs,[25] where science is an expression of it). The very notion of a base/superstructure disjunction allows for the errors of theoretical idealism and economic reductionism.

Bhaskar's suggestions for a restructuration of Marxian discourse are of critical interest. He argues that there is something very misconceived in the traditional Marxian manner of lumping together all ideas, indiscriminately, to form a bloc termed a superstructure, as distinguished from a "material" base. Quite simply, even purely economic activity necessarily has an inalienable ideational component; all activity, economic or otherwise, necessarily carries with it the presumption of some conception carried by the agents as to the what and the why of their

The Foundations of Economic Analysis: Toward Realism

actions. The Marxian error in this regard may be located quite unmistakably; Marx provided a decisive critique of the Hegelian error of positing the autonomous existence of the ideal (aside from arguing for the primacy of the material over the ideal), but the Hegelian thesis can hardly be inverted. There can be no grounds for arguing for a purist autonomy of the material in social existence, since the material sphere is inextricably bound up with ideas—to the extent that we are speaking of human society. It follows, then, that the distinction between base and superstructure, as originally formulated, is false and misleading, specially so in the hands of immature and rash Marxists eager to apply instant formulae to the diversity of history.

The suggested alternative procedure then, closer to the inspiration of Marx if not the letter, is to conceive instead of different (multiple) ideologies associated with different practices, these different and varied practices having autonomous "bases" of their own. Different ensembles of practices generate their own rationalizing ideologies. In this view, then, religion is a real social practice with its own justifying ideology enjoying a real autonomy from other practices such as politics, despite the fact of linkages, connections, and homologies between them and other ideologies. The material conditions for the reproduction of these practices may still be traced to the social economy that sustains all social life. But this is not to imply any determination of the practices themselves. The point is of extraordinary significance for Marxian theorizing: ideational structures are not reflexes of an all-determining material "base"—in fact, the idea of a material determination is devoid of content altogether. Away from the stasis of a fixed "base," Bhaskar offers the dynamics of social practices as the ultimately "determining" agency, for ideologies bear determinant links with practices.

At the next remove, Marx's ideas come in for castigation on account of their flirtation with elements of positivism—the idea of "laws of motion," for example, so cheerfully repeated by generations of Marx scholars. The Marxian critique of idealism, so thoroughly made in *German Ideology*, was never followed through with a similar critique of empiricism, despite many apprehensions of the importance of the latter critique. Again, law-like regularities are only characteristic of closed systems (the assumption of positivism) but society, being an open system, is not subject to such immanent "laws." Much of the nonhistorical accounts in *Capital*, for instance, need therefore to be dropped (and also the scenarios of anticipation of an indeterminate future, such as the visions of communism and the "withering away" of the state, etc.). It is in such accounts that Marx comes close to fetishizing economic categories with a kind of naturalism (the cost of trying to subvert the classical economics from within) that simply cannot be sustained given the ontology of societies. "Laws" such as the "falling rate of profit" simply cannot be taken as such, and it is small wonder that Marxian economists—armed with econometrics, that special tool of positivism—operating in that area are such devotees of positivist methodology in practice. The point can be made quite simply; prediction, in an open system, is virtually impossible (which is why neither Friedmanite neoclassicals nor positivist Marxians have ever displayed anything but a sorry record in this regard). The social sciences, at best, can only aspire to explanation, not prediction, for social life has to do with meanings, and meanings can only be understood, not measured. This precision in meaning assumes the place of accuracy in measurement (as an *a posteriori* arbiter): to quote Bhaskar, "Language here stands...to social science as geometry stands to physics."[26]

All in all, then, a good bit of Marxian baggage gets jettisoned, having to be trimmed (a) in the light of ontological realities of society, and consequently (b) in the light of a methodology appropriate to (a). The tremendous content gain for Marxism despite this radical surgery is in the salvation—beyond criticism—of its central insights into social life at the cost only of abandoning unsustainable flourishes that do violence to reality. The sophisticated Marxian will now have to accept the fact that social phenomena are conjuncturally determined, requiring explanation with respect to a multiplicity of causes, with no place for either determinism or historicism, social life needing to be grasped as a totality, a totality whose configuration is continually changing. The different moments of this totality will need, of course, to be asymmetrically weighted, "primed," as Bhaskar puts it, "with differential causal force," depending on the issue in question. Truly, then, realism encompasses Marxism and surpasses it as a genuine critique would and should.

~

As a competent methodology in the social sciences radically current in its apprehension of the discoveries of modern-day philosophy of science (something that neither neoclassical economics nor conventional Marxism can lay claim to), it would seem as if transcendental realism would need no further justification, no other strengths with which to parade its potency as a devastating critique of the ruling pretensions in social science.

But Bhaskarian realism offers more than a sedentary methodology of science. It offers also a perspective on human emancipation that is solidly based on the underlabor of science. "The philosophers," complained Marx in a well-known statement, "have only interpreted the world; the point, however, is to change it."[27] For too many Marxians, this declaration has led to the denigration of the cognitive enterprise, flinging themselves into the struggle for change, perhaps, at some cost in terms of missed cognitive apprehensions. Realism strongly insists on the view that science is, ipso facto, revolutionary or emancipatory in that it helps to pierce the necessary veil of illusion that envelops social practices. Thus, for Bhaskar, no a priori, subjective declaration of the emancipatory agenda is needed as a preface to science, for science itself, if taken seriously and carried through, counteracts ideology and provides enlightenment. By a similar token, even work preceded by reactionary motives can unwittingly serve emancipation, provided the scientific program has not been wantonly abridged in the process.

Of course, the emancipation that science provides is of a *cognitive* nature, and, as Bhaskar frankly concedes, "dissonance not liberation may be the immediate result of enlightenment";[28] This dissonance could just as easily lead to revolutionary activity as to plain and simple "despair." There is a logical gap, Bhaskar reminds us (contrary to the chiliastic hopes of many a Marxist) between "knowing and doing," and no science can—logically—lead an individual from one to the other. Although this very well-founded skepticism is a sane counsel for caution, nonetheless Bhaskar argues for the general emancipatory potential of explanatory knowledge which "increases the range of real (nonutopian) human possibilities," swinging the balance of the "argument" against the *status quo*. In this respect, the dominated and exploited classes, peoples, etc., are deemed to have (should have?) an interest in knowledge as a necessary condition for emancipation. In keeping with ontological realism, Bhaskar is careful to preclude any necessary scenarios of liberation. Unlike the fancies of some forms of Marxism, knowledge may not be either a necessary or a sufficient condition for social change.

By any token, transcendental realism poses a real challenge to the long reign of positivist intuitions (be it logical or empirical positivism) in economic science, whether of the Marxian or neoclassical variety. It does so, in each case, by explicitly denying the possibility in a social science of making arbitrary ontological assumptions (something ruled as a methodological virtue in Friedman and a practical inevitability in Max Weber). It does so, in each case, by denying that an adequate epistemology is possible upon the basis of an inaccurate ontology. The rather desperate—though not necessarily waning—Ricardo-Robbins[29] tradition of arguing for an economics based only on a radical *a priorism* of inspired introspection is likely to meet, in this critique, rather fatal objections to its clumsy pretenses. On the other hand ultraempiricism, or the "instrumentalist" variant of mainstream economics, is likely to see its positivist rudder flounder quite hopelessly—at least on a logical plane—in the face of its own revealed myopia and counterfactuality. In this respect, it is important to remember that transcendental realism provides a correction and a critique both to ruling epistemologies and the ontologies they conceal. Neither positivist-inspired monism nor its obverse, a plural neoKantian hermeneutics, live up to the ontological demands of social reality. Monism fails for not recognizing the transitive dimension in social science, the causal interdependency between subject and object in the social production of knowledge. Hermeneutics, for all its correct emphasis on the *Verstehen* idea, implying that in social life we are always dealing with a pre-interpreted reality, nonetheless fails to come through for its misapprehension of the intransitive dimension of society. In other words, the presence of causal interdependence does not contradict the possibility of the existential intransitivity of the social object of investigation. Put in Bhaskar's words:

> ...although the processes of production may be interdependent, once some object exists...however it has been produced, it constitutes a possible object of scientific investigation. And its existence (or not), and properties, are quite independent of the...process of investigation...even though such an investigation...may radically modify it.[30]

The point, made against both positivism and hermeneutics, could not be clearer: the human sciences can be sciences in "exactly the same sense, though not in exactly the same way," as the natural ones. Realism, therefore, demands a series of necessary modifications in the nature of economic theorizing, specially with regard to the nature of "assumptions" made about the human units of analysis, both with respect to intentions and activities. Both predicates of purpose and action need to be derived from a legitimate specification of the matrix of social relations in which they arise and exist. Motives can neither be ascribed nor assumed; they need to be derived, in all their defying complexity, from the structure of social relations within which their meanings are realized. Stated simply, the challenge to neoclassical theorizing consists in demanding that it get its anthropology and its political sociology right in a real world of unequal strata, power differentials, exploitation, and unequal access. Even apologetics needs be based, it would seem, on sound conceptions of the social order. This vital ontological correction reveals both the strength and the limitations of the realist challenge; for realism does not—perhaps cannot—provide a substantive economic theory, although it can point to the construction of a stable scaffolding upon which such a social economics may be erected. (The very term "economics" itself, of course, betrays an irrealist fragmentation of the unity of social life.) At this stage, at any rate, realism offers more a critique than a complete reconstruction of economic categories. But it is a critique that shares little of the wishful thinking common to both Marxian and neoclassical visions, basing itself instead on logically and empirically sustainable propositions.

The foregoing necessarily implies that the ruling currents are unlikely to be displaced by the sheer strength of the logical critique of realism. The great strength of paradigms—as tested in my own work on Ricardo[31]—has less to do with logical rigor than with conformity to the ruling perceptions of order. In that respect, realism is unlikely to supplant—except at the fringes—the main body of erroneous doctrine, the kiss of realism leaving asleep (but not undisturbed) in dogmatic slumber the wayward princess of mainstream political economy.

The mechanics of paradigm-shift have to do with material, not logical truths.[32] But, though socially and materially inspired, paradigms in social theory still need to shore up their logical apparati. It is in this regard that the realist challenge will impose enormous strain on the main corpus of economic theory by way of the requirement for readjustment of its defenses. The monist variant of positivism, in qualified retreat ever since the hermeneutical tradition launched its critique of naturalism, may well be further sequestered by the realist assault. However, it is likely that the

ECONOMICS AND EPISTEMOLOGY: TOWARD MATERIALISM

neoKantians[33]—within the ruling orthodoxy—might be the early beneficiaries of this waning of positivist influence. Similarly, at a different pole, a cautious institutionalism[34] might receive a renewed lease on life, since they were among the first to recognize indeterminacy and overdetermination in social life, bringing them a step closer to accurate ontological apprehensions than either the neoclassicals or the vulgar Marxists.

In this respect, realism can probably only register vicarious triumphs, as it helps prod social thinking to more closely approximate the domain of the real. To use a metaphor drawn from Bachelard, it will be a while—if ever—before the nocturnal philosophy of realism can overshadow the diurnal practice of positive science: a pity—but then again the owl of Minerva was never intended, perhaps, to fly at dawn.

Notes

1. The Friedman variant of positivism actually went to the extent of denying any need for a realist scrutiny of assumptions on the doubtful grounds that predictive efficiency neutralizes any errors in the prior specification. In fact, in what Samuelson characterized as the "F-Twist," Friedman almost implied that predictive accuracy was related in a simple fashion to the degree of *irrealism* of the assumptions. For a discussion of this issue, see M. Blaug, *The Methodology of Economics*, 1980, pp. 103-114.

2. Max Weber's explicit directives on method are to be found in M. Weber *The Methodology of the Social Sciences*, 1949. A more contemporary discussion is available in A. Giddens, *Capitalism and Modern Social Theory*, 1971.

3. The *Capital* controversy between the two Cambridges might well be treated as a case in point.

4. T. S. Kuhn, *The Structure of Scientific Revolutions*, 2nd ed., 1970. For a fuller statement on the Kuhn debate, see I. Lakatos and A. Musgrave, eds., *Criticism and the Growth of Knowledge*, 1970.

5. For arguments in this vein, see D. Hindess and P. Hirst, (1975) *Precapitalist Modes of Production*, 1975. Not dissimilar is the orientation of H. Cleaver, *Reading Capital Politically*, 1979.

6. On the mainstream tradition of Positivism, see L. Kolokowski, *Positivist Philosophy from Hume to the Vienna Circle*, 1972. For a discussion of Positivism in relation to social theory, see A. Giddens, ed., *Positivism and Sociology*, 1972. As regards Economics, see the Friedman classic, *Essays in Positive Economics*, 1966, and A. Coddington, "Positive Economics." *Canadian Journal of Economics*, 5, 1972. In the area of Philosophy, see A. J. Ayer, *Language, Truth and Logic*, 1952. As for classical Humean sources of positivist and many neo classical utilitarian ideas, see D. Hume, *Essays Moral and Political*, 1875; also, see Hume's *A Treatise on Human Nature*, 1967.

7. In the Marxian variant, the revisionism of the Second International, some aspects of Bolshevik thinking, and of course Stalinism, all represented Marxism as an empirical science of social engineering. See, in this regard, Otto Neurath, *Empiricism and Sociology*, 1973; also see N. Bukharin *Historical Materialism: A System of Sociology*, 1926, and G. V. Plekhanov, *In Defense of Materialism*, 1972. More recently, the work of John Roemer and Jon Elster is illustrative of this tendency, given in their embrace of analytic philosophy.

8. Friedman, op cit.

9. K. R. Popper, *The Open Society and Its Enemies*, 1962.

10. E. Durkheim, *The Rules of Sociological Method*, 1964. For a more current appraisal, see A. Giddens, op cit., 1971.

11. P. Berger and T. Luckman, *The Social Construction of Reality*,1967. London.

12. G. Bachelard, *The Philosophy of the New Scientific Mind*, 1958; also see *Le Rationalisme Applique*, 1949. For the Bachelardian influence on Marxian views, see D. Lecourt, *Marxism and Epistemology*.

13. P. Feyerabend, *Science in a Free Society*, 1978.

14. R. Bhaskar, *Reclaiming Reality*, 1989.

15. R. Bhaskar, *Scientific Realism and Human Emancipation*, 1986, p. 6.

16. Ibid., p. 26.

17. R. Bhaskar, op. cit., 1989, p. 51.

18. R. Bhaskar, *The Possibility of Naturalism*, 1979, p. 35.

19. In striking consonance, Keynes argued the case for the paradox of thrift. In fact, much of Keynesian economics is based on the rather simple—yet important—proposition that a macroeconomics may not be

constructed as a simple extension of micro-propositions. It is in this regard that Keynesianism is a step closer to realism than the neoclassical system it tried to criticize.

20. R. Bhaskar, op. cit., 1979, p. 37.

21. The theory of consumer behavior is a good example of a completely axiomatized deductive system unable to predict (surprisingly, given the emphasis placed on prediction as a necessary function of science) virtually any case of empirical consumer behavior, although ready to "explain"—post factum—any given instance of behavior. Stated simply, the law of demand boils down in practice to the proposition that anything is possible: quantity demanded may rise, fall, or remain stationary, given an original change in price. All these disparate behaviors may subsequently be titled as "rational," depending upon the premise used to justify each instance separately. In this case, the attribution of "rationality" to all possible behaviors makes the concept a caricature.

22. R. Bhaskar, op. cit., 1989, p. 61.

23. Auguste Comte, *The Positive Philosophy*, 1893, pp. 37-38.

24. L. Althusser, *Lenin and Philosophy*, 1971; also see V. Gerratana, "Althusser and Stalinism," *New Left Review*, 1077, 101-102; also P. Hirst, "Althusser and the Theory of Ideology." *Economy and Society*, 5:4, 1976, p. 396.

25. See G. Oldrini, ed., 1979; also, G. Lukacs, *History and Class Consciousness*, 1971; and G. Stedman-Jones, "The Marxism of the Early Lukacs," *New Left Review*, 70, November-December, 1971.

26. R. Bhaskar, op. cit., 1979, p. 59.

27. K. Marx, "Theses on Feuerbach," in F. Engels *Ludwig Feuerbach and the End of Classical German Philosophy*, 1888.

28. R. Bhaskar, op. cit., 1979, p. 112.

29. An excellent discussion of this and other methodological controversies in economics may be found in M. Blaug, op. cit., 1980.

30. R. Bhaskar, op. cit., 1979, p. 60.

31 See R. Kanth, *Political Economy and Laissez-Faire: Economics and Ideology in the Ricardian Era*, 1986.

32. See R. Kanth, "The Decline of Ricardian Politics: Some Notes on Paradigm Shift in Economics," *European Journal of Political Economy*, Summer 1985, pp. 157-187.

33. The neo-Kantian writ runs large upon contemporary theory; see P. Winch, *The Idea of a Social Science*, 1958; see also G. Myrdal, *Value in Social Theory*, 1959, and *Objectivity in Social Research*, 1970. For a placement of the *Verstehen* tradition in social science, see W. Outhewaite, *Understanding Social Life*, 1975.

34. See W. Samuels, ed., *Institutional Economics*, 1988.

11
~
Science, Class, and Theory:
The Elusive Anatomy of Social Discourse

One of the distinctive aspects of the mature, postEnlightenment view of science was the apparent conflation of natural and social science within a single framework of positivism (as with Comte), within which a natural science of society could be deemed equally as feasible as a natural science of nature. In some regards, of course, this is quite possible, indeed perhaps even desirable; for, in the approach to the subject matter, in the techniques of study involved, and in what might be termed the essential *existential intransitivity*[1] of the object studied, there is much common ground between the two orders of science. However this commonality, while obviously important, must not be allowed to obscure the fact that, although social factors may well influence the selection of areas of investigation even in the natural sciences (in the so-called "applied" areas), both the subsequent process of science and the generation of specific conclusions therefrom, are far less tendentious and carry, ultimately, a more relatively neutral impact on society itself than is true in the social sciences. The discovery of Halley's comet, for example, or the prediction of its return, is unlikely to affect or be affected by (an important dualism) the sectoral sympathies of either the scientist or the "school" he or she represents. Not so, however, in the examination of social periodicities where, for example, a field of study such as trade cycles has long suffered from the direct ideological intrusion of social partisanship. That is to say, while the object of study may well be

~145~

ECONOMICS AND EPISTEMOLOGY: TOWARD MATERIALISM

intransitive, in the social sciences one faces the phenomenon of what might be termed *causal interdependency* between subject and object. Stated simply, in the social sciences, the adjective is as important as the noun, the scientist being the active and reactive part of the organism under study. This is a qualitative difference ignored by positivism in much the same way that the idea of society as an intransitive object is ignored by the Weberian[2] neoKantians and other brands of subjective idealists.

It is this latter phenomenon—i.e. causal interdependency—that raises the question of a science of society compellingly: how scientific is social science, one might ask, given such a demonstrable interdependency? In what follows, I offer some suggestions for a clear understanding of both science and society, not merely by making abstract pronouncements, but with specific empirical recourse to the Ricardian period, using the Ricardian "science" (of political economy) as an illustration of the difficulties in this area.

~

First, to offer a definition of social science as "problem-solving" activity; this, of course, amends Kuhn's definition of science (bearing in mind that all of Kuhn's[3] models automatically equate natural science with science itself) as "puzzle-solving" activity. The difference in emphasis will be readily apparent: in Kuhn, the flavor is one of intellectual "puzzles" internally generated within the process of science (something only true for the "pure" aspect of natural science, but not at all true for the "applied" fields), whereas the notion of a "problem" is more general, and inclusive of vital practical and theoretical concerns. In this view, if science, in general, is problem-solving activity, then social science must be involved in solving social problems. But who decides—one might ask—what constitute societal problems and, just as importantly, how they are to be resolved?

Clearly, "official" social science is constituted by, and beholden to, the ruling establishment. Consequently, on average, both diagnosis and cure are usually on behalf—if not the behest—of the ruling perception of "order." Viewed thus, the instrumentality of social science becomes readily apparent. In the rather blunt phrase of Bukharin: "...science or theory is the continuation of practice by other means,"[4] implying that social science is simply inseparable from the social practice in which it is located. However, the establishment (no matter how constituted) is not coterminous with society as a whole; invariably, there are other contending interests. In this regard, one can easily foresee entirely legitimate disagreement over the ruling definition of both problem and solution, particularly since "problems" which appear as such in one discourse may be quite invisible in another. Only one example is the Marxian notion of exploitation, which is simply excluded, on a priori grounds, by most neoclassicists in the field of economics in favor of the idea of mutually beneficial exchanges between individuals and "factors."

It is this lack of a shared perception—when interests diverge—that underlines the principal difficulty of a social science within a stratified society, for then both the latent existence and the manifest (historical) emergence of more than one social science "perspective"—depending upon the material interest accommodated and point of view embraced—become entirely conceivable. Speaking concretely, in nineteenth-century England for instance, there were, in the area of economics, at least three distinct political economies self-consciously apart from each other: the world view of landowners expressed, however imperfectly, in the works of Lauderdale, Malthus,[5] and Jones; the resentment of workers, openly captured in the ideas of Thompson and Hodgkin;[6] and, finally, the initiatives of the manufacturers as reflected in the texts of Ricardo and others. Obviously, then, there were as many coherent political economies as there were independently definable socio-economic orders in the evolving socio-economic formation of nineteenth-century England. Which one, one might well ask, had the larger purchase on truth?

~

The answer to this question—and it is quite astonishing how many traditions in the history of thought have fudged both the question itself and the answers to it—is decidedly complex, moving at several levels, and involving various necessary stages. In a simple sense, of course, the answer to the question raised might be seen to depend—in relativist fashion—on the specific societal interest one is trying to accommodate. When interests diverge—it might be argued—who is, neutrally, to decide which plan is best? This view is also bolstered by the fact that it is by no means clear that it is the intellectually valid (even were that to be definable unambiguously) position that automatically reaps top honors, for that would be to share the rather unsustainable faith (yet shared by many, nonetheless) that issues of validity in a social science can be settled within the internal domain of science itself. In point of fact, in early nineteenth-century England, the political economy that succeeded socially was the one that won the social struggle between the various orders concretely, i.e. in material practice. Manufacturers won (and this should surprise no one), by dint of force, the right to impose their policies on other segments of society, and, thereby, Ricardo prevailed (temporarily, of course) so that workers and landowners, with separable interests of their own, were ultimately assimilated (temporarily again) into the great sweep of the Ricardian mainstream.[7] Given all this, of course, at least a preliminary case may be said to exist for the class relativity (if not other kinds of relativity) of what we have called "science," and the very practical basis for the issue of "validation" (quite apart from any notion of scientific "correctness").

If we were, accordingly, now to admit the plurality of social science (a different pluralism than the pluralism of mainstream social theory, à la Weber) with the historical example of economics in mind, then the immediate issue might be whether (or not) the term "science" is at all appropriate in this context. Are we not, perhaps, dealing, rather, with firmly articulated social ideologies?[8] If theory, as in Bukharin's aphorism, is simply practice by other means, then it is possible that social science may only be, perhaps, a scheme of practical ideology, rationalizing and organising the world from a given point of view. What becomes, then, of the distinction between science and ideology, and how are we now to assert the common presumption of the inferiority of the latter?

~

The Popperian[9] tradition has maintained, of course, that the demarcation issue is rather simply resolved: that science is at least potentially falsifiable, whereas pseudo-science is not. This idea, interestingly, suggested that it was possible (desirable?) to rule on the issue of scientificity not with respect to the empirical content of theories, but only in regard to the modes of proof and disproof proffered. This was a novel, even a daring, idea. But, practically, it shifted the burden of resolution in such matters to proof and disproof. However, the new orthodoxy, under

Science, Class, and Theory: The Elusive Anatomy of Social Discourse

Lakatosian impulse, rejects the Popper criterion as naive, it being now taken as "proved" that there is no logic of proof or disproof that is conclusive. All scientific theories, says Lakatos,[10] are equally unprovable. But then how are we to rescue the pretensions of "science"? Sciences, he argues, are only research programs and a progressive research program is one that is able to predict some hitherto undreamt of "novel" fact; indeed, it is this ability that distinguishes, for Lakatos, a "progressive" research program from a "degenerating" one. Implicit also in this view is the idea that scientists eventually latch on to superior programs while abandoning degenerating ones that lag behind reality. Needless to add, of course, all Lakatosian illustrations are drawn, without exception, from the natural sciences.

But can this typology be fitted to economics? I submit that this is difficult for, in the policy sciences, we have for the most part what may be termed "political research programmes"[11] tied to particular interests and specific schemes of social organization. Accordingly, the "success" of specific perspectives may have less to do with empirical accuracy, and/or predictive ability, than with the triumph of a given, sectarian interest in social practice.

Stated differently, *social science is social policy*—or research linked with it—reflecting the practice situated in a given structure of domination. Neoclassical economics survives, for instance, one might hypothesize, not because of its spectacular predictive successes but because it implicitly supports—and enjoys the support of—the established order of modern-day capitalism. No doubt, official Marxism, in the erstwhile socialist world, similarly rationalizes (or rationalized) the status quo.

So, quite contrary to the Lakatosian presumption, scientific research programs are not replaced automatically by more embracing, or better, predictive systems, but in fact change only when material conditions—including class orderings—undergo alteration in history. Again, using the example of economics, Ricardian economics was succeeded by neoclassicism in the last third of the nineteenth century not because it could predict some novel, hitherto inexplicable "fact," but because it fit the policy environment of mature capitalist society better. That is to say, neoclassicism was more serviceable than Ricardian economics, given the altered social relations and the changed social agenda of late capitalism. Modes of social science "degenerate", to employ Lakatosian usage, because either the power sustaining them in society has lost its force, or because the particular need they answered originally has ceased to be. This, as I will try to show, was the reason why Ricardian economics fell from grace when it did in the middle of the nineteenth century.

To return, thereby, to the original issue raised: can science and ideology be clearly demarcated in an absolutist sense, given that both derive from the same governing provenance of practice? This matter can be addressed indirectly, yet concretely, by means of a close examination of classical (Ricardian) political economy.

~

By any reckoning, David Ricardo is one of the outstanding economists of the classical period, if not indeed the greatest of them all. Certainly, Ricardo's fame and general intellectual reputation in the first third of the nineteenth century in England compares favorably with that of Adam Smith in the last quarter of the eighteenth. His theories, though most likely little understood—except in their implications (both assumed and real)—attracted the attention of a very wide audience, well beyond the few specialists in the field. As a wealthy stockbroker (and one dare not discount this very handy badge of material success), a member of Parliament, and a key founding member of the Political Economy Club—a virtual shadow government of economic policy, counting amongst its members prominent personages within the political elite—Ricardo exercised enormous influence both within the so-called "new school"[12] of political economy (that took its name from him) and upon the making of policy by the political establishment of his day.

Although granted more than his share of detractors and critics, for reasons that should become clear, he was nonetheless generally regarded as having attained the pinnacle of classical accomplishment in his *Principles*, published in 1817. And yet, despite this achievement, barely a decade or so after his untimely death in 1823, his star went on the descendant; and, by the middle of the century, he had been all but repudiated, to be buried by a rapidly evolving discipline that he had done so much to place at the center of national attention. Rarely had someone so mighty fallen from grace,[13] so quickly—a fact that cries out for explanation. Indeed, in the history of economic thought, we are possessed of at least two powerful analyses—though opposed to one another—that have tried to account for the phenomenon of the fall of the house of Ricardo.

Science, Class, and Theory: The Elusive Anatomy of Social Discourse

One interpretation, borrowed from Marx and tendered by Marxians thereafter, incidental subtleties apart, accounts for the demise of Ricardianism by recourse to politics and ideology: it is claimed that the Ricardian emphasis on class conflict, and its attachment to a "labor theory" of value proved much too dangerous a set of ideas for the ruling order, particularly since these ideas had been adopted for their own by a growing working-class movement with radical ambitions. Hence, with apologetics in mind, the new neoclassical representatives of the bourgeoisie steered economics away from these subversive aspects of Ricardianism. And so the theoretical legacy of Ricardo was allowed to expire, gradually, having first been retired from active discourse by the new switching of rails.[14]

The competing version is rendered by the neoclassicals who focus, instead, on the putatively erroneous nature of Ricardianism—such as its embrace of the labor theory of value—as the reason for its abandonment. This is to say that an "incorrect" theory of value and distribution was ultimately—and quite naturally—replaced by a correct model, as it was to be constructed in the deliberations of the postRicardians. And so, in this account, the rejection of the Ricardian model is viewed as an appropriate and expected eventuality in the long march of analytical progress in the discipline. The eclipse of Ricardo is here seen completely as an issue internal to the science (unlike the Marxian account, with its stress on the external environment), without any need to refer to any other operative social determinations. False theory, runs the facile argument, is always replaced (if only eventually) by true theory.[15]

These contrasting views have constituted the rival, enduring orthodoxies on the issue of the dissolution of the Ricardian school, and yet each is guilty of rather singular misperceptions. The Marxian thesis[16] seems to be predicated too closely upon a conception of class conflict within capitalism in general, i.e. in the abstract, being deafeningly silent on the question of the specific needs accommodated by the Ricardian enterprise. Equally, it fails to specify (in fact, seems almost unaware of) the practical agenda underlying both Ricardian and postRicardian paradigms. To point to a further shortcoming: it would also seem—in this rendering—that mainstream economics is, pure and simple, little more than a defensive, class-conscious ideology serving no other function than the suppression of models premised upon class conflict, along with issues potentially hostile to a harmonious vision of capitalism.

ECONOMICS AND EPISTEMOLOGY: TOWARD MATERIALISM

The mainstream version, on its part, fails to specify any social determinations altogether, arguing as though fundamental shifts in the social sciences are purely internally generated within the process of science itself. This apart, the notion of analytical progress it espouses is quite spurious; one can measure progress and regress unambigously only when the object of the discourse is unarguably unaltered. But the object of study of Ricardian and neoclassical economics is anything but the same: they ask different questions; they are interested in different issues; and they have different practical objectives[17] in mind. Additionally, it needs be noted that, even if the theoretical object of study were the same for both of these schools, the real historical object would nevertheless still be different, for social relations in England had arguably changed between the epoch of Ricardo and the age of Jevons. Therefore, the assertion of a "superior" analytical framework in the case of postRicardian economics is both vacuous and misleading. But even were it to be possible to establish such "superiority," it would not follow that such analytical strength by itself guaranteed its preeminence as against Ricardianism. In the real world, virtue—even of the academic kind—sad to say, does not triumph quite so easily; worldly success, alas, being contingent upon many other factors, as well.

The mystery of the displacement of Ricardian economics, therefore, has not really been solved, either by the mainstream or the Marxian tradition, although unquestionably some incidental aspects of the process have been identified, by the Marxists, most notably. What follows is a more coherent explanation for the declension of Ricardianism that confirms, in the process, a larger thesis of the practical foundations of economic theory—and, indeed, of social knowledge generally.

~

Now to sketch the vital historical backdrop against which the Ricardian model evolved.[18] The period with which we are concerned, speaking broadly, is 1800-1850; a little more accurately one might place its location between 1815 and 1846—1815 being the year of Waterloo, the passage of the first post-war Corn Law, and Ricardo's *Essay on Profits*, and 1846 being the year when the Corn Laws were finally repealed. Or, to mark it between important texts, between the *Essay on Profits* and the *Principles*, penned by J. S. Mill in 1848. Within this envelope, there are two definable phases: a phase that might be termed *Ricardo ascendant*, lasting until the Reform Act of 1832, and a phase best termed *Ricardo decadent*,[19] covering the remaining years. The meaning of such a categorization will unfold as we proceed; but, first, to establish the significance of this period in the evolution of English capitalism.

With Napoleon having been granted his final sabbatical in 1815—i.e., with England's last surviving commercial and military rival securely disposed of—from the point of view of the industrial and manufacturing classes, there were but three prime issues that appeared to stand in the way of England becoming the workshop and foundry of the world. Firstly, the Poor Laws,[20] as amended in 1795, for having interfered with the capitalist work "incentives" and having stemmed the flow of "surplus" rural labor into the welcoming channels of industry, owing to their provision of the dole, which enabled a modicum of survival outside of the preferred wage-labour nexus. Secondly—and once again regarded from the same vantage point—there were the Corn Laws, which were perceived as having raised wages and lowered profits by preventing cheaper imports of foreign corn, also thereby inhibiting the emergence of a foreign market for domestically produced manufactures (as corn imports would have provided the outside world with purchasing power which could then be expected to return to England as a duly constituted demand for industrial goods). Thirdly, there was the "Reform" question, which, in some respects, was perhaps even more immediate since it was a "Parliament of Landlords" that, of course, stood in the way of "reforming" policies (such as the Poor and Corn Laws) in the direction more favorable to industrial interests. For instance, important emergent manufacturing centers such as Manchester, Birmingham, and Sheffield had no representation in either House. To state matters bluntly, without a reform of the existing suffrage, the manufacturing order simply could not directly make policy in defense of its interests vis à vis the commercial and landowning aristocracy.

So, among a host of other minor matters, these three issues seemed to constitute—again, from the vantage of a specific stratum—the principle obstacles to an England ready to rush headlong on the path to a mature industrial capitalism. It is not necessary to aver that these problems were, indeed, the sort of insuperable obstacles to economic growth as they were made out to be. In fact, growth was quite continuous throughout the period, despite the presence of these alleged obstructions, as it was indeed afterward when the path was cleared of such "debris." More importantly, it was the manufacturing order which perceived itself (perhaps not inaccurately) as being disadvantaged by these factors, and—through a variety of means—it managed to disseminate this perception quite effectively amongst a large corpus of opinion.

~

The foregoing "practical necessities"—as discerned by an enlightened industrial interest—have now been sketched; now to examine how classical political economy—in its decisive Ricardian phase—responded to these "challenges."

The "involvement" of postSmithian political economy in the issues just defined was direct and relentless. In 1795, the so-called Speenhamland declaration amended the Tudor Poor Law by sanctioning, implicitly, what Karl Polanyi was to call the "right to live"[21] of workers, regardless of market conditions, granting—in effect—a socially guaranteed subsistence. By 1798, before the dust had settled, as it were, Malthus had both penned and published his famous *Essay on Population*—or rather, to call things by their proper names, his *Essay on the Poor Laws* (which were, of course, the real subject of his attentions). The first classical blow against Speenhamland had been struck: poverty was now being described as a "natural" condition created by the poor—of their own volition—owing to their incurable propensity to multiply like bacteria on a petrie dish. Charity, as it was to be called, toward the poor was now deemed a great error, for the dole only exacerbated—or so it was held—the original condition of poverty. "Natural" laws were not to be interfered with—so Speenhamland had to go! Not only had Malthus "shown" the retrograde nature of the Poor Laws, he had also managed to put his prejudices on a "scientific" footing; for, it might be noted, his "theory" depended heavily on the alleged differential in the mathematical rates of growth of food production and population[22] (the latter outstripping the former exponentially). The spurious math was the secure basis of his confident appeal to "science." As Hume had already said, in the same century, if a piece of analysis involved no reasoning concerning "quantity or number," it was best to "commit it then to the flames!" It was the vaunted ratios that constituted Malthus's trump card of scientism, revealing, incidentally, the early marriage between positivism and quantitative analysis. Those who may have otherwise distrusted Malthusian motives and policies would, nonetheless, have been rendered impotent by the seeming ineluctibility of his time series! Of course, the entire apparatus, both theoretically and empirically, as we know—or should know—was bogus. But it did not matter: Malthus was perceived, by the votaries of the new order, as having "scientifically" defended the case for repeal of the Poor Laws.

Although James Mill had attacked the Corn Laws[23] in an earlier pamphlet (in 1804, in response to an 1804 Corn Law), the first really significant "classical" cannonade directed against the Corn Laws came from the pen of Ricardo in 1815 (responding to the Corn Law of 1815), with his *Essay on Profits*.[24] Ricardo takes great pains, in this pamphlet, to establish the "fact" that agricultural profits depress the general rate of profit across the economy. But why are agricultural profits surmised as declining, in the first place? Because of diminishing returns in agriculture runs the argument. But why do returns diminish in agriculture? Because the protectionist Corn Laws necessitate recourse to poorer, marginal lands (implying, of course—an important assumption—that new lands are less fertile than the old). And why do we have the Corn Laws? Because landlords, in defense of their unconscionably selfish interests, are holding society to ransom, And thus we see that the manufacturers' discontent with the aristocracy on economic and political matters gets a "scientific" airing—almost. But the *Essay* didn't go far enough; its many logical deficiencies (and its ill-concealed practical intent) was immediately spotted by the astute Malthus who, on this issue, was protective of the landed interest. And so we get, in 1817, the expanded version of the *Essay*, the definitive (if analytically equally deficient) bible in the crusade against the landowners and their Corn Laws, but somewhat neutrally titled (for economics had, in the end, to be a science!), *Principles of Political Economy and Taxation*, the pinnacle of the Ricardian—some would say classical—theoretical achievement. A purely topical policy issue had spawned a "theoretical" epic of classical political economy.

As for the Ricardian embroilment in the Reform movement, suffice it to say that it was total. In fact, Ricardo purchased a seat in Parliament (as only a Ricardo could), and was a key spokesperson for the so-called Radicals within. Outside of Parliament, he and his comrades amongst the political economists, Mill, McCulloch, Tooke, and Torrens included, campaigned actively on behalf of Reform in as many forums as were to be found available. All things considered, then, the engagement of the political economists in the Ricardian fold in matters conforming to manufacturing, middle-class interests, in their charter for economic advancement, was complete. More importantly, it was effective. In fact, one might even say that the totality of the class interests of the manufacturing order was—as is quite frequent in such things—better understood by the Ricardians than by their own kind (the famous Merchants' Petition, for instance, was drawn up by Tooke). It is in this respect that one might speak of the Ricardians as constituting the intellectual vanguard of the manufacturing order. Be that as it may, it is easy to see the simple correspondence between the institutional needs of a particular stratum within a specific situational conjuncture—early nineteenth-century Britain in the aftermath of Waterloo—and "scientific" articulation of those needs in the "theory" of classical political economy.[25] But the story is still not told; so to examine, now, the theoretical basis of the Ricardian model, reviewing its implications for a Ricardian "science."

~

To recapitulate, the *Principles* was in reality an extended, amended version of the *1815 Essay* (which itself was a salvo fired against the 1815 Corn Law), designed to make a strong, indeed ironbound, case against the Laws.[26] Ricardo's objectives were quite clear, and also quite simple. He was trying to establish, as solidly as possible, the following propositions: first, that the relative price of corn and cotton (to use these highly symbolic goods) were moving in a way antagonistic to the industrial interest; second, that the rate of profit was falling, owing to the resort to less fertile lands made inevitable by the Corn Laws, initially in agriculture, and then (by an inference itself built upon certain very strong premises) elsewhere (indeed everywhere!) in the economy; and third, that the so-termed "stationary state" (that mythical day of doom where all of the net produce was soaked up by rents, leaving profits at zero. In exact symmetry, Ricardo had argued, in Parliament, that the Poor rates—which subsidized the embryonic "welfare" system sanctioned by Speenhamland—would soon swallow up the entire net product.

References to such imagined threats were quite frequent in the popular pronouncements of the Ricardians), ever impending, was not to be foiled until the Corn Laws had been abolished. All this, of course, would confirm the Ricardian view that the interest of the landlords was opposed to all other interests; but how, one might ask, could "science" achieve all this for Ricardo and the manufacturers?

It could only perform thus, we shall see, by means of a carefully chosen, selectively applied set of assumptions[27] (in this Ricardo was only the grand pacesetter; economics remains, to this day, a science of assumptions). In point of fact, the sheer economy in the fundamental assumptions adopted by Ricardo is possibly quite sufficient to make him the greatest "economist" of all times! The two principal assumptions employed by Ricardo—only two were sufficient!—were, firstly, the so-called "law of population" (borrowed from Malthus, in the main, although, admittedly, such ideas enjoyed widespread popularity in this period), and secondly, the so-called "law of diminishing returns" (coupled, of course, cautiously, with the idea of the differential fertility of land) in agriculture. It is of interest to see how the fledgling science of political economy invoked its own theoretical "laws" to battle the more practical laws of the landowners' state: the "law" of population was sufficient to attack the Poor Laws, and the "law" of diminishing returns was enough to assail the Corn Laws! At any rate, both, taken together, make up the basis of the Ricardian model: the law of population gives, essentially a constant real wage, while the law of returns gives a declining net product at the margin of cultivation. Now bring in a very cautiously employed labor standard of measurement, and Ricardo, with the further aid of a dozen other ancillary—but nevertheless equally doubtful—subassumptions had almost (but for the gimlet eye of Malthus) proven his case.

This merits a second glance at the apparatus, so skillfully constructed. Malthusian population theory—misspecified in logic, false on empirical grounds—is in fact one of the axial supports of the model. The second piece of vital scaffolding is the idea of diminishing returns in agriculture, premised upon a dearth of technical progress in agriculture and on the equally doubtful proposition that new lands brought in, as the margin of cultivation is extended, are always less fertile than the old. Whenever the fact of technical progress is admitted, it is "assumed" to be overrun by the strength of the forces making for diminishing returns; this, it will be noted, in a country that was the envy of Europe on account of its rational agriculture—indeed one that had undergone an agricultural revolution before its industrial transformation! Assume these remaining propositions and then—with the aid of the invariant standard of measurement (invariant, that is, to changes in distribution)—you can "show," as Ricardo did, that rents rise and profits decline with capital accumulation, i.e. landlords gain, in both absolute and relative terms, vis à vis their suffering manufacturing cousins. Given his "assumptions,"[28] and given the perfectly invariant standard—which Ricardo was ultimately unsuccessful in developing—of course, Ricardo had bent "science," successfully, in service to his will:[29] but, and here is the million dollar question, were these assumptions correct? Stated simply, the truth of Ricardo's assumptions, much like the presumption of equality in the preamble to the American Declaration of Independence, was considered—or held—to be self-evident.

The Ricardians, in effect, defended these assumptions steadfastly. Ricardo himself made no effort to conduct an empirical inquiry, despite the provocation (even if a desire to seek the whole truth were not provocation enough) posed by pamphleteers across the country, claiming evidence to the contrary, evidence that directly challenged his "theory" of distribution. It was argued, for instance, that profits and rents had both risen simultaneously, that the rate of profit had fallen, that wages showed little fixity, and so on. But the Ricardians turned a deaf ear and a blind eye toward all criticism (it must be borne in mind that the case against the Corn Laws would have collapsed completely if these assumed truths were to be admitted as being false). And so Ricardo carried the day in the ascendant phase of the Ricardian age. (DeQuincey, a friend and admirer of Ricardo, was to blissfully characterize Ricardo's truths as being akin to the certainty of geometric theorems, thus affirming the lofty credentials of the science of political economy.) And 1832 (but a few years after Ricardo's untimely demise) saw the first triumph of the Ricardian industrial agenda: the Reform Act was duly passed. Within two years of passage, the Poor Laws had been "reformed" in ways consistent with the capitalist mandate for labor, so well understood by Bentham and Ricardo: the workhouse "Panopticon" was vigorously reinstated and relief was made, to use Bentham's pregnant phrase, "less eligible," i.e. wretched, miserable, and inadequate. Only a decade later,

Science, Class, and Theory: The Elusive Anatomy of Social Discourse

as a foregone conclusion, in 1846, the Corn Laws were repealed. The Ricardian agenda had now achieved total success.

~

The practical success of the Ricardian agenda was contingent upon a vast paraphernalia of means of persuasion; the propaganda side was pursued with great vigor in clubs, debating societies, journals, newspapers, colleges, in the "nursery pap" of Jane Marcet, and the secular preachings of Harriet Martineau, etc. This overwhelming deluge of inspired propagation rested as much on Ricardo's quasiscientific theories of political economy as on the quasitheoretic slogans of "free trade" and "laissez-faire" (as significant to the Ricardian revolution as "liberté, égalité and fraternité" had been to the French), which gave them even wider currency for being simple, accessible, and readily identifiable ideas. No doubt, as in all crusades, belief in these ideas may have been quite sincere (after all, as Nietzsche had it, the true visionary lies to himself, not to others). But it became no less clear, after the victory of Reform, who the real intended beneficiaries were. Workers who had formed the naive, if enthusiastic, allies of the middle classes found themselves excluded from the franchise (as always!) now extended to their former friends. And, to compound the injury, the new Poor Law struck deep and hard at their traditional sense of the social compact, at their very "right to live," in fact. The Ricardian promise had been, if a promise at all, a trickle-down promise: certainly no immediate benefits, even by way of cheapened corn, came the way of the workers. Instead, they learned the hard way not to be led by the rhetoric of their manufacturing overlords, who betrayed them just as easily (and perhaps with even less compunction) as the aristocracy was alleged by the Ricardian warriors to have dispossessed workers in the context of the Corn Laws.

The enthusiasm generated by the Ricardians was, of course, not for the internal dialectics of the Ricardian model but for the Ricardian cause, the Ricardian policy imperative. (In his own lifetime, Ricardo felt that there were only about twenty-five souls in the length and breadth of England who really understood what he was saying in theory—possibly an overstatement!—aside from the policy implications, in his model.) It was this specifically-directed euphoria that also carried the case high in the popular middle-class mind. Hence, it was the external environment that made of Ricardo a celebrity. On matters internal to the theory, there was little agreement—even within the Ricardian school; but, in Ricardo's own lifetime, it was felt, tactically, that it was best not to publicize these differences, so as to maintain a necessary, united front against aristocratic and landlord pretensions. It is this phenomenon of a Ricardo riding the popular crest that explains, also, why the opposition could not win the hearts and minds of the public. Malthusian objections to Ricardo's schemes, for instance, were not "wrong"—although open to the same charge of partisan inspiration—but his ideas, along with Lauderdale's, ultimately lost the struggle, in a manner of speaking, because the landed interest lost the class struggle, having first lost the mass base of workers. The mass bass of workers were inveigled by the propaganda of the manufacturing order (the Anti-Corn Law League) into opposing the landed interest and supporting the free trade cause. The Ricardian system, accordingly, to use a phrase of Keynes, had a "complex of suitabilities" that conquered England in much the same way that the Inquisition had conquered Spain (even Keynes was probably unaware as to how apt this metaphor was). A more potent clue to the viability of paradigms in the social sciences can hardly be more evident.

~

Paradoxically (and the matter is instructive for students of science particularly) it was this very practical success that, in fact, spelled the doom of the Ricardian model. With the Poor Laws and the Corn Laws repealed, with free trade authorized and laissez-faire accepted, what further, instrumental, purpose could the model serve? Virtually all of the conclusions of the Ricardian analysis, it needs be remembered, were tied to the existence of the Corn Laws; with the laws set aside, stripped of its critical connection—of its very raison d'être—the theory went, of a sudden, bankrupt! So we can now appreciate the real reason for the fall of the classical house of Ricardo: it had become, rather abruptly, practically irrelevant. The manufacturer-led state that replaced the landowners' state had no further need for that custom-designed, function-specific, apparatus; the Ricardian "theorems," being contingent formulations in the main, became functionally obsolete.

Slowly, the tools fashioned by Ricardo were withdrawn, softened, or simply abandoned. They had done their duty and earned their bread,

Science, Class, and Theory: The Elusive Anatomy of Social Discourse

and, much like old soldiers, they were now retired, but not without due ceremony. Landlords were now looked upon with benevolence, for a certain kind of class struggle had been won, and the former antagonists were now sought as propertied allies in the conjoint struggle to tame working class agitation. Ricardo had defined political economy as the study of "distribution," and he could not have given a clearer expression to the nature of the real imperatives of the time, for that particular phase within English capitalism involved a bitter struggle between landlord and manufacturer for control over the state, the direction of economic policy, and the establishment of a "proper" hierarchy in the distribution of the net product between rents and profits. The very object of study of the science of political economy, as in the Ricardian definition, had a direct practical and material determination. Reality, at times, one may venture, is far more vulgar, even, than an inept Marxism.

After 1846, itself made possible by the victory of 1832, the distributive struggle had, in effect, been won: profits, not rents, had been placed in undisputed command. There was no further institutional necessity for a "distributive" focus for political economy. The Ricardian object of analysis, much as the Ricardian agenda, had become defunct. It is quite easy, therefore, to understand the eclipse of the Ricardian paradigm: it had "solved" its historically given "problem." So we can appreciate the rise of neoclassicism, defining, as it was to do, economics anew, within a novel focus, indeed with a new problematic: it was indeed a new discipline trying to solve problems contemporary to its genesis, bearing little connection with either the Ricardian period, or its own classical ancestry.

~

Now to look at the methodological features of the Ricardian project in the light of the foregoing analysis. We have noted that the "model" itself was constructed on the basis of tendentious reasoning involving, as pointed out, a very selective choice of assumptions intended to confirm the case being argued. The Ricardians, by and large, were to reify Ricardo's own calculatedly dogmatic stubbornness into a duly designated "methodology" of science. Thus, political economy, as per Nassau Senior's boast, claimed that it "is not greedy of facts; it is independent of facts."[30] (Could

ECONOMICS AND EPISTEMOLOGY: TOWARD MATERIALISM

there be a more telling indictment of a "science"?) The truths of economics, such as they were, were said to be gleaned through inspired introspection that quite placed them, almost, beyond the vulgar reach of falsification. As J. S. Mill[31] was to magisterially announce, writing in 1836, economics was a "mental," "abstract" science based on the "a priori" method—its assumptions, thereby, could be wholly "without foundation in fact," even while its truths were likened to those of "geometry" and, hence, "true in the abstract." Perhaps, it might be held, Mill—like the Ricardians—had in mind Smith's description of the Newtonian method, whereby we assume certain ideas as "primary or proved in the beginning," from which we then deduce a chain of other arguments (the hypothetico-deductive method of modern parlance). But this approach, as Mill might have known, was highly disingenuous—it seemed hardly credible, even in Mill's own time, to place arguments about a given historical society, such as England, on par with the axiomatic revelations of geometry. Far more to the point, in fact, was the opinion of a perceptive critic who noted, wisely, that the "strength of economists" lay in their keeping a safe "distance from the facts."[32]

The purely defensive nature of this revulsion to facts was only too obvious. Even one as intellectually generous as J. S. Mill was not above fudging in this respect; facts were allowed the rather apologetic role of verification and corroboration, but were never permitted the critical function of disproving the introspectively derived truths of economics. And, in the Ricardian era, never was a science more contemptuous (and not merely ignorant) of empirical evidence. Ricardo never provided a shred of empirical evidence—direct or indirect—for his own introspective revealments, even while systematically disregarding all evidence proffered by others, evidence that contradicted, whether potentially or actually, his own chosen conclusions.

But the case against Ricardo can be taken further. It would appear to be merely the logical duty of a science—constructed purely on assumptions, as it were—to investigate, however partially, the potential strength, validity, and significance of counterarguments which could, in the period concerned, have been just as easily (some would say much more realistically) proposed for consideration. He might have, for instance, from purely heuristic considerations alone, considered the case for increasing returns in agriculture, coupled with the suggestion that food production might be increasing faster than (or even just as fast as)

Science, Class, and Theory: The Elusive Anatomy of Social Discourse

population (instead of the Malthusian inversion of the variables)—both of which, incidentally, could arguably be considered the more likely situation at the time. But then—and how could his incisive intelligence have missed this apprehension?—Ricardo would have constructed almost a classical antiRicardian model for a crusade against his own system. The rate of profit would not have declined, then, for Ricardo's reasons, and the necessary conflict of interest between landlords and the rest of society would have vanished into thin air. That is to say, the "scientific" basis for the crusade against the Corn Laws would have, then, duly evaporated. It is this notable failure to consider an entirely legitimate alternative mapping of assumptions that most directly weakens the strong case for a detached Ricardian "science." It indicates, additionally, the trivial (but nonetheless true) fact that, contrary to Max Weber, assumptions are never arbitrary in the social sciences; rather, they always embody—rightly or wrongly—powerful predeterminants of the subsequent analysis.

~

It is this matter, of course, that brings us to the present day. Milton Friedman,[33] in an early discourse on method which has since become the conservative catechism on the subject, has argued, in the manner (albeit later) of Lakatos, that it is only the predictive value of theory that is of import; issues of the validity of assumptions, and even of their possible counter-factuality, being of no primary concern to the scientist as much as to the project of science. As he put it, in the much celebrated essay (an index of the intellectual sophistication of the science), "...to be important...a hypothesis must be descriptively false in its assumptions," something which Samuelson was to characterize as the "F-Twist." It should be understood that Friedman was not merely saying that assumptions are irrelevant; he was also implying that, somehow, the chances of accuracy in prediction are linked to the degree of falseness of the assumptions! We can now appreciate Friedman as only a latter-day representative of the original Ricardian tradition, which continued in the second half of the nineteenth century—after Ricardo—through Cairnes. Cairnes went on to argue that the premises of economics were not hypothetical, but rather were based on the "indubitable facts of human nature and of the world," and further, that "the economist starts with a knowledge of ultimate causes. He is already, at the outset of his enterprise, in the position which the physicist only obtains after ages of laborious research."

This tendency—dignified with the appellation of radical *a priorism* in the literature of economics—continued into the twentieth century with the work of Lionel Robbins who, in 1932, in essence, repeated the argument of Cairnes in his famous essay on the nature of economic science, culminating finally in the neoAustrian treatise of Von Mises who, in 1949, argued confidently that, in economics, "the particular theorems are not open to any verification or falsification on the grounds of experience." Of course, in so doing, Von Mises was—much as Friedman—implicitly defending the well-known (for their paucity, emptied as they are of any realist content) assumptions of neoclassicism about the nature of capitalist society and economy which, in well-heeled Ricardian fashion, rationalize very specific policy orientations. In the light of the hazards of such an approach—as highlighted in the case of Ricardo—I would urge that this piece of cryptomysticism be abandoned as a sound principle of prudent method. As with the case of Ricardo, assumptions are not merely the keys to the scientific kingdom: they also powerfully predetermine the subsequent conclusions and analysis. So, to excise the critical study of the criteria employed in the preliminary choice of assumptions from the general purview of scientific scrutiny is to renege on scientific responsibility at the very doorstep of scientific inquiry. Such transparently shallow methodological defenses should now be seen for what they really are—"immunizing strategems," as Popper might have referred to them, invented and reinvented to protect a doubtful model from the certainty of destructive criticism which it would almost inevitably provoke.[34]

Similarly, without wishing to set the agenda for what, socially, may pass for science, it is easy to see that to overemphasize (or worse, to solely emphasize) the predictive capability of a science, to the detriment of its explanatory capability, is to voluntarily disembowel the intellectually informative content of the science. In other words, the Friedman-Lakatos[35] criterion of "predictive" value imposes an unnecessary poverty on the scope of the scientific project. Besides, prediction is not explanation in reverse (as is sometimes implied in positivist discourse) and, in fact, can be contemplated quite independently of a real knowledge of any causal connections whatsoever. Indeed, no more is

Science, Class, and Theory: The Elusive Anatomy of Social Discourse

explanation prediction in reverse, for in the social sciences, given the transformational nature of social relations, the business of prediction will always be, at best, problematic and, at worst, vacuous. In fact, the Friedmanite approach to prediction always displays the structural weakness of the positivist collation of nature with society (monism). Social science is always incomplete for purely ontological reasons, leading to the well-known phenomenon of both the past and future being redefined constantly.

~

To a certain extent, it is quite possible to treat Ricardo as a metaphor for the practice of modern economics, which departs from Ricardo only in minor details. Thus, the question, was the Ricardian enterprise science, or was it ideology? can also be turned against today's mainstream theorizing with almost as much meaning. (This is a far cry from the Schumpeterian view, wherein the "modern" era is exclusively "scientific," as opposed to all of the perversions extant in Ricardian, physiocratic and, indeed, any and all pre-neoclassical economics.) And so the study of the past, in human society, can only illuminate the present. But to raise the issue, first, of the "scientific" credentials of the Ricardian variant of classical political economy, as it is interpreted in the Marxian tradition.

In a much quoted passage, Marx implied that, so long as the class struggle was "latent," political economy functioned as "science," whereas with the sharpening of working class political consciousness and open class hostilities—in the second third of the nineteenth century—political economy degenerated and turned, ultimately, "apologetic." This would seem to establish an existential reason why a distorted perspective becomes "necessary," objectively speaking. But, a little later on, Marx makes another distinction between classical and vulgar economics (of course, by way of clarification, it needs be remembered that Marx, in this passage, is not thinking of the later neoclassical tradition, à la Jevons, but rather of the postRicardians such as Senior). To quote:

> When I speak of the "classical political economy" I mean all the political economy since W. Petty which has been devoted to the study of the real interrelations of bourgeois production in contradistinction to "vulgar economy." The "vulgar economists" are content to elucidate the semblance of the interrelations of bourgeois production; like ruminants, they

spend their time chewing the cud of materials provided in days long past by scientific political economy seeking thence to extract for bourgeois daily food plausible explanations for the most obvious phenomena; and, for the rest, they are satisfied with systematizing in pedantic fashion, and proclaiming as eternal verities, the most trivial and self-complacent notions which the agents of bourgeois production entertain with regard to their own best of all possible worlds.[36]

What is not instantly clear, in both of these suggestions, is the issue of whether "vulgar" economics is self-conscious propaganda, or merely unwitting self-deception (the latter, of course, would exonerate the "vulgar" economists from the charge of being merely subjective liars). This, of course, has remained the key problem of the Marxian theory of ideology because Marx does, seemingly, drift between unselfconscious and self-conscious versions of what might be termed "false consciousness" (or of what may be termed negative and positive conceptions of "ideology"). And indeed, matters are made no clearer when J. S. Mill is cleared of "apologetic" intent, as in this passage:

> ...to avoid misunderstanding, I wish to point out here that though such men as John Stuart Mill deserve criticism on account of their contradictions between their obsolete economic dogmas and their modern tendencies, it would be utterly unjust to confound them with the ruck of apologists belonging to the school of vulgar economics.[37]

The issue, in this posing of it, quite simply, seems to revolve around intellectual honesty or dishonesty, which has little, directly, to do with the larger issue—raised most fundamentally in Marx's work—as to how we are duped by reality.

At any rate, Marx's meaning[38] was that Ricardo, "fearlessly," makes no attempt to conceal conflicts of interest within capitalism, whereas "apologists" such as Senior "disguised" those struggles within an essentially harmonious conception of economy and society. Prima facie, this is a tempting view—for Senior's contempt for the indigent was quite unqualified—but I would argue that such a categorization seriously misreads and misspecifies the Ricardian contribution. In point of fact, what Marx finds attractive (aside from Ricardo's celebrated intellectual—and personal—honesty) in Ricardo is his apparent admission of class

Science, Class, and Theory: The Elusive Anatomy of Social Discourse

conflict (obtaining most fundamentally for Ricardo, of course, to make matters clear between landowners and all others and—in a lesser key—between manufacturers and workers on the single issue of the substitution of fixed capital for living labor), and his (qualified) adoption of a "labor theory" of value. It is this set of attributed that establishes, in Marx's eyes, the scientific credentials of Ricardo.

But this attribution is quite problematic. For Ricardo always maintained that capitalism is quite a harmonious system once the Corn Laws (and landlords) had been deposed and policy had become securely geared to the manufacturing interest, thereby placing capital accumulation above all considerations. So the class struggle referred to in the Ricardian schema (with the caveats already noted) was only a temporary and contingent feature. With free imports of corn, as Ricardo tirelessly reiterated, the rate of profit would be perpetually buoyant, and accumulation—thus assisted—would thereby function as a smooth and beneficent process. Similarly, it becomes quite clear that Ricardo's attachment to a "labor" theory of value (and even his understanding of the latter concept) is of quite a different order than that of Marx. For Ricardo, the labor-embodied criterion was sufficient (almost) to establish the long-run differentials in the prices of agricultural and industrial products; that is to say, it was relevant, primarily, to a consideration of relative values over time (quite apart from any search for the "secret" of profits, as in the case of Marx). And, most importantly, it was the only value theory (given the extant choices) that enabled him (again, almost) to establish the results of his delicate constructions in theory. (In point of fact, up until this realization, forced upon him by the criticisms of Malthus, Ricardo had been quite content with the Smithian legacy in value theory.)[39]

So, as may now be appreciated, it is quite problematic to sustain the idea of Ricardo as a rarefied scientist so long as we are also attempting, simultaneously, to suggest that Senior[40] was an ideologue. Both shared, it is vital to remember, a similar platform, and both supported the same political policy agenda. Ricardo's allegedly "abstract" science was as ideological, or rather it was as equally motivated, as Senior's more ingenuous, direct, and "honest" propaganda. In fact, in what may seem a strange inversion of traditional perspectives, it is Senior who is the more direct and "honest" propagandist, whereas Ricardo's exertions consisted in presenting the air of a detached and disinterested generality (and what could—still can—convey scienticity more effectively?) to a rather transparent policy position. So, in effect, the possibility of characterizing a corpus of work as either "scientific" or "apologetic" seems not to turn primarily upon whether the class struggle is latent or manifest, as Marx—upon occasion—imagined: the criterion of science needs a fuller specification than the specific Marxian insight would seem to afford.

~

The foregoing helps to situate our discussion more sharply. Is an objective social science possible given contending societal interests and world views? Interestingly, if not surprisingly, both Marxism and neoclassicism opt for the same answer, in the affirmative, each claiming the titular distinction of "science" for itself even while designating the other as an ill-founded nonscience (or even, occasionally, as nonsense). A preliminary case exists, then, for a relativist understanding of social science. But relativism needs be understood with some care, especially two distinct variants of this position: *epistemic relativism*,[41] which holds that all social knowledge is socially produced and historically transient,[42] on the one hand, and *judgmental relativism* (with which the former is often confounded), which suggests that all beliefs are equally valid, on the other. Clearly, it is the former sense that is in context of my usage, and not the latter, although even the notion of epistemic relativism (in itself quite innocuous and almost undeniable) can be (and has been) interpreted so broadly as to constitute a vague and vacuous truism. In fact, I shall propose that class relativism is central to the issue of epistemic relativism, so long as it is understood that we are speaking of sources of production of societal knowledge, rather than bases of validation of that knowledge. But first, to prepare the groundwork.

Before knowledge of society—i.e. an epistemology—can be legitimized, an understanding of the ontology of societies, no matter how preliminary, becomes an imperative. Questions of ontology become fundamental in any science, because ontology defines the object of study, which only thereafter suggests appropriate means and mechanisms for a proper epistemological capture. A definition of the nature of the social object is therefore a vital preliminary because, ultimately, ontological limits set bounds to epistemological possibilities. Only one requirement of the object of science becomes a further necessity: it needs be irreducible or, if not, needs be referred to that further level of the irreducible.

In this "realist" understanding, the true subject matter of a social science (i.e. a system that investigates real causes and real determinations) is neither the domain of actions (or even interactions) nor events; not behaviors, nor structures, nor systems. For, although all these social forms are real enough, they constitute epiphenomena, i.e. that which needs to be explained. *The true subject matter of a social science, rather, is relations and relations between relations; these are the irreducible phenomena, the ultimate object-data phenomena and, therefore are more primary in the causal chain.* Society—an ensemble of these relations—is the ever present condition and outcome of all of these phenomenal forms. Our actions, behaviors, etc., never really create society, ab initio, however they do reproduce and transform it, for social practice—based on relations—is nothing other than the continuous production and reproduction (if in transformed ways) of all such conditions of existence. Activity is conscious, of course (how could it be otherwise?), but works its effects quite unconsciously, and often in opposition to intentionality. So practices, and the roles constituting relations within them, form the link between human resolve and social structure, individual and society, serving as the mediating agency between these two orders, bridging the ontological gulf between them. Although its effects are knowable empirically, however, the *totality* of society can only be grasped *theoretically*. The enterprise of social science is a qualitative one, for the search is for meaning: relations are not susceptible to measurement.

Our ontological set is now complete. Society is a set of relations which both define the parameters of social activity and are transformed by it. These relations constitute a totality—the totality of society—forming the site of various and varying social practices. These different practices, then, give rise to different views of the world, for consciousness can only be the consciousness of a given material existence.[43] However, a further clarification: in the general set of social relations, production relations are important, for they are fundamental to the material reproduction of all relations (including themselves). It is this kind of primacy which makes of class relations, and class practices based thereon, the magnetic locus of collective outlooks. And these outlooks, in an evolving—for being challenging as much as challenged—historical sense, will, of course, be class relative.

ECONOMICS AND EPISTEMOLOGY: TOWARD MATERIALISM

The idea that social knowledge is filtered through class prisms—by no means either a novel or an unacceptable idea—affords the possibility that there are (or may be) at least as many perspectives as there are class locations and practices. (However, one must note, in qualification, that there are practices other than class-mediated ones; nonetheless, it is arguable that the outlooks engendered in these practices are nonbinding and are, in fact, adaptive to class expressions, owing to the primacy of the material.) If this is so, the question endures: how are we to adjudicate the validity of a given class-predicated view as against another, since each class outlook may be presumed to be "appropriate" to the class practice/location in question?

At first blush, the issue seems to dissolve itself into a morass of what has been termed "judgmental relativism," but actually—and arguably—matters are not entirely hopeless. In any given set of social relations, there is a material equivalence in the capacities or propensities of different classes to generate worldviews. However, it does not follow that different classes—owing to this material equivalence—have an equal grasp on the ontology of the whole, principally because their respective interests vis à vis the whole are likely to diverge and vary. It is this ontologically real divergence of interests that determines the relative "truth content" of the respective class outlooks, a content that will itself vary as the class struggle, historically, takes on different forms.

In general, the ruling classes will have a stake in distorting, or concealing, the reality of unequal access to the means of production and consumption, while the subaltern orders have every objective interest in exposing the real state of affairs in their demand for justice. (Although, obviously, for the subaltern orders a subjective understanding of its existential situation has to ripen—and does seem to develop—at those historical junctures of ferment, when the "veils" over such relations are shred, either by virtue of individual insight or social struggle.) Mannheim's distinction between "ideology" and "utopia" has a fine bearing on this matter. It is only in this qualified sense that the challenger class(es)—and its (or their) champions—acquire a vested interest in the truth, for a revealment of the latter itself is its best means of propaganda. The more science they generate, in other words, the better off they are. The dilemma for the ruling order(s) is, then, easy to fathom: it must generate enough objective information so as to conduct its own affairs, while also generating enough misinformation—gloss—so as to confuse its opposition, the balance between fact and fantasy depending upon the nature and intensity of the threat from below.

An important qualification is necessary at this point. While it is both easy and fruitful to generate such a rationalist account of class imperatives, it is less clear whether—in a materialist sense—i.e. in an ontologically realist sense—such an outcome is to be expected. Essentially, the answer to this question turns on our understanding of the nature of false consciousness: is this phenomenon produced, for instance, behind our back, or is it the creature of an instrumental self-consciousness?[44] (This is, of course, to ask which conception of ideology[45] we adhere to, a "positive" or a "negative" one? As in many other matters, Marx had an ineradicable dualism with regard to this question.) Although both versions appear in Marx, it is clear that the Marxian tradition, broadly, has taken the "positive" route of ideology as deliberately induced false consciousness. In this latter view that is ultimately less consistent with historical materialism, our problem is simplified in the extreme: the subaltern classes are systematically duped by an all-knowing propaganda machine operated by the ruling class. However, taking up the "negative" conception of ideology poses the greater challenge, for now the burden of proof is upon us to show how the ordinary processes of life—in a given, antagonistic mode of production—generate the false consciousness that cements society together, unifying antagonistic interests while also producing—at times of tension and transition—the means by which the subordinate classes "see through" the veils of illusion.[46]

~

The "class outlook"—an outlook based on practices within determinate material relations—will necessarily contain both "scientific" and "ideological" elements, i.e. both facts as well as prejudices and wishful thinking; this much would be true for the rulers as much as the ruled, for neoclassicism as much as Marxism. Indeed, in societies where Marxism—of a sort—is the officially sanctioned worldview, at least of the governing strata, it is easy to see the apologist, propagandist elements come to the fore, to the detriment of any scientific pretensions. In a class society, such as socialism, it would be more surprising if it were otherwise. In formal terms, therefore, the existence of a class-divided society (even in the simplest sense of a radical divide between the rulers and the ruled) raises the ever present possibility of an official science rationalizing the status quo. Can we, then, in the context of modern capitalism, simply assimilate neoclassicism as a ruling class ideology, pledged to defend the social and economic regime of capitalism?

The answer, unambiguously, would be in the negative, because the content of any outlook is an historically concrete detailing that needs be defined and understood, most particularly in the specifics. Just as importantly, even an officially sanctioned social science must "perform," i.e. it must identify, study, and solve real, given "problems."

The primary Marxian concern is the issue of exploitation (class domination), in keeping with its pedagogy of revolt that is basic to the aspirations of all subaltern classes, although Marxism poses and "resolves" this issue uniquely—i.e. historically. All of its categories are constructed around this unique "problem-orientation." The implicit bias toward order of neoclassicism prevents its appropriation of exploitation and class domination as "issues" in much the same way as the bias toward "justice" enables Marxism to virtually sidestep all of neoclassical concerns (rightly, possibly) as not fundamental to its purpose.

But the two biases (class relevant in the main) cannot simply be equated to one another; for the presumption toward order objectively diminishes the explanatory content of neoclassical theory by consistently ignoring reappearing historical regularities, thereby overlooking matters of relevance to its own object of study. This cannot be said of Marxian economics; the latter's omission of neoclassical concerns does not weaken its analysis as applied to its own chosen object of study, nor is it detrimental to its own purpose. As remarked earlier, Marxism has, a priori, a greater vested interest in unmasking reality. It is this focus that gives it an enduring relevance and a continuing vitality in capitalist societies, where its critical role is automatically assured. This despite all its medley of theoretical propositions always remaining logically and empirically questionable and open—always—to sensible, sometimes devastating, criticism (as evidenced in the "economics" of the great confused epic: *Capital*). A fact not always appreciated by the average Marxist economist, Marxism seeks to explain more, much more, than neoclassicism; its scientific ambitions are far greater (than perhaps its concrete achievements would warrant). This adds, inevitably, an audience of inquiring minds to the constituency of ethically sensitive ones that are drawn to it. But, sad to say, in its mix of demonstrable truths and wishful thinking, it is—like neoclassicism—ultimately a blend both of science and acute idealism.

A caveat, though: there is an important sense in which the Marxian explanatory schema transcend the neoclassical perspective decisively. In any critique, it is insufficient merely to point out the falsity of a given paradigm; it is just as necessary to be able to demonstrate the necessity, in spite of the falsity, for the existence of a rival paradigm. Marxism, in its own terms, can not only point to the "falsity" of the neoclassical view of capitalism, but can—importantly—go further and suggest why, nonetheless, neoclassical theory survives and thrives; neoclassical theory, on its part, in its own terms, can point to the falsity of Marxian theorizing, but is unable to account for the emergence and persistence of Marxism as a rival corpus of theory. This is a major, and significant, difference in intellectual attainments; by any token, Marxism comes out the more encompassing a theoretical framework of the two. The stark failure, at this level, of neoclassical theory is explained by its total ignorance of history, and its equally complete innocence of any concept of ideology.

~

The Ricardian case is one of the clearest instances of the rise and fall of paradigms connected to issues of practical relevance and material suitabilities, illustrating the thesis of the practical foundations of social theory almost too perfectly. But Ricardo, to withdraw credit where it is undue, was no radical innovator in this respect; for economic theory, whether mercantilist, physiocratic or Smithian, similarly generalized topical, practical agendas into high theory. (Ricardo, of course, set impossible standards in this respect; indeed, so much so that the most practically inspired economist who ever lived—David Ricardo—could still come to be visualized, by Marxist[47] and mainstream alike, as the most abstract theorist of them all.) Indeed, in the policy sciences, it could not be otherwise. Here, paradigms change owing to altered agendas, changed material conditions, and transformed social relations; and the various paradigms are not, strictly speaking, comparable: we cannot assess the question as to whether there has been scientific progress between, say,

Smith, Ricardo, and Keynes, because their preoccupations were with different moments—and facets—of the developing accumulation process. Again, the contrast with the natural sciences could not be clearer. In the latter, such "progress" is better defined, more or less unequivocally, because the object of the discourse is relatively static. (How different is the moon today, for example, compared to the way it was in 1066 AD, and yet how very different is English society within the same time frame?) Further, in the natural sciences the social location of the perceiving subject is not a significant factor disturbing the data.

But again, despite these ontological limitations vested in the societal form, and stemming from its historically transformational character, there is, nonetheless, an intransitive (if nonempirical, in the sense that it can only be known indirectly, through its effects rather than in any vulgar, positivist observational context), theoretically definable object called society which, through its causal powers, allows for the possibility of a social science—nonpredictive and nonhistoricist—though one that is forever doomed to be incomplete for its focus on an open, evolving system. Invariant empirical regularities simply do not obtain. Contrary to the Neo-Kantians,[48] the existence of a causal interdependency and class relativism do not vitiate the search for true explanations of real phenomena; and, contrary to the positivists, there is no privileged domain for either science or the scientist; the capacity for intransitive study is itself given by the specifics of the social process.

But more than one case study of a paradigm is indicated, for meaningful conclusions in social sciences can only be historically specific, not formally general; *the practical foundations of economic theory (and social theory) need to be established and reestablished continuously.* The fire of social knowledge, in Promethean fashion, cannot be appropriated just once and for all time; more like Sisyphus—but a little more successfully—we have to try and try again, a project involving ongoing research into other and all paradigms. This form of research has not been undertaken by the mainstream,[49] for obvious reasons, nor by Marxists, for less obvious reasons. The practical provenance of the great neoclassical eruption in the 1870s,[50] for instance, remains essentially unexplored, despite some attention paid to it recently as an intellectual problem. Early official Marxism dismissed it, routinely, as bourgeois ideology[51] (although Bukharin[52] did spare some effort to specify it, more carefully, as the outlook of the rentier class), a stance of blanket dismissal is quite inadequate and utterly ahistorical, for, within limits, it can similarly be shown that Ricardian, Jevonian, and even Keynesian economics are all variants of such a "bourgeois" perception. How, then, can one explain the tremendous differences within the same "bourgeois" outlook—as recognised internally by these schools themselves—with respect to the object of study, the ordering of variables, the attribution of causality and so on (i.e. differences in theories of value, distribution, growth, etc.)? Clearly, even common class standpoints do not mechanically generate the same theoretical schemes if only because, as referred to earlier, history and society, ever dynamic and protean, produce new problems that render the old obsolete and irrelevant.

Therefore, the designation of a class reference is never enough to establish either the external stimulus or the internal detail of a specific paradigm. A concrete, historical examination of the practical urges of a period is vital before the specifics—and not surface appearances—can be gleaned and placed in context. Neoclassical theory, for instance, has now boiled down to being a normative theory of "efficient" action, a praxiology (as Lange[53] once called it) employing the calculus of maximization—essentially neither right or wrong, in social terms. Strictly speaking, neoclassical theory, then, does not venture to be a social science at all, although its models are often premised upon what, in a loose sense, could be termed an abstract, idealist sociology. It deals primarily with the allocation problem (in an exchange framework) in general, defined as the maximization of net advantages. And the set of tools it forges (taken from mathematics) in this quest are of relevance, indeed, to both market and nonmarket societies. This aspect would represent its "science" content, for it "solves," with given supplies—and a given set of behavioral assumptions—the allocation of expenditures between different ends, making that the fundamental object of its investigations, no less legitimate (if not as exciting) than the matters investigated—in the heroic epoch of capitalism—by a Smith or a Ricardo.

While the problem-solving nature of the neoclassical enterprise now becomes clear, there is still much to recommend the view that it is really more a technology (again, something understood by Lange) of optimal resource management than a science that seeks to explain real relations between enduring social entities. But even here, neoclassicism does focus on at least one permanent aspect of social relations, i.e. relations of exchange. This field of inquiry is not always fully specified in other paradigms, including Marxism—though here, as well, neoclassicism studies the problem in terms of a priori assumptions of rationalism and the stress on "free and voluntary" exchanges rather than in any concrete, historical manner. But whether as a science or a technology, while the object of neoclassical interests is clear and definable, the origins of this theoretical interest, in disparate geopolitical settings in the last third of the nineteenth century, still remain to be explored and established, a task that can be accomplished in the kind of program outlined here.[54] This essay's revealment of Ricardo is the first, hesitant, and possibly inadequate, step in that general direction.

Notes

1. This is a term I borrow from the work of Oxford philosopher R. Bhaskar (1979); my comments on the ontology of society I owe much to his framework of transcendental realism.
2. Max Weber's explicit directives on method are to be found in M. Weber, *The Methodology of the Social Sciences*, 1949. A more contemporary discussion is available in A. Giddens, *Capitalism and Modern Social Theory*, 1971.
3. T. Kuhn,
4. N. Bukharin, 1931, p. 20.
5. See Paglin (1961) for an account of this brand of anti-Ricardian fervor, a perspective that was to be, almost literally, *outclassed*!
6. For the working-class based rejection of Ricardo, see Lowenthal, 1911; also, Stark, 1943, pp. 51-148.
7. By far, the fullest account of the Ricardian period is still the rendering of Blaug, (1958).
8. Stark (1944) makes a strong case for considering these various philosophies in terms of their own historical and social context; otherwise, we normally get, in the history of economic thought, "grid readings," which can only misread the originals, be they neoclassicist or Marxist in inspiration. See Stark (1944).
9. See K. Popper, 1965; also Blaug, 1980.
10. A short, but revealing paper on the Lakatosian viewpoint is available in his radio address given in 1973, subsequently published in I. Lakatos, "Introduction: Science and Psuedo Science," 1978, pp. 1-7. But, as Bhaskar writes, if every theory, interpreted empirically, is

false—Popper maintained, for instance, that the mathematical probability of all theories being true, regardless of evidence, was zero—then "no theory can ever be falsified" R. Bhaskar, 1979, p. 63.

11. A term employed by Blaug in M. Blaug, 1980.

12. It is probable that Malthus was the key designator of this term, applied by him to mark off the Ricardians as distinctly different from the old tradition of Adam Smith. Malthus, of course, was treated rather roughly by this "new school."

13. Details of this account are available in M. Blaug (1958).

14. See R. Meek, 1950, as well as M. Dobb, 1973 for an elaboration of this account.

15. See J. A. Schumpeter, 1954, and Stigler, 1950 for this view.

16. The original Marxian reference is spelled out in Marx and Engels, 1970a; see also Marx, 1970b.

17. For a confirmation of the differing projects of classical and neo-classical theories, see A. Dasgupta, 1985.

18. The social history of the period is covered well in Halevy (1961) and Trevelyan (1967); the economic history, in Hobsbawm (1968) and Ashton (1968).

19. The late Ricardian "softening" becomes apparent, for instance, in the work of Senior and McCulloch.

20. A history of the Poor Laws is available in Poynter (1969); but, their true significance, particularly of the Speenhamland provisions, is best sketched in Polanyi (1957); for the views of the political economists on this question, see Cowherd (1978) and Kanth (1986).

21. Polanyi, op. cit., 1957.

22. The empirical and theoretical fallacies in Malthus are the proper subject of *undergraduate* study; briefly, he confuses fertility with fecundity, ignores technical progress in agriculture, and, falsely, gives the static proposition of diminishing returns a dynamic, long-run operativeness: his "ratios" were, of course, pure nonsense. Small wonder that Marx terms his ideas a "libel" on the human race.

23. The chronicler of the Corn Laws is Barnes (1961); see Kanth (1986) for an account of Ricardian involvement in such issues.

24. A good review of the *Essay* is to be found in Peach (1984).

25. A full account of the period may be found in Kanth (1985; 1986).

26. The entire Ricardian model is beautifully dissected in Blaug (1958); the significance of the so-called "invariable standard" is discussed in P.

Sraffa's "Introduction" to the *Collected Works* of Ricardo (1951-1973); the Sraffian interpretation, in turn, is criticized in S. Hollander (1979), and T. Peach (1984); for all of these separate evaluations in a handy volume, see G. A. Caravale, ed. (1985).

27. Blaug places the entire issue of method in perspective in M. Blaug, 1980, pp. 55-86.

28. Pasinetti (1974) finds Ricardo's assumptions "very crude," and puts this aspect of Ricardo's analysis down to his "naiveté" (pp. 21-22); clearly, at issue is Pasinetti's naiveté, not Ricardo's.

29. In a perceptive article written in 1824 for the *Quarterly Review*, Malthus, instructively, compares Ricardianism to physiocracy, indicating their common features as being tight reasoning, apparently mathematical demonstrations, and conclusions based on assumed data. Malthus, of course, was critically aware of the extra-scientific strengths of the Ricardians—see Paglin (1961), pp. 157-65, for a discussion of this point—and their extended public outreach; however, he remained convinced—and history has borne it out—that the Ricardian doctrines would not "stand the tests of examination and experience."

30. As quoted in A. Toynbee, 1920, p. 9.

31. These references to Mill's ideas are taken from J. S. Mill (1967).

32. This droll view is attributed to William Maginn, a contemporary of Ricardo, by DeMarchi, 1974, p. 124.

33. Friedman, 1953.

34. See Latsis (1972) for a detailed commentary on neoclassical assumptions within a Lakatosian matrix.

35. For the full Lakatosian thesis on "research programs," see Lakatos (1978).

36. Marx, 1967, pp. 14-15.

37. Ibid.

38. Although Ricardo's defense of manufacturers is never doubted by Marx, he still maintained that Ricardo did so "...only because and in so far as, their interests coincide with that of production" (Marx, 1969, part II, p. 118). Ricardo is seen as defending economic progress simultaneously in his defense of manufacturers as the prime movers of the process; this, for Marx, exonerates him from a "negative" class prejudice. "When the bourgeoisie comes into conflict with them," Marx goes on to say, "he is just as ruthless toward it as he is at other times toward the proletariat and the aristocracy." Aside from the fact that there are no ready examples

Science, Class, and Theory: The Elusive Anatomy of Social Discourse

of Ricardo's "ruthlessness" toward manufacturers, the problem with this line of reasoning is that it assumes that "free trade/*laissez-faire*," or the Ricardian way forward, *was the only viable option for material advance*: there is simply no historical way of "demonstrating" the truth of such a proposition.

39. Dissatisfaction with Smithian value theory is expressed in the *1815 Essay* (see Peach, 1984); however, the reason for the dissatisfaction is best expressed in Sraffa's "Introduction" to Ricardo's works; Smithian "adding up" theory would simply not demonstrate the fall in the rate of profit owing to a rise in the value of corn, i.e. it was inadequate from the point of view of Ricardo's desired conclusion.

40. Senior's mature views—on all things—are to be found in Senior (1928).

41. Much of this section is based on the work of Bhaskar (1979).

42. The original Marxian notion of ideology has turned, in modern times, into the full-blown field of study called the "sociology of knowledge," which admits to this proposition as almost axiomatic. See Mannheim (1960) and Stark (1958) for a view of the topology of this terrain.

43. Again, Bukharin makes the point well when he tells us that, although the question of how cognition is possible is frequently asked in history, the question of how *action* is possible is never asked; so, we have burgeoning schools of epistemology, but not schools of what he, jocularly, calls "praxiology."

As he puts it, theory and practice are steps in the joint process of "the reproduction of social life" as, historically, the sciences grew out of practice, with the production of ideas detaching itself from the production of things. But, of course, in this, he is only paraphrasing Marx and Engels, who wrote, in *German Ideology*:

> Division of labor becomes a real division of labor only when a division of material and spiritual labor begins. From that moment, consciousness may, in reality, imagine that it is something other than the consciousness of existing practice. From the moment that consciousness begins really to imagine something, without imagining something real, from that time onwards it finds itself in a position to emancipate itself from the world and proceed to the formation of "pure theory," "theology," philosophy, morality etc.

ECONOMICS AND EPISTEMOLOGY: TOWARD MATERIALISM

The sole preoccupation with the issue of cognition detached from practice is itself, therefore, a reflection of an historically specific constitution of the division of labor in society; small wonder, then, that today's thinking class finds so much kindred in the works of the thinking class of ancient times: Greek philosophers, for instance, who were similarly cut off from material practice in the form of being an idle, slave-owning class of "comtemplators"; the class division between mental and manual labour was as complete in Greek society as it is in contemporary society, providing the essential continuity between the ancients and ourselves. At any rate, it is instructive to the philosophical solipsists among us to note that, in the area of practice, there are, in the words of Bukharin, "...no agnostics, no subjective idealists."

44. In the Marx-inspired tradition—other than Max Weber—Lukacs (1971) and Mannheim (1960) have paid much attention to this aspect of the sociology of knowledge.

45. The issue of "ideology" in the Marxian tradition—like so many other issues in that tradition—is a complicated one; put simply, it is possible to discern a "positive" and a "negative" view of ideology in the writings of Marx and Engels, with the bias toward the latter: i.e. ideology as the distortion produced by a deceiving reality that helps to gloss over real contradictions between classes, thereby assisting the domination of the ruling class. It is not the deliberate product of a class initiative; and it is always opposed to "science" that is defined negatively and critically toward it. However the later Marxist tradition, unaware of the existence of *German Ideology* (published only in 1924), veered toward a more positive, instrumental, and activist conception of ideology, as for instance in Lenin.

As I see it, the two interpretations are not mutually exclusive—the two occur historically in a definite sequence—since there is evidence for both in everyday life. In this paper, I have taken the activist slant as far outweighing the involuntary aspect as far as this is reflected in the works of the partisans of capitalism: as in the neoclassical economics of the J. B. Clark variety, perfectly aware of the "need" to counter Marxist views on the subject. This, of course, does not preclude other aspects of neoclassical theory—and other neoclassicals—from being innocent and unconscious of any need for the imposition of the hegemony of capitalism. At any rate, for more on the Marxist idea of ideology, see Larrain (1983).

46. I want to stress the purely formal, hypothetical nature of these

general statements of sociology; the truth of these needs be demonstrated, historically, in every instance. Unlike the pronouncements of the idealists, we cannot hold these truths to be self-evident in a priori fashion; history must reveal the truth of such ideas: the "truth" cannot be used to reveal history.

47. The Marxian tradition views Ricardo as the culmination of a century of "classical thinking," beginning with Petty (to be surpassed only, of course, by Marx, as he himself saw it); Rubin (1979) echos the sentiment well when he writes that "His [i.e. Ricardo's] book marks the highest point that the classical school was able to obtain." (p. 232).

48. Weber's thesis of there being only particular, or "one-sided," knowledge, is thus both true and false; the intransitivity of the totality of social relations obviously escapes him, drowned as he is in the idea of causal interdependency. That the real exists and can be accurately perceived remains a fact, despite the concept-dependent, activity-dependent, and space/time-dependent nature of the social.

49. An improperly specified attempt, in this direction, does already exist, of course, in the shape of Rogin's work (Rogin, 1971).

50. An entire conference devoted to an examination of the "Marginal Revolution," was held in Bellagio, Italy, in 1971, without any definitive, new discoveries being made, either in evaluative or in interpretive terms. See R. D. C. Black, et al., eds., 1973.

51. Oddly enough, this is not merely a Marxist view; in a recent paper, Latsis has defined the "metaphysical core" of the neoclassical research program as the "assumptions" of: (a) profit maximization; (b) perfect knowledge; (c) independence of decisions; and (d) perfect markets. These are held as "assumptions" not subject to verification. Next, we have a "protective belt" of auxiliary assumptions, such as: (a) product homogeneity; (b) large number of buyers and sellers; (c) free entry and exit, which are subject, in principle, to verification, etc. Latsis concludes, on the basis of Lakatosian criteria, that neoclassical theory qualifies as a "degenerating paradigm."

52. Bukharin did take time off to deal with this new phenomenon (Bukharin, 1927); no Marxist since has cared to even emulate, let alone improve upon, his example.

53. O. Lange, *Political Economy* (1963).

54. My interpretation necessarily departs from the recent vogue of identifying "two" traditions in all economic theory since Adam

Smith—one, the so-called "surplus" approach, and the other the "supply-demand" framework, with Smith-Ricardo-Marx representing the first, and Smith-Malthus-Jevons the second (see Dobb, 1973; also Bharadwaj, 1986). Any taxonomy is only as good as the taxonomic principle selected, and many other such "divides" can be identified; but such interpretations always remain ad hoc constructions, inherently neither true nor false. But the line I am drawing is not merely a rationalist, "intellectual" one, servant to my own interests and fancies, but one that is given practically and historically. No such historical justification exists in the Sraffa-Dobb view, which is, additionally, also a teleological "grid" reading that has been the bane of so-called "histories of thought." On the general issue of "grid" readings in the history of economics, see K. Tribe, (1978).

12

Political Economy and Philosophy: Tensions in Orthodoxy

Marxism is nothing, Lukacs has written, if not method. And perhaps the issue of method is the best place to begin in tracing the complex, if not wholly abstruse, issue of the relationship between Marxian political economy and philosophy. Engels, for instance, tells us that the question of method was indeed a problem to be dealt with before an analysis of political economy could at all begin:

> Which scientific method should be used? There was, on the one hand, the Hegelian dialectics in the quite abstract "speculative" form in which Hegel had left it, and on the other hand the ordinary, mainly Wolfian metaphysical method, which had again come into vogue, and which was also employed by the bourgeois economists to write their bulky, rambling volumes. The second method had been theoretically demolished by Kant and particularly by Hegel, so that its continued use in practice could only be rendered possible by inertia and the absence of an alternative simple method. The Hegelian method, on the other hand, was, in its existing form, quite inapplicable.[1]

The Hegelian method was found to be "quite inapplicable," mainly because in its existing form it was idealist, taking as its point of departure pure thought: a method which, in its own terms, came "from nothing

ECONOMICS AND EPISTEMOLOGY: TOWARD MATERIALISM

through nothing to nothing." But, idealist as it was, in the given state of logic, it was the optimal point from which a departure could be made toward a real comprehension of history. Accordingly, we are told, the founders of classical Marxism took it upon themselves to meet this errant method head on: to carry through a scientific critique of it, prior to launching the study of political economy itself. On the other hand, Hegel's idealism stood apart from other bourgeois "ideologies" because, no matter how abstract and idealist the form employed, his evolution of ideas always ran parallel with the evolution of universal history, even though the latter, in typical Hegelian fashion, was always adduced as proof of the former. Hegel was the first great thinker, concedes Engels, who tried to demonstrate that there is "an evolution, an intrinsic coherence in history..." It was this monumental conception of history that impressed Marx and Engels:

> This epoch-making conception of history was a direct theoretical pre-condition of the new materialist outlook, and already this constituted a connecting link with the logical method, as well.[2]

Here, then, perhaps, lay a true Hegelian paradox: that the basic materialist conception of history, this theoretical precondition of materialism, was derived from the work of an idealist philosopher—and freely acknowledged as such by the founders of classical Marxism. It was the exceptional historical sense in Hegel's writings that seems to have suggested the celebrated "historical" method that was to be used with such epoch-making consequences in the Marxian study of political economy. This working out of the method underlying Marx's critique of political economy was the fruitful result of the critical encounter with Hegel's writings.

All this was clear enough to Marx and Engels, and they deserved to think, as they did, that in all finality they had consigned Hegel to the dustbin of history, while retaining nonetheless—indeed perfecting—the dialectical method free from all idealist trappings. But, contrary to the faith of Marx and Engels, their lineage in recent times is less certain of the matter—the problem of the relation between Marx and Hegel still remaining a matter of some contention.

One point may, however, be made at the outset; the problem itself may be situated in one of two ways: either it is a question of examining

Political Economy and Philosophy: Tensions in Orthodoxy

the historical relationship between Marxist political economy and Hegelian, even neoHegelian, philosophy—Marx and Hegel serving as proxies for political economy and philosophy, respectively (easy enough to trace, given Marx's early and well-known preoccupation with Hegelian studies)—or it is a matter of investigating the intrinsic relationship between political economy and philosophy, which is far less obvious. In the many writings on the issue, the critical distinction between the two approaches is not always recognized, a considerable failing because the two methods are far from being identical. But we'll return to that later; first to review a sample of writings that situate Marx in relation to Hegel. Avineri (1973), for instance, tells us that Marx's fascination with Hegel was provoked by his "wish" to "realize philosophy" and, thus, to "close the gap between social life and its theoretical criteria...it was the realm of social life that caused Marx's adoption...of Hegel's system"; further, that ultimately Marx's socialism can "make no sense" outside of the "specific tradition of Hegelian political philosophy, and that, in a way, Marx sought to actualize the ultimate postulates of Hegel's *Philosophy of Right*." And, for Avineri, even the basic technique of Marx's critique of *The Philosophy of Right* is internal: "seldom, in the annals of philosophy, has a systematic edifice been so bored from within" (Avineri, 1973, p. 4). In this viewpoint, affinities with Hegel are stressed against any possible or actual "break" with Hegel. As yet another, Irving Fetscher, affirms that:

> Marx agrees with Hegel on a number of essential assumptions concerning the philosophy of history...it is worth emphasizing the coincidence between the two anthropological assumptions: for Hegel and for Marx alike, man is a being who realises his own potential, who turns himself, by his own activity, into a man...[3]

Often, these "affinities" with Hegel (real enough as affinities, as attested to far more powerfully in Marx's own writings) are sketched with a view to dissolving Marx in Hegel totally, or even to using Hegel as a foil against Marx. Here, an instance of the latter, in the work of Schroyer:

> Marx's form of critical theory is thus in some ways less dialectical than Hegel's "idealistic" one. Hegel's philosophy united theory and history in a radically new way...Hegel's radical combination of philosophical and

ECONOMICS AND EPISTEMOLOGY: TOWARD MATERIALISM

social analysis is usually overlooked, especially by Marxists who polarize materialism and idealism, Hegel's critique contained a theory of cultural alienation...[it] is a more fundamental theory of alienation more sensitive to socio-cultural processes. Marx's critical theory has underestimated the socio-cultural...[4]

Let us ignore the suggestion that it is only Marxists who polarize materialism and idealism, or that this opposition was in some sense invented, for purposes unsavory, by their perverse genius. What is more striking is that some version of Stalinism is usually the preferred strawman standing in for Marx, who is accused of having underestimated this or that aspect of social life. At any rate, returning to the point, Marx is seen as not only immersed in "Hegelianisms" of all variety, but also with the very language of Hegel:

The reading of Hegel may have been accidental but the influence of Hegel went deeper...The most striking passage of the *Grundrisse* in this respect is the draft plan for Marx's *Economics*, which is couched in language (such as the distinction between essence and appearance) that might have come straight out of Hegel's *Logic*.[5]

Affinities in language and idiom are hardly surprising; after all, it was Marx himself who wrote that the "tradition of all the dead generations weighs like a nightmare on the brain of the living," and Marx had spent much time, in his early years, immersed in the critical study of Hegel. But what is more fundamental is not the use of similar concepts (the form), but their specific content in the Marxian lexicon. By way of analogy, liberty, freedom, and equality are terms belonging to the "language" of the great French Revolution (and many others besides); but the fact that such ideas resurfaced during the makings of the Russian Revolution does not make the content of the two revolutions the same, or even similar.

The same terms can signify different things, in different social epochs—a simple materialist truth recognized, only in the breach, by idealist thinking. Whatever the judgment of later reviewers, the divide between Hegelian philosophy and Marxism was more obvious to Marx and Engels themselves:

The great basic question of all philosophy, especially of the modern philosophy, is that concerning the relation of thinking and being...the relation of spirit to nature... which is primary, spirit or nature...The answers which the philosophers gave to this question split them into two great camps...idealism and materialism...[6]

Quite unambiguously, Engels then places Hegel in "the camp of idealism." So when Lenin writes that, "as the most comprehensive and profound doctrine of development, and the richest in content, Hegelian dialectics was considered by Marx and Engels the greatest achievement of classical German philosophy,"[7] he is only affirming the views of classical Marxism: that Hegel's achievements in philosophy went beyond anything that classical German philosophy had produced until then (referring to the "time-bound" nature of his "advances," which may well become irrelevant at a later date), despite false premises (idealism) and reactionary conclusions (political apotheosis of history in the Prussian state etc.), by virtue of his method (dialectics): it is only this method of dialectics that is carried over (rescued) by Marx. The point is simple and profound simultaneously.Now to take up the other possible approach: to look for intrinsic connections between political economy and philosophy. Perhaps there is an a priori need for clarification, as in this comment:

> The question of Marxism's relation to philosophy is inescapable for an exploration of Marxism's conceptual status if only because "philosophy" is the discipline, par excellence, which has reserved to itself the right of debating issues of a categorical and conceptual kind.[8]

Since Marxism is doubtless based on clearly enunciated materialist premises, the question may well be asked: is there, perchance, a Marxist philosophy? Here, too, the scope for controversy is rich. Althusser, to name only one important modern-day critic, credits Lenin with the fundamental discovery that:

> Marx's scientific theory did not lead to a new philosophy (called dialectical materialism), but to a new practice of philosophy, to be precise, to the practice of philosophy based on a proletarian class-position in philosophy.[9]

This Leninist position on philosophy, as presented by Althusser, has the following elements:

1. Philosophy is not a science; it has no object like science.
2. Philosophy is an act of political intervention carried out in theoretical form.
3. It intervenes in two domains: in the class struggle, and in the effects of scientific practice.
4. In essence, it is produced by the conjunction of these two domains.
5. It intervenes politically.
6. All that philosophy expresses is a class position.
7. It represents a rejection of idealist philosophy.[10]

Barring the many sophistries in this presentation, the principal problematic of Althusser is clear enough: that it is the *XIth Thesis on Feuerbach* that has captured his attention, though he interprets it to mean that the true philosopher is the practitioner—i.e. the agent of revolutionary change—which may well be an overstatement of the *Thesis* itself.

Engels seems to offer some support for this position in his *Anti-Duhring* (written with the approval of Marx), in which he writes that "modern materialism," i.e. Marxism, no longer required any philosophical standing above the sciences, for, as soon as each separate science "is required to get clarity as to its position in the great totality of things and of our knowledge of things," a special science dealing with this totality becomes superfluous. Yet, dialectical materialism as initiated by Engels nonetheless, but developed as catechism by later Bolshevik orthodoxy, did precisely aspire to become a new, total, inexorable, overriding philosophy of everything imaginable. Boundaries between science and philosophy, as traditionally understood, were quite lost in the process, as evidenced in this comment by Cornforth:

> Dialectical materialism is a method...with dialectical materialism begins a new stage of philosophy as a science...dialectical materialism is a scientific philosophy...it is the philosophy of the struggle for socialism...it is not the philosophy of a school...[11]

Political Economy and Philosophy: Tensions in Orthodoxy

Almost like Althusser, though possibly less consistently, the argument here is that science and philosophy fuse with Marxism, their earlier separation dissolved in the new system. It is this fusion argument that enables neoHegelians to seize Marxism by the throat: if Marxism is philosophy (albeit a fused one!), then it must bear the imprint of Hegel, "one way or other." The argument, though the obverse of Conforthian error, can be compelling: if Hegel was reactionary, then so was Stalin:

> The state with Stalin as its leader and the party as the state organisation is established as the criterion of truth...It became an analogy of Hegel's absolute idea...as the philosophy and ideology of the absolute state, Marxism degenerated into Hegelianism...[12]

But this is simply to prostitute history for the sake of cheap analogies that ignore more than they reveal; Stalinism is not Marxism, but it is just as far from being "Hegelianism," as well. The thesis of this paper may now be stated, with the benefit of the foregoing discussion, in the following three propositions: (1) that classical Marxism—in its own self-perception, at least—is not Hegelianism, not even a simple stood-on-the-head Hegelianism; (2) that Marxian political economy is—at least explicitly—not philosophy as commonly understood and certainly not as understood by Marx; and (3) that Marxist social theory—historical materialism is not a new philosophy, scientific or otherwise.

To turn first to Marx and Engels, now, in *German Ideology*:

> German criticism has, right up to its latest effort, never quitted the realm of philosophy. Far from examining its general philosophical premises, the whole body of its inquiries has actually sprung from the soil of a definite philosophical system, that of Hegel. Not only in their answers but in their very questions there was a mystification...It has never occurred to any one of these philosophers to inquire into the connection of German philosophy with German reality, the relation of their criticism to their own material surroundings...[13]

The suggestions are quite inescapable: that philosophy, both in its questions and its answers, is a mystification; that philosophy and reality are not necessarily identical. In opposition to the philosophical premises criticized above, Marx and Engels then set forth their own fundamental premises, which they insisted were real, not arbitrary:

> The premises from which we begin are not arbitrary ones, not dogmas, but real premises from which abstraction can only be made in the imagination...they are real individuals...these premises can thus be verified in a purely empirical way...[14]

In the *Economic and Philosophical Manuscripts*, written a year before *German Ideology*, in 1844, we find a similar sentiment expressed by Marx while discussing Feuerbach and Hegel. Singling out Feuerbach as the only one who had a serious, critical relation to Hegel's dialectic, and who, moreover, is said to have been the "conqueror" of this "old philosophy," Marx writes that:

> Feuerbach's great achievement is: 1. The proof that philosophy is nothing else but religion rendered into thought and expounded by thought, hence equally to be condemned as another form and manner of existence of the estrangement of the essence of man; 2. The establishment of true materialism and real science, since Feuerbach also makes the social relationship "of man to man" the basic principle of the theory...[15]

Here is a definition that is not flattering to Hegelians and philosophers alike! In yet another work, *The Poverty of Philosophy*, written in 1847, there is an even more explicit recognition of the inverted relationship between political economy and philosophy.

Finding a Proudhon, hopelessly trapped in speculative philosophy, transforming "relations of production into a dialectic of abstractions" (a succinct and prescient critique of both structuralist and postModernist philosophies extant today!), Marx writes:

> Economic categories are only the theoretical expressions, the abstractions, of social relations of production. Holding things upside down like a true philosopher, M. Proudhon sees in real relations only the incarnation of these principles or categories which were slumbering—M. Proudhon the philosopher again tells us—in the bosom of the "impersonal reason of humanity..."[16]

At another remove, Gramsci suggests that "Marxism is Hegel plus Ricardo," providing a counterpart in economics to what we are by now accustomed to in bourgeois philosophy. Marx becomes a neoRicardian in economics much as a neoHegelian in philosophy (ignoring, thereby, both the epistemic break with Hegel and the theoretical split with Ricardo).

If this were true, then Marx would have been advancing backward. To make but a simple point, Marxian political economy "suspends" and goes beyond Ricardo (to borrow a phrase from Martin Nicolaus), else Marx indeed would have been the "minor postRicardian" that Samuelson makes him out to be.

Further, it can be shown, at least logically within Marxist discourse, that the categories of political economy as laid out in the *Critique* and *Capital* are not philosophical categories, nor do they give rise to philosophical problems *per se*. Political economy is the anatomy of civil society, a study of the mode of production of capitalist society, this mode itself being an articulated combination of a specific mode of appropriation of nature and a specific social mode of appropriation of surplus, of a given dyad between forces and relations of production.

The categories of political economy, commodities, capital, labor-power, etc., are not philosophical abstractions but rather real, determinate social forms embedded in real relations between real social beings. As such, philosophy can neither reconcile nor resolve (though it can, obviously, reflect upon) the contradictions arising from such social relationships. Only revolutionary social practice can (note we are referring to a process, not an event called "the revolution");—that is the true meaning of the *XIth Thesis on Feuerbach* (and again, we are referring to the internal context of meaning within the classical Marxian edifice, not to matters of the validity of these ideas, which is a separate issue). Philosophy can only fail to go beyond these relations, because it is a child of its time, occupying a definite space in the division of labor of bourgeois society it reflects upon: i.e. it becomes a part of the ruling ideology, sharing the illusions of the epoch.

Even when the developing social crisis gives philosophy a radical tinge, the crisis itself cannot be resolved in that domain—problems of social practice being amenable only to practical engagement. *Marxism is not a theory of society, but a theory of praxis*. As Gunn puts it:

ECONOMICS AND EPISTEMOLOGY: TOWARD MATERIALISM

...by understanding theorisation as linked to—as forming a unity with—practice...Marx can unify theory and metatheory, thereby dispensing with the need for "philosophy"...the answer lies in what I...term "practical reflexivity.[17]

In contradiction to this idea, it is often suggested, in neoMarxian and bourgeois discourse, that capitalist social relations give rise to problems of a philosophical nature: alienation, reification, fetishism, etc. (here, one can discern the movement from Marx to Hegel, and even Freud): but this is to grant, in Marxian terms, an illegitimate permanent ontological status to a specific socio-historical problem. Perhaps even more to the point, even if practice originates philosophical injuries, they can hardly be healed at the level of philosophy alone, as Colletti put it, (with reference to Lukacs's *History and Class Consciousness*):

> The analysis of capitalist fetishism is expounded in this work in the terminology of the Hegelian critique of the materialism of the scientific intellect and common sense. The division which capital introduces between the laborer and the objective conditions of labor is replaced by the distinction which the "intellect" introduced between the subject and object...that is the "fetish" is not capital or commodities, but natural objects external to thought...[18]

Lukacs, at least, admits as much in his self-criticism; but bourgeois ideologists are not quite so self-critical: Daniel Bell,[19] who led the tide of the "end of ideology" school in the sixties, for instance, is astonished that what is a legitimate ontological problem has been given a "false" social content by Marx, as against German philosophy (Hegel). This is, for him, quite an "extraordinary thing," Marx being accused of locating falsely the problem of alienation in property relations, and the social order generally (carrying the dubious assumption that philosophical disorders can only be corrected—endured?—philosophically).

The materialist conception of history and the so-called "dialectical method" which fuse in the Marxist study of political economy were never conceived as philosophical tools, even though, under Stalinist scholasticism, they begin to appear in that light. As Deutscher once put it, dialectics is only the grammar of Marxist thinking, and like all grammars, mastery is evidenced not in mulling over its formulae or reciting its rules,

Political Economy and Philosophy: Tensions in Orthodoxy

but in living speech. These tools are not ends in themselves, but only a means to process economic and socio-political raw material.

Intrinsically, then, there is no essential relationship between philosophy and political economy (the former being a meta-theory or second-order theory, as opposed to the latter being a first-order theory), at least within classical Marxism. Marxism is in no need of a separate meta-theory when it alone offers not merely a theory—like other political economies—but a theory of theory, as well: as a contemporary critic has it:

> My contention...will be that the (Marxist) left has no need for a philosophy: there is no conceptual gap within Marxism which "philosophy" might fill...Marx saw Hegel as the paradigmatic "philosopher" but, I would urge, he was never more Hegelian than when the critique of philosophy is present as a figure of his thought.[20]

Indeed, the irrelevance of philosophy can be posed even more starkly as in this comment:

> ...I believe we must recognise the priority of substantive science and politics over philosophy. When looking for positive guidance from philosophy we must rest content with some vague generalizations about the need to be specific.[21]

But this is not to say that other variants of classical political economy were not contaminated—infiltrated—by a philosophical tint; witness, for instance, Proudhon's *Philosophy of Poverty*. It was precisely this superfluous taint that was sought to be overcome by Marxian analysis, by the latter's location of the subject matter of political economy in the real, historical matrix of social relations. Of course, as a fact of real history, Marx was inspired by Hegel—inspired, that is, to place the refutation of Hegel as the very first task of criticism, even before commencement of a study of political economy.

Now many commentators have gone out of their way to prove that a Hegel stood on his head (or on his feet)—as in the Marxian critique—is still a Hegel intact.[22] But that is only a comment on the nature of Hegelian philosophy itself, which seems to grow mightier through negation. The critique of Hegel, and the strong emphasis on the importance of such a critique in Marxian writings, only testifies to the nature of the bitter ideological struggle conducted by Marx and Engels against German ideology in all its corruptions—and against reactionary and idealist philosophy generally, a vital part and parcel of the European class struggle against reaction to which they were so avidly committed.

A century later, it seems still necessary to conduct such struggles, at least within the matrix of western Marxism. Having emasculated any concept of real political praxis in this tradition, the revival of purely philosophical battles—to no particular end—seems almost predestined to be played out in all its vacuousness. In this sense, a radical philosophy (even if only a "Hegelian" radicalism) may well become a substitute for radical practice, homologically equivalent to a Hegel substituting for Marx. If so, the defeatism of western Marxism, nurtured systematically for decades now, my well prove to be a self-fulfilling prognostication. A Marx that is seen as a minor footnote to Ricardo in political economy and as an afterword to Hegel in philosophy is, after all, no Marx at all.

Notes

1. F. Engels in K. Marx, *A Contribution to the Critique of Political Economy*, 1970, p. 223.
2. F. Engels in K. Marx, op. cit., p. 224.
3. Irving Fetscher, *Marx and Marxism*, 1971, pp. 46-56.
4. Trent Schroyer, "Introduction" *The Critique of Domination*, 1973, p. 32.
5. David McClellan, "Introduction" *Karl Marx, The Grundrisse*.
6. F. Engels, *Ludwig Feuerbach and the Outcome of Classical German Philosophy*, 1941, pp. 20-21.
7. V.I. Lenin, *The Three Sources and Three Component Parts of Marxism*, 1969, p. 19.
8. Richard Gunn, "Marxism and Philosophy: A Critique of Critical Realism", *Capital and Class*, 37, Spring 1989, p. 88.
9. L. Althusser, *Lenin and Philosophy*, 1971, p. 107.
10. These seven points simply paraphrase Althusser's discussion in *Lenin and Philosophy*, 1971, pp. 107-108.
11. M. Cornforth, *In Defence of Philosophy*, 1950, pp. 55-61.

12. H. Lefebvre, quoted by Irving Fetscher in *Marx and Marxism*, op. cit., 1971, pp. 45-56.
13. K. Marx and F. Engels, *The German Ideology*, 1970, p. 40.
14. Ibid. p. 42.
15. Karl Marx, *The Economic and Philosophical Manuscripts of 1844*, 1964, p. 172.
16. Karl Marx, *The Poverty of Philosophy*, 1973, p. 95.
17. Richard Gunn, op. cit., p. 92.
18. Lucio Colletti, *From Rousseau to Lenin*, 1972, pp. 133-134.
19. Daniel Bell, "The Rediscovery of Alienation" in Schlomo Avinieri, ed., *Marx's Socialism*, pp. 59-79.
20. Richard Gunn, op. cit., pp. 88-89.
21. Alan Chalmers, "Is Bhaskar's Realism Realistic?", *Radical Philosophy*, 49, Summer 1988, p. 23.
22. See, for instance, the essays by Avineri and Lichtheim in Avineri, op. cit., 1973.

FIVE

~

EuroMarxism and Third-Worldism: Toward Autonomism

> In general the word *materialistic* serves many of the younger writers in Germany as a mere phrase with which anything and everything is labeled without further study; they stick on this label and then think the question disposed of. But our conception of history is above all a guide to study, not a lever for construction after the manner of the Hegelians. All history must be studied afresh, the conditions of existence of the different formations of society must be individually examined long before the attempt is made to deduce from them the political, civil-legal, aesthetic, philosophic, religious, etc., notions corresponding to them. Only a little has been done here up to now because only a few people have got down to it seriously. In this field we can utilize masses of help, it is immensely big, and anyone who will work seriously can achieve a lot and distinguish himself. But instead of this too many of the younger Germans simply make use of the phrase historical materialism (and *everything* can be turned into a phrase), in order to get their own relatively scanty historical knowledge (for economic history is still in its cradle) fitted togther into a neat system as quickly as possible, and they then think themselves something very tremendous.
>
> —F. Engels, Letter to Conrad Schmidt (1890)

13

~
EuroMarxism and "Dependency":
A Portentous Disjunction

Western Marxism, as Perry Anderson has noted, has—with few exceptions—been marked with defeatism and retreat ever since the failure of European working-class uprisings following upon the First War. With Stalinism soon consolidated in the East, the gulf between socialist intellectuals and working-class praxis in the West—a gulf unthinkable in classical Marxian vision—became almost institutionalized. The retreat of theorists from any mass connections—usually, but not always, into secluded academic havens—took many or all of the following forms: (a) an ongoing flirtation with idealist and bourgeois theoretical schemes; (b) an exaggerated focus on method and constant reinterpretation of historical materialism; (c) a turning away from economics and politics toward cultural and aesthetic critiques; and (d) a transition to a posture of healthy skepticism as to the possibility of revolutionary change. As Anderson[1] suggests, method signified impotence, art became consolation, and pessimism translated into quiescence. In the hands of these neoMarxists, the fairly unremarkable conceptual terrain of Marxism became a wonderland game of croquet played, as Koestler[2] once put it, with "mobile hoops." Being primarily defensive, bad faith was not long in following, and Marxism became a species of the genus of inventing a private language and then complaining that it had been misunderstood, a strategy that Popper,[3] in the philosophy of science, would later categorize as a resort to "immunizing stratagems," testifying only to a real intellectual bankruptcy. Far from any intellectual originality, even the sheer political and moral courage of a Luxembourg, a Lenin, or a Trotsky was simply not to be duplicated in the West after that generation.

Marxism always, of course, has had two components, inextricably linked: a sociology of knowledge—i.e. a theory of theory—and an exhortation to practice. Having abandoned any pretense to the latter, western Marxism turned increasingly to the role of a passive sensor, a (not always reliable) recorder of history—after the fact—rather than a prime mover and maker of it, with textual exegesis substituting for political engagement. Engaged instead in refinement and re-refinement of the sacred texts, it was the word that became the bread and butter of many a comfortably ensconced academic Marxist praying (in more heartfelt terms, perhaps) for tenure before socialism. In this competitive context, the game was to be more Marxist than thou, not perchance in revolutionary action nor even original conceptualizations within a schema of social change, but in quotational class conflict, argument by rote, and debate by catechism. Intellectual default could not but follow the abject political surrender, and Marxism was increasingly presented as an apology for economic growth, as a paean to the success of capitalist production, often even as a stirring defense of both colonialism and imperialism, the latter ultimately being construed as brave medicine for the wretched of the earth at the iron heel of European powers. Thus Bill Warren,[4] could sternly ask for more not less imperialism to be meted out to the Third World. After all, as another distinguished western Marxist, Kay,[5] had suggested, the workers and peasants in these societies simply had not been exploited enough! In the works of these Marxists, every neoclassical (mainstream), right-wing policy and attitude towards the Third World was to be duplicated—without even the saving grace of that mild garnish of hypocritical guilt, as usually qualifies the more liberal writings in this area. In Bill Warren's hands—as with Stalin—it was a fetishism of the forces of production that paraded as Marxism; forces of production give us capitalism, better and bigger forces will deliver us socialism. And so the legacy of Marx was to be perverted with bowdlerized or unformed (or simply uninformed) statements of Marx being gleefully recruited to sanction imperialism, capitalism, and—the truth must be told—racism.

It is against this background of infamy in western Marxian currents that one must evaluate the efforts of highly original intellectuals, though composing utterly minority strands within western radicalism, such as

Euromarxism and "Dependency": A Portentous Disjunction

those of André Gunder Frank,[6] and others working within his so-called "dependency" paradigm. Stated simply, stemming this ignoble tide of rhetorically rich but intellectually misconceived and practically worthless (aside from being morally corrupt) "Marxism," in the tradition of Paul Baran,[7] Gunder Frank returned us in the West to the true legacy of Marx and Lenin, betrayed for all practical purposes by those who nonetheless used their names as symbols in a retreating, defeatist discourse. He returned us to revolutionary Marxism, to political Marxism, to an activist Marxism, to a Marxism once again infused—after a long and bleak period of reaction—with a moral fervor matching the zeal of the founding figures of Marxian social theory. Frank was fighting against apologists for capitalism on both the left and the right: Stalinists and reactionary Marxists on the one hand; Arthur Lewis[8] and Bauer[9] on the other. In fact, apologetic Marxism had so thoroughly sold out its birthright that only the discriminating few could discern the difference between passages penned by Lord Bauer, on the right, and by Bill Warren, allegedly on the left. The point could not be simpler: one can be truer to the spirit of Marxism without benefit of authorized slogans and official buzzwords; and one can just as easily be a reactionary hypocrite while still paying elaborate lip service to all of the variable sounds of Marxian discourse. The summary dismissal of the Frankian inspiration by the principal current in western Marxism, the incestuous group built around the editorial board of the *New Left Review* in the name of a fictionalized European "history," and using a mechanized Marxist vocabulary, must rank as among the more shameful episodes in the history of the European left. Small wonder the *New Left Review* published, quite appropriately, the work of Warren and rallied to the work of Brenner and Laclau (the latter, quite typically, was to abandon Marxism altogether at a later date, the Marxian "purism" wearing off quite suddenly).

Especially for those for whom something has to be "Marxist" before it can be true, the convincingly Marxist essence of Frank and his "dependency" logic—much abused by textual Marxists with their superior finesse for purely verbal subtleties—is as follows: (a) it provided a much-needed modern complement to Lenin's aging theory of imperialism virtually abandoned by western Marxism (with nothing to lose thereby); (b) it exposed the reactionary nature of Stalinists, and official communist parties, forever postponing the struggle for socialism; (c) it warned against the dangers of class collaboration with the exploiters; (d) it revealed historically the role of colonial plunder and despoliation in the mechanics of European metropolitan advancement; (e) it showed exactly how the colonies provided some of the means for the primitive accumulation thesis sketched by Marx; (f) it pointed to the retrograde social relations often imposed in the colonies by metropolitan capital; (g) it pointed to the forcible retardation of productive forces and indigenous development in the colonized areas, providing therefore a theory that explained the "backwardness" of much of the Third World, unlike the reactionary Marxists who could, in grand tautology, only suggest that they were backward because they were backward; (h) it thereby challenged the mechanistic formula thesis parroted by western Marxists drawing on the European experience that capitalism always destroys precapitalist formations by showing that, in the colonial experience, metropolitan capital lived quite peaceably with all manner of precapitalist institutions, often even reinventing retrograde and obsolete forms of labor exploitation—such as slavery—as and when it suited them. Notice the difference here between saying that capitalism, via colonialism, always stabilized reactionary formations (there are certainly exceptions to this), as compared with saying that after the colonial experience it can never be taken as given—that capitalism indeed does carry out social revolution wherever it goes; this, with special reference to the oft-cited Marxian dictum that the colonized nation simply reproduces—at some indeterminate point, of course—"progressive" social relations in the "image" of the advanced colonizer) (i) it also showed up the narrow Eurocentrism[10] of western ideologues, Marxist or otherwise, and their hasty deductions about the nature of capitalism, generalized from north European capitalist experience (is there a western Marxist who does not, in some degree, believe that European civilization is indeed the repository of all "modernism"—i.e. all (capitalist) culture and progress? Had Frank made but even one of these several points, his contribution to a genuine Marxist analysis of the third world would be well secured for history. The Frank version of dependency theory, for all of the impatient writing, the ad hockery in definitions and the indulgence in terms, is closer to the spirit of classical Marxism than anything which has come from the ranks of the mechanistic, Eurocentered, formula Marxists to date—and far richer in content and relevance as well.

Dependency was, quite simply, the living Marxism of the colonized periphery, in the first flush of self-discovery, reflecting not the abstract

Euromarxism and "Dependency": A Portentous Disjunction

theorems—uncontaminated with any exposure to reality—as with Warren and Brenner et al., but the concrete, lived experience of the impoverished two-thirds of humanity, sequestered in the cheerless periphery of international capitalism, victims of both domestic and foreign exploiters. The textbook Marxists, in their arrogance, never quite understood this aspect of what they would contemptuously term "third-worldism."

In this regard the initial critique of Frank by Brenner, in a notorious paper, to recall a history that might otherwise be forgotten, is a useful case in point.[11] Running true to the distinguishing traits of that tradition, his critique of Frank, by his own admission, was primarily based on "method," of getting the "word" right (by method, of course, is meant getting the European—or more narrowly, the English—sequence of capitalist development right, abstracting this history into Marxian "theorems," and then applying them uncritically to the world at large!). But Laclau,[12] of course, had actually beaten Brenner to this task in "correcting" Frank on matters of definition. Indeed, Laclau, like Kay (among others), had already assured this completely barren scriptural "triumph" of Marxism (or so matters were to be portrayed) with Brenner arrived only to round off the utterly vacuous celebration. It is indeed high time that this celebration, which still upholds the reactionary current in Marxism, was defused just a jot; for these are perilous times and, should Marxists not clarify their own agendas (especially that remarkably enduring trait of crass opportunism), they run the certain risk of losing the interest—not to speak of loyalty—of the peoples of the third world, much as they have lost it in eastern Europe (to say nothing of western Europe!). With this in mind, to turn—briefly—now to the early Brenner contribution, widely believed to have buried the "third-worldist" challenge of dependency theory, and considered something of a landmark in such studies at the time.

First, we learn from Brenner that it is relations of production that are central to a Marxian analysis, the implication being that Frank has missed their significance: of course this was old hat, for Laclau—among others—had already criticized the allegedly "circulationist" (and therefore, amazingly, irrelevant!) definitions of Frank. Further, argued Brenner, class structures, once established, determine the course of subsequent development. (What a grand, suprahistorical generalization possessed of a sweep that all but ignores the real specifics and the conjunctural detail of a nonconjectural history of societal modes!) But this will not quite do. Focusing on the relations of production instead is not quite the ultimate correction to focusing on the forces of production. True, the forces of production must not be fetishized, but they cannot, equally, be ignored (a dozen passages in Marx have made this point, explicitly, but I will not quote; it is correct because it "makes sense"). Class relations can only do their thing when several intermediate moments in the forces of production are in place. The mode of production is made up of both, not either/or, their interconnection being an historical matter and not a logical inference from some Marxian model situated apart on Martian terrain.

Second, we are told that "capitalism has a systematic tendency to unprecedented economic development...to the expansion of relative surplus value without recourse to the methods of increasing absolute surplus labor, extension of working days, etc." Really? Where do we get this universal sounding statement from? From Somalian capitalism? Bangladesh perhaps ? No, Brenner is drawing on European history once again—if not simply from passages of *Capital*. But there is no capitalism in the abstract, only "isms" that require separate historical study; one "blueprint" alone—drawn from a tired old European example—will simply not suffice. The north European or, or even more specifically, the English historical example, cannot generate subsequent histories, after its own fashion, purely by definition. Besides, the living history of peripheral capitalism suggests the ongoing relevance of "primitive accumulation," not to mention its import even within metropolitan capitalism as feminist scholarship—if nothing else—continually reminds us: the enclave of the "primitively" exploited is, emphatically, not a shrinking one.

Third, Laclau's alleged Marxist critique of Frank was equally rather simple. Frank had not located capitalism in production, he argued, only in exchange. Let us note, however, that capitalism lives on at both levels—and one of the more dramatic failures of Marxist analysis is in its neglect of exchange paving the way for a virtual neoclassical monopoly of the field in political economy. But how does Laclau define capitalism itself? Capitalism is a mode of production based on wage labor. This sounds very Marxist of course (aside from being *simpliste* in the extreme!) and Laclau garnered a lot of EuroMarxist support for having shown up, thereby, the deficiency of Frankian discourse. But is it sufficient as a definition? Do we have capitalism wherever—and whenever—we find wage labor? In that case we would have capitalism in southern Gaul in

Euromarxism and "Dependency": A Portentous Disjunction

the first century of the Roman empire (not to mention instances drawn from ancient India, China, and Egypt: the famous, if always silent, "Other"[13] of European theorizing), where pottery was so organized. Brenner might have heeded the work of Banaji;[14] relations of production may not be confused with relations of exploitation. The same error that deduces feudalism from serfdom deduces capitalism from wage labor. Stated simply, wage labor in conditions of simple reproduction has existed at many points in history without leading to that tumultuous, self-reinforcing expansion that so fascinates Brenner and his ilk. Indeed, one should take note: the framework of ever-expanded reproduction seems to require all manner of intermediate conditions including "circulationist" exchange and other multifaceted "market" phenomena. So, having the "class relations in place" is far from sufficient. Furthermore, it becomes significantly evident that Brenner's critique of so-called "neoSmithian" ideas is trivially false for being completely inadequate. Stated simply, Smith did not get matters wrong when he stressed the importance of exchange and market-related phenomena in the context of expanded reproduction—*relations of production do not automatically generate such momenta on their own*. Indeed, it is quite astonishing to see such production-centered thinking ignore the contribution of mercantilism in the context of late feudalism carving—by force—a captive, colonized world market without which the most model set of class relations could never have given us that fateful ascendancy of European capitalism.

Fourth, Brenner argues that it is impossible to accept the thesis that the development of underdevelopment has anything to do with the subordination of the Third World under the European heel. Of course, no historical survey of the Third World, nor its contribution to first world dynamism, either in the past or present, appears in the article to substantiate this idea—because we realize it is quite unnecessary (it is in the nature of the "Other" to remain silent). It is almost self-evident to western Marxism that European colonialism could only civilize and uplift and "modernize" the nonEuropean world. So logic alone does the trick, without the distraction of anything quite so vulgar as evidence. Sartre's critique of Stalinism thus also applies pointedly to the Brenner position:

> The Marxist claims to discover the object in the historical process and the historical process in the object. In actuality, he substitutes for both alike

EUROMARXISM AND THIRD-WORLDISM: TOWARD AUTONOMISM

a collection of abstract considerations which immediately refer to principles.[15]

Instead of Marxism being a means to gain knowledge, it becomes the handbook of scriptural knowledge itself. No wealth of historical materials need be brought in. The stunning ignorance in western traditions as to the real socio-economic histories of nonEuropean civilizations such as India and China is to be seen to be believed;[16] (this in perfect parallel with the neglect—indeed, *denial*—of the contribution of Black Africa (Egypt) to the civilization of classical Greece, the cradle of European culture.[17] *Where prejudice is the rule, assertion is proof.* Similarly, the surplus drain from the captive colonial markets, such as India, had little to do with England's sudden takeoff into industrial supremacy; it was just the Magic of Relations of Production alone! So, armed with this scriptural confidence, we shall have to wait to see Somalia take off, similarly. Rostow[18] must be as right as Brenner. Indeed, where's the difference? But the facts (in all their stubbornness) are otherwise, and available to those who need to consult ongoing research prior to making historical overstatements. To satisfy the characteristic craving for quotes from Marx *(for nothing is true—to the kind of Marxist in question—that did not appear in one or other of the classical scriptures)*:

> rents in kind may assume dimensions which seriously imperil reproduction of the conditions of labor, of the means of production themselves, rendering the expansion of production more or less impossible and reducing the direct producers to the physical minimum of means of subsistence. This is particularly the case when this form is met with and exploited by a conquering commercial nation such as the English in India.[19]

Of course—and this is a serious point in any real conception of method—this would have been true *even had Marx not said it*, because it was *real*, i.e. it can be substantiated not by recourse to general principles but with respect to historical evidence. *It might be instructive for Marxists to recall that Marx himself had no such scriptures at hand to gain his knowledge of social matters*, or indeed to validate it; he learned from history much as we can. But for his epigones, regrettably, the Good Book stands in the way of a direct appropriation of reality.

Euromarxism and "Dependency": A Portentous Disjunction

The colonial mode of production had a retrograde effect in many contexts; especially in India, but also in North Africa and South America, leading to all manner of distortions.[20] These include (but are not limited to): (a) thwarting of industrialization, generally; (b) a drain of capital; (c) the constriction of home markets; (d) a channeling into unproductive forms of capital; (e) the creation of an unemployable *lumpen* or semiproletariat; (f) a total destruction of traditional food production in favor of commercial export crops engendering the chronic "famine" syndrome as in Bengal; (g) the creation of a super exploited, pauperized peasantry on dwarf holdings in conditions of technical backwardness, and overall wretchedness. *To be exploited without being developed* (as Banaji felicitously phrases it): that was the colonial legacy in a country that exported manufactured goods before British savagery reduced it to its present disarticulated Third World status. All of this can only be grasped when the function of the colony is conceptualized within the imperial scheme of metropolitan capital in a serious, historically mindful way. Far from providing answers, however, the Brenner tradition is unaware that there even is a problem to be studied here, for any such admission would discount heavily their version of the "rise of the West."

Indeed, the most stinging part of Brenner's critique of Frank is that, through him, horror of horrors, we are led into that biblical den of iniquity, namely "Third World" ideology. How terrible that Marxism embraces the sufferings of the hopeless, the poor, and starving, the "wretched of the earth," as Fanon called them. Materialist machismo à la Warren and Brenner requires that we speak metallically, and abstractly, of forces and relations—the language of compassion being considered either feminine, third-worldist, or simply weak and ineffectual. And the "rantings" of a peripheral radical—such as Fanon—of course, are not admissible as "Marxian," in much the same way as the protests of feminists were ignored for the longest time as distractive of the class struggle. For western Marxism is class triumphant, race and gender to be "fitted in" at some time appropriate, after the primal deed of "revolution." The tale of western Marxism internalizing, in all security, the prejudices of European bourgeois civilization yet remains to be told in all its disquieting detail. We shall, rather, be steadfastly "first world" in our ideology, where the benefits of advanced capitalism abound—provided that one is male, white, and, preferably, Republican. Shall we hold with Brenner and Company then? If so, the Third World is no place to seek either data or ideas, when we might comfortably betray Marx, turning his plea for a general human emancipation into sanction for a self-appointed mandarinate, secure in the newest set of self-validating convictions of European civilization, officially engaged in either endless textual criticism of texts and texts within texts—be it in the spirit of construction or deconstruction; all this while the world continues to be transformed by the struggles of peoples without the aid of these "Marxists," or even their knowledge (but occasionally, if catastrophically, caving in on their very heads).

A Chinese proverb says that, when the finger is pointed to the moon, the idiot looks at the finger. Classical Marxism was fashioned, always, as a tool pointed at changing the world. Let us stop endlessly reexamining the tool, and begin thinking instead of how it might be practically and politically employed, in the manner, yet, of Frank, the "un-Marxist" Marxist, and other committed antiimperialist scholars generally, in what is now self-consciously beginning to be understood as the field of subaltern studies, where the newest revolts of the *sans-culotte* are in the making. The urgency of this reorientation is underscored by the recent collapse of the second world, leaving the world divided all the more dangerously between an incredibly powerful, rapacious, and self-satisfied North (the recent butchery of Baghdad and its environs—a mere two hundred and fifty thousand dead!—symptomatic of the new western lease on an old, imperialist brutishness toward nonEuropean peoples) and a rather vulnerable and a prostrate South, the masses within which are still forced to do battle for bread and sub-basic needs. The relative harmlessness of western Marxism in the context of the old world order, where the progressive elements of the third world could look to the East for relief, is now transformed—given present conditions—into something far more deadly. For this is a Marxism that allies itself with western capitalism and imperialism against the peripheral societies and revolutionary movements therein. This craven political capitulation is already written in the slow theoretical erosion of the fundamentals of Marxism in western traditions. Only the latest in a series of defaults is the gleeful embrace of bourgeois analytic philosophy on the part of Brenner, Roemer, Elster, et al.,[21] an embrace that sets the stage for a final dissolution of the rather faint, progressive residual that might still have been supposed to endure. Here, instead, is an invitation to radical, antiimperialist, nonEurocentric scholarship to join the struggle to expose the growing reactionary elisions in the western tradition; and to the latter, a plea to rediscover the meaning of classical Marxism before it is too late, in a renewal of support for Third World struggles, the struggles of women, of minorities, of ecological activists, of autonomist movements for self-determination worldwide, instead of retreating into a purist priesthood, simply because "we" have the word and "they" do not. A welter of oppressive regimes, fraudulently invoking the formulae of Marx, while turning entire societies into Kafkaesque fortresses built on falsehoods, big and small, have just collapsed, like a house of cards, the little good therein buried with their much more formidable evils. No Marxist alive can dare pretend that there is nothing to be learned from the colossal failure: about socialism and power, about capitalism and liberty, and, perhaps, most of all, about Marxists themselves—their economism, their sectarianism, their opportunism, and their near-fatal, hegemonic lust for absolute power at cost, always, to the ever-forgotten masses, whose own impotence, ignorance, and apathy (now carefully cultivated) continue to remain the time-honored basis of class rule. It is time—and the lesson is writ rubric on the walls of East Europe—such Marxists learned to serve the cause(s) of peoples in their struggle for self-determination; instead of hoping, simply, to rule over them in a phony, hapless, stultifying "utopia" built of a grim, arid, lifeless materiality.

Notes

1. Perry Anderson, *Considerations on Western Marxism*, 1976, p. 93.
2. A. Koestler, *Bricks to Babble*, 1980, p. 63.
3. K. Popper, *The Unended Quest*, 1976, pp.42-44.
4. See chapter entitled "Progressive Imperialism...," in Bill Warren, *Imperialism: Pioneer of Capitalism*, 198, pp. 1-10.
5. See G. Kay, *Development and Underdevelopment*, 1975, p. x.
6. A. G. Frank, *Capitalism and Underdevelopment in Latin America*, 1967.
7. Paul Baran, *The Political Economy of Growth*, 1957.
8. A. Lewis, *The Theory of Economic Growth*, 1955.
9. P. T. Bauer, *Dissent on Development*, 1976.
10. And, now, better late than never, a book on the subject by Samir Amin: *Eurocentrism*, 1989.
11. R. Brenner, "The Origins of Capitalist Development: A Critique of Neo-Smithian Marxism," *New Left Review*, 104, 1977, pp. 25-92.

12. E. Laclau, "Feudalism and Capitalism in Latin America," *New Left Review*, 67, 1971.
13. See Johannes Fabian, *Time and the Other*, 1983; also, E. Said's *Orientalism*, 1978.
14. J. Banaji, "For a Theory of Colonial Modes of Production," *Economic and Political Weekly*, 1972:52.
15. Jean-Paul Sartre, *Search for a Method*, 1963, p. 135.
16. For an extended statement on the nature of such omissions, see George Gheverghese Joseph, Vasu Reddy, and Mary Searle-Chaterjee, "Eurocentrism in the Social Sciences," *Race and Class*, 31 (4), 1990.
17. See Basil Davidson, "The Ancient World and Africa: Whose Roots?" *Race and Class*, XXIX, 2, 1987.
18. W. W. Rostow, *The Stages of Economic Growth: A Non-Communist Manifesto*, 1960.
19. K. Marx, *Capital*, Vol. III, 1967.
20. Among a host of Indian historians addressing these issues, see the work of Amiya Bagchi, Bipan Chandra, Irfan Habib, Romila Thapar etc.
21. For a stirring critique of analytic philosophy, see Ali Shamsavari, *Dialectics and the Logic of Capital*, 1991.

Bibliography

Althusser, L. *Lenin and Philosophy* (London: New Left Books, 1971).
Amin, S. *Eurocentrism* (New York: Monthly Review Press, 1989).
Anderson, P. *Considerations on Western Marxism* (London: New Left Books, 1976).
———, *Lineages of the Absolutist State* (London: Verso, 1979).
Andreski, S., ed., *Max Weber on Capitalism, Bureaucracy and Religion: A Selection of Texts* (London: George Allen & Unwin, 1983).
Ashton, T. *The Industrial Revolution, 1760-1830.* (London: Oxford University Press 1968).
Avineri, S., ed., *Marx's Socialism* (New York: Lieber-Atherton, 1973).
Ayer, A. J. *Language, Truth and Logic* (New York: Dover, 1952).
Bachelard, G. *The New Scientific Spirit* (Boston: Beacon Press, 1984).
Banaji, J. "For A Theory of Colonial Modes of Production," *Economic and Political Weekly.* 1972: 52, pp. 2498-2502.
Baran, P. *The Political Economy of Growth* (New York: Monthly Review Press, 1957).
Barnes, D.G. *A History of The English Corn Laws from 1660-1848.* (London: Routledge and Kegan Paul 1930).
Bauer, P. T. *Dissent on Development* (Cambridge: Harvard University Press, 1976).
Bell, D. "The Rediscovery of Alienation," S. Avinieri, ed., *Marx's Socialism* (New York: Lieber-Atherton, 1973). pp. 59-79.
Berger, P. and Luckman, T., *The Social Construction of Reality* (New York: Doubleday, 1967).
Bharadwaj, K. "Ricardian Theory and Ricardianism," *Contributions to Political Economy*, 2, 1983, pp. 49-77.
Bhaskar, Roy. *The Possibility of Naturalism* (Brighton: Harvester, 1979).
———, *Scientific Realism and Human Emancipation* (London: Verso, 1986)
———, *Reclaiming Reality* (London: Verso, 1989).
Black, R.D.C. et.al. eds. *The Marginal Revolution in Economics.* (Durham: Duke University Press 1973).
Blackburn, R., ed., *Ideology in Social Science* (Suffolk: Fontana, 1972).
Blaug, M. *Ricardian Economics.* (New Haven: Yale University Press 1958).
———, *The Cambridge Revolution: Success or Failure?* (London: Institute of Economic Affairs 1975)

BIBLIOGRAPHY

——, *Economic Theory in Retrospect*. (Cambridge: Cambridge University Press, 3rd edition, 1978).
——, *The Methodology of Economics*. (Cambridge: Cambridge University Press 1980).
Bottomore, T.B. *Elites and Society* (Harmondsworth: Penguin Books, 1966).
Brenner, R. "The Origins of Capitalist Development: A Critique of Neo-Smithian Marxism," *New Left Review*, 104, 1977, pp. 25-92.
Brown, B. *Marx, Freud and the Critique of Everyday Life* (New York: Monthly Review Press, 1973).
Bukharin, N., *Historical Materialism: A System of Sociology* (New York: International Publishers, 1926).
——, *The Economic Theory of the Leisure Class* (London: Martin Lawrence 1927).
Bukharin, N. ed., *Science at the Crossroads* (London: Kniga, 1932).
Cannan, E. *A Review of Economic Theory*, 3rd ed. (New York: A.M. Kelley, 1964).
Caravale, G.A., ed., *The Legacy of Ricardo* (Oxford: Basil Blackwell, 1985).
Chalmers, A. "Is Bhaskar's Realism Realistic?" *Radical Philosophy*, No. 49, Summer 1988, pp. 18-23.
Cleaver, H. *Reading Capital Politically* (Austin: University of Texas Press, 1979).
Coats, A. W., ed., *The Classical Economists and Economic Policy* (London: Methuen and Co., 1971).
Coddington, A. "Positive Economics," *Canadian Journal of Economics*, 5, 1972, pp. 1-15.
Colletti, L. *From Rousseau to Lenin* (New York: Monthly Review Press, 1972).
Comte, A. *The Positive Philosophy*, 2 Volumes (London: Kegan Paul, 1893).
Corbridge, S. *Capitalist World Development* (Totowa: Rowman and Littlefield, 1986).
Cornforth, M. *In Defense of Philosophy* (London: Lawrence and Wishart, 1950).
Cowherd, R. *The Politics of English Dissent: the Religious Aspects of Liberal and Humanitarian Reform Movements from 1815 to 1848*, (New York: New York University Press, 1956).
——, *Political Economists and the English Poor Laws* (Athens: Ohio University Press, 1978).
Dahl, R. *Who Governs?* (New Haven: Yale University Press 1961).

Dahrendorf, R. *Class and Class Conflict in Industrial Society* (Stanford: Stanford University Press, 1959).
Dasgupta, A. *Epochs of Economic Theory*. (Oxford: Basil Blackwell 1985).
Davidson, B. "The Ancient World and Africa: Whose Roots?" *Race and Class*, XXIX, 2, 1987, pp. 1-15.
DeMarchi, N.B. "The Success of Mill's Principles," *History of Political Economy*, 6:119-157, 1974.
Dobb, M. *Theories of Value and Distribution Since Adam Smith* (Cambridge: Cambridge University Press 1973).
Dorfman, R. "Thomas Robert Malthus and David Ricardo," *Journal of Economic Perspectives*, Vol.3, Number 3 (Summer 1989) pp.153-164
Draper, H. *Karl Marx's Theory of Revolution* (New York: Monthly Review Press, 1977).
Durkheim, E. *The Rules of Sociological Method* (New York: The Free Press, 1964).
Engels F., *Ludwig Feuerbach and the Outcome of Classical German Philosophy* (New York: International Publishers, 1941)
Fabian, J. *Time and the Other* (New York: Columbia University Press, 1983).
Fetscher, I. *Marx and Marxism* (New York: Herder and Herder, 1971).
Feyerabend, P.K. *Against Method*. (London: Verso 1975).
———, *Science in a Free Society*. (London: Verso 1978).
Foucault, M. *La Volonte de Savoir* (Paris: Gallimard, 1976).Frank, A. G. *Capitalism and Underdevelopment in Latin America* (London: Monthly Review Press, 1967).
Friedman, M. *Essays in Positive Economics*. (Chicago: Chicago University Press 1953).
Gerratana, V. "Althusser and Stalinism," *New Left Review*, 1977, pp. 101-102.
Gerth, H.H. and Mills, C. Wright. *From Max Weber: Essays in Sociology* (New York: Oxford University Press, 1958).
Giddens, A. *Capitalism and Modern Social Theory* (Cambridge: Cambridge University Press, 1971).
Giddens, A., ed., *Positivism and Sociology* (London: Heinemann, 1974).
Gold, D., Lo, Y. H., and Wright, E. "Recent Developments in Marxist Theories of the Capitalist State, Part One," *Monthly Review*, No. 5, Oct. 1975, pp. 29-43.
———, "Recent Developments in Marxist Theories of the Capitalist State,

Part Two, *Monthly Review*, No. 6, Nov. 1975, pp. 36-51.
Grampp, W. D. *The Manchester School of Economics* (Stanford: Stanford University Press, 1960).
Guerin, D. *Anarchism* (New York: Monthly Review Press, 1970).
Gunn, R. "Marxism and Philosophy: A Critique of Critical Realism," *Capital and Class*, No. 37, Spring 1989, p. 88.
Halevy, E. *A History of the English People in the Nineteenth Century*. 6 Vols. (New York: Barnes and Noble, 1961)
Harcourt, G.C. *Some Cambridge Controversies in the Theory of Capital* (Cambridge: Cambridge University Press 1972)
Hindess, D. and Hirst, P. *Precapitalist Modes of Production* (London and Boston: Routledge and Kegan Paul, 1975).
Hirst, P. "Althusser and the Theory of Ideology," *Economy and Society*, 5:4, 1976, pp. 385-412.
Hobsbawm, E.J. *Industry and Empire* (Harmondsworth: Penguin 1968).
Hodgskin, T. *Labor Defended Against the Claims of Capital* (London: Hammersmith Bookshop, 1964).
Hollander, S. *The Economics of David Ricardo* (Toronto: Heinemann 1979).
Hume, D. *Essays Moral and Political* (London: Longmans and Green, 1875).
———, *A Treatise on Human Nature* (Oxford: Oxford University Press, 1978).
Joll, J. *The Anarchists* (London: Eyre and Spottiswoode, 1964).
Joseph, G., Reddy, V., and Searle-Chatterjee, M. "Eurocentrism in the Social Sciences," *Race and Class*, 31(4), 1990, pp. 1-26.
Kanth, R. "The Decline of Ricardian Politics: Some Notes on Paradigm-Shift in Economics from the Classical to the Neo-Classical Persuasion," *European Journal of Political Economy*, 1/2, 1985, pp.157-187.
———, *Political Economy and Laissez-Faire: Economics and Ideology in the Ricardian Era* (Totowa, New Jersey: Rowman & Littlefield Publishers 1986).
———, "The Social Foundations of Political Economy" in Kanth, R. & Hunt, E.K. (eds.), *Explorations in Political Economy* (Savage, Md: Rowman & Littlefield, 1990).
Kay, G. *Development and Underdevelopment* (London: Macmillan, 1975).
Keynes, J. M. *Essays in Persuasion* (London: Macmillan and Co., 1972).
Koestler, A. *Bricks to Babble* (London: Picador, 1980).

Kolokowski, L. *Positivist Philosophy from Hume to the Vienna Circle* (Harmondsworth: Penguin Books, 1972).
Kornhauser, W. *The Politics of Mass Society* (Glencoe, IL: Free Press, 1959).
Kuhn, T. S. The Structure of Scientific Revolutions (Chicago: University of Chicago Press, 1962).
Laclau, E. "Feudalism and Capitalism in Latin America," *New Left Review*, No. 67, May-June 1971, pp. 19-38.
Lakatos, I. "The Methodology of Scientific Research Programmes", *Philosophical Papers*, eds. Worral, J. and Curry, G. Vols. 1 & 2. (Cambridge: Cambridge University Press 1978).
Lakatos, I., and Musgrave, A., eds., *Criticism and the Growth of Knowledge* (Cambridge: Cambridge University Press, 1970).
Lange, O. *Political Economy*. (Oxford: Pergamon Press, 1963).
Larrain, J. *Marxism and Ideology* (London: Macmillan Press 1978).
Latsis, S.J. "Situational Determinism in Economics," *British Journal for the Philosophy of Science*, 1972, 23:207-245.
Lecourt, D. *Marxism and Epistomology* (London: New Left Books, 1975).
Lenin, V. I. *The State* (Peking: Foreign Language Press, 1965).
Letwin, W. *The Origins of Scientific Economics*, (New York: Doubleday & Co, Inc., 1964).
Lewis, A. *The Theory of Economic Growth* (London: George Allen and Unwin, 1955).
Lipset, S.M. *The First New Nation* (New York: W. W. Norton 1963).
Lukacs, G. *History and Class Consciousness*. (Cambridge: MIT Press 1971).
Malthus, T.R. *Principles of Political Economy Considered with a View to Their Practical Application*, 2nd ed., 1836, with an Introduction by Morton Paglin (New York: Augustus M. Kelley, 1964).
———, *An Essay on The Principle of Population and a Summary View of the Principle of Population*, Anthony Flew, ed. (Harmondsworth: Penguin, 1970; reprinted 1982).
———, *First Essay on Population* (London: Macmillan & Company 1926).
Mannheim, K. *Ideology and Utopia* (London: Routledge and Kegan Paul 1960).
Marcuse, H. "Max Weber," *New Left Review*, No. 30, 1965.
Marx, K. *The Economic and Philosophic Manuscripts of 1844* (New York: International Publishers, 1964).
———, *Capital*, Vol.1. (New York: International Publishers 1967).

BIBLIOGRAPHY

———, *Theories of Surplus Value Part 2* (London: Lawrence and Wishart, 1969)
——— and Engels F. *Selected Correspondence* (New York: International Publishers, 1935)
———, and Engels, F. *The German Ideology*. (New York: International Publishers 1970[a]).
———, "Preface" to A Contribution to the Critique of Political Economy, in *Marx-Engels, Selected Works in One Volume*. (London: Lawrence and Wishart 1970[b]).
———, *The Eighteenth Brumaire of Louis Bonaparte* (Moscow: Progress Publishers, 1972).
———, *The Poverty of Philosophy* (Moscow: Progress Publishers, 1973).
———, *Marx and Engels, Collected Works* (New York: International Publishers, 1983).
Meek, R.L. "The Decline of Ricardian Economics in England", *Economica*, n.s., 1950 17:43-62.
Meisel, J. H. *The Myth of the Ruling Class: Gaetano Mosca & the Elite* (Ann Arbor: University of Michigan Press, 1958).
Michels, R. *Political Parties* (New York: Dover, 1959).
———, *First Lectures in Political Sociology* (New York: Harper and Row, 1965).
Mill, J.S. *Collected Works: Essays on Economy and Society*. ed. J.M.N. Robson. (Toronto: University of Toronto Press, vol. 4. 1967).
Mosca, G. *The Ruling Class* (New York: McGraw-Hill, 1939).
Myrdal, G. *Value in Social Theory* (London: Routledge and Kegan Paul, 1958).
———, *Objectivity in Social Research* (London: Gerald Duckworth, 1970).
Neurath, O. *Empiricism and Sociology* (Dordrecht: Reidel Publishers, 1973).
Outhewaite, W. *Understanding Social Life* (London: George Allen and Unwin, 1977).
Paglin, M. *Malthus and Lauderdale: The Anti-Ricardian Tradition*. (New York: A.M. Kelley 1961).
Pasinetti, L. *Growth and Income Distribution*. (Cambridge: Cambridge University Press 1974).
———, *Lectures on the Theory of Production* (New York: Columbia University Press, 1977).

BIBLIOGRAPHY

Peach, T. "David Ricardo's Early Treatment of Profitability: A New Interpretation", *Economic Journal*, 94 (Dec. 1984), pp. 733-751.

———, "David Ricardo and the Invariable Standard", unpublished paper presented to the 1987 U. S. History of Economics Conference, Boston.

Plekhanov, G. V. *In Defense of Materialism* (New York: International Publishers, 1972).

Polanyi, K. *The Great Transformation*. (Boston: Beacon Press 1957).

Popper, K. R. *The Open Society and Its Enemies* (London: Routledge and Kegan Paul, 1962).

———, *The Logic of Scientific Discovery* (New York: Harper Torchbooks 1965).

———, *The Unended Quest* (London: Fontana, 1976).

Poulantzas, N. "The Problem of the Capitalist State," Blackburn, R., ed., *Ideology in Social Science* (Suffolk: Fontana, 1972).

———, *Political Power and Social Classes* (London: New Left Books, 1973).

Poynter, J.R. *Society and Pauperism*. (London: Routledge and Kegan Paul 1969).

Ricardo, D. *The Works and Correspondence of David Ricardo*, 11 Vols., P. Sraffa, ed. (Cambridge: Cambridge University Press, 1951-73).

———, *Principles of Political Economy and Taxation*, Donald Winch, ed. (London: Dent, 1974).

Robbins, L. *The Theory of Economic Policy* (London: Macmillan and Co., 1953).

Rogin, L. *Meaning and Validity of Economic Theory*. (New York: Books for Libraries Press, 1971).

Rostow, W. W. *The Stages of Economic Growth: A Non-Communist Manifesto* (London: Cambridge University Press, 1960).

Rubin, I.I. *A History of Economic Thought*. (London: Ink Links, 1979).

Runciman, W.G. *Social Science and Political Theory* (Cambridge: Cambridge University Press, 1965).

Said, E. *Orientalism* (New York: Pantheon, 1978).

Samuels, W., ed., *Institutional Economics* (Aldershot Edward Elgar, 1988).

Sartre, J-P. *Search for a Method* (New York: Alfred A. Knopf, 1963).

Shamsavari, A. *Dialectics and the Logic of Capital* (London: Merlin Books, 1991).

Schroyer, T. *The Critique of Domination* (Boston: Beacon Press, 1973).
Schumpeter, J.A. *Imperialism and Social Classes* (Oxford: Basil Blackwell, 1951).
———, *A History of Economic Analysis*. (New York: Oxford University Press 1954).
Senior, N. *Industrial Efficiency and Social Economy*, 2 Vols. ed. Leon, S., (New York: Henry Holt & Co. 1928).
Smith, A. *The Glasgow Edition of the Works and Correspondence of Adam Smith* (Oxford: Clarendon Press, 1976).
Stark, W. *The Ideal Foundations of Economic Thought*. (London: Kegan Paul, Trench, Trubner & Co. 1943).
———, *The History of Economics in its Relation to Social Development*. (London: Kegan Paul, Trench, Trubner & Co. 1944).
———, *The Sociology of Knowledge* (London: Routledge and Kegan Paul 1958).
Stedman-Jones, G. "The Marxism of the Early Lukacs," *New Left Review*, #70, Nov.-Dec. 1971, pp. 27-64.
Stigler, G.J. "The Development of Utility Theory", *Journal of Political Economy*, 1950, 58: 307-396.
Sweezy, P. *Theory of Capitalist Development* (New York: Monthly Review Press, 1970).
Therborn, G. *Science, Class and Society* (London: Verso, 1980).
Thompson, W. *Inquiring into the Principles of the Distribution of Wealth* (New York: Augustus M. Kelley, 1963).
Toynbee, A. *Lectures on the Industrial Revolution of the Eighteenth Century*, (London: Longmans, Green & Co., 1920).
Trevelyan, G.M. *English Social History, A Survey of Six Centuries* (London: Pelican Books 1967).
Tribe, K. *Land, Labour and Economic Discourse*. (London: Routledge and Kegan Paul, 1978).
Tucker, R. "Marx as a Political Theorist," S. Avineri, *Marx's Socialism (New York: Liber-Atherton, 1973)*.
Warren, B. *Imperialism: Pioneer of Capitalism* (London: New Left Books, 1980).
Weber, M. *Theory of Social and Economic Organization* (Glencoe, IL: Free Press, 1947).
———, *The Methodology of the Social Sciences* (Glencoe, Illinois: Free Press, 1949).

BIBLIOGRAPHY

———, *The Protestant Ethic and the Spirit of Capitalism* (New York: Charles Scribner's Sons, 1958).
Winch, P. *The Idea of a Social Science* (London: Routledge and Kegan Paul, 1958).
Wright, E.O. *Class, Crisis and the State* (London: New Left Books, 1979).
Zeitlin, I. *Rethinking Sociology* (New York: Polity Press, 1973).
———, *Ideology and the Development of Sociological Theory* (Englewood-Cliffs: Prentice Hall, 1968).

Index

Almond, Gabriel 75
Anderson, Perry 199
Anthropomorphism
    taint of, on the social
        sciences 128
Anti-Duhring 188
Antinuclear movement 42

Baran, Paul 201
Bauer, Lord 201
Bell, Daniel,
    and the end of ideology
        school 192
Biological heredity 3
Bolshevik Revolution 29, 68
Bonaparte, Louis, of France 30
Bourgeoisie
    economic power of, in
        Europe 58
Bureaucracies
    and dehumanization 20
    virtues of 20
Bureaucracy
    as agent for class rule
        according to Marx 32
    Czarist 29
    internal structurings of 33
    Marx's ideas on 29
    as means of social control 20
    and the modern state 25
    and the monopoly of routine 38
    in Stalin era 31
    superiority of 27
Bureaucratization 26
    and the concentration and
        centralization of
        executive power 40
    and concentration of means of
        production
    and management 20
    process of 26
    and Weber's philosophy of
        history 17

Capital 87, 172
    circulating vs. fixed 98
Capitalism 27
    and bureaucracy 28
    and class denomination 30
Capitalist fetishism 192
Capitalist state
    relative autonomy of 30
Caste
    and theory of caste-conflict 12
Causal interdependency 146
Charisma
    as antidote to routine 28
    as challenge to societal
        routines 14
    Weber's faith in concept of 22

INDEX

Class conflict 11
   and minority rule 48
Class consciousness 11
Class domination 7
Class interest 11
Class outlook
   scientific and ideological
     elements of 171
Class relations
   as property relations 71
Class struggle
   and dictatorship of the
     proletariat 74
Classless society
   socialist goal of 62
Coleman, James 75
Communist Manifesto 70
Comte, Auguste 134
Corn Laws in 1846 86, 153
   and class conflict theory of
     Ricardo 85
   as form of protectionism 88
The Crisis 104
Critique of the Gotha Programme 70
Culture
   and science 9

Dahl, Robert 63
Democracy
   as ideal form of capitalist
     rule 13
   and oligarchy 50
Democratic self-control
   and opposition movements 42
Despotism 7
Development
   and subordination of the
     Third World 205

Dialectical materialism
   of Engels 188
Dialectics
   Marxist grammar of thinking 192
Dilettantism
   and bureaucracy 27
Disorganized Capitalism 73
Domination
   class, function of 30
   legitimation of 7

Economic and Philosophical Manuscripts 190
Economic materialism 5, 186
The 18th Brumaire 70
Elites
   Mosca-Pareto school of 72
   specification of 35
Elitist ideology
   vs. democratic thought 58
Elitist theory
   and the expanding middle
     classes 63
   historical basis for 34
   and limiting activities of
     the masses 65
Enlightenment
   dissonance as a result of 137
Epistemic relativism 129, 168
Epistemology
   and the transitive dimension
     of studies of the world 128
Essay on Population 104, 112, 154
Essay on Profits 85
Essay on the Poor Laws 154
Eurocentered analyses
   Weber's theme of 29
EuroMarxism 197

INDEX

Existential intransitivity 145
Exploitation
    as primary Marxian concern 172

Feudal absolutism
    and French Revolution 17
Feudalism 7
    and elitist theory 34
Fiscal Crisis of the State 77
Foucault, 11
Frank, Andre Gunder 201
    and dependency theory 202
French Revolution of 1789 17, 47, 186
Friedman, Milton 163
Friedrich Wilhelm III 30
Functionalism, 69

Gasset, Ortega y 63
Genetic fallacy, theory of 57
The German Ideology 70, 75
Germany
    and bureaucratic despotism 29
Great Depression 68
Grounds of an Opinion 109
Grundrisse 186

Historical materialism
    basic tenets of 76
    Marxian method of 95
    reinterpretation of 199
History and Class Consciousness 192
History
    intrinsic coherence of, according to Hegel 184
Hitler, Adolph 29
Human perfectibility
    Mosca's disavowal of 63

Idealism
    of Hegel 184
    Marxian critique of 135
Imperialism
    American, and interests of the state 73
Industrial capital
    age of 116
Industrialization
    in postrevolutionary Russia and Ricardian struggle 99
Inquiry into the Nature of Progress of Rent 109
Introduction to Ricardo's Principles 109
Iron cage, politics of 29
Iron Law of Oligarchy 49, 52

Judgmental rationality 129
Judgmental relativism 168

Kontrartheorie 100

Laclau, E.
    and definition of capitalism 204
Laissez-faire
    and classical economics 83
    as protector of manufacturers 88
Lakatos, I. 149
Landlords
    economic importance of, according to Malthus 116
Language of compassion
    vs. materialist machismo 207
Leadership
    and relations to oligarchical forms 53
    and gulf between ranks 36

INDEX

Lenin, V. I. 31
Lewis, Arthur 201
Logic 186

Machinery
   as detriment to working class 97
Malthus, T. R. 85, 104
   championing of agrarian interests 115
   Ricardian attack on 121
Mannheim's "intellectual stratum" 61
Marx, Karl 3
   and irrationality of state 11
Marxian analysis 11
   and class conflict 11
   and class consciousness 11
   and class interest 11
   superstructures in 76
Marxism 3, 4
   as apology for economic growth 200
   classical 67, 78
   classical, and comtemporary academics 67
   classical, as theory of radical transformation 69
   classical, rediscovering meaning of 209
   as exhortation of practice 200
   as method 183
   as science of emancipation 14
   as sociology of knowledge 200
   as theory of praxis 191
   shaken faith in, European tradition of 68
Materialism 6, 197

Materialist machismo
   of Warren and Brenner 207
Means of production
   concentration of 28
Mediation
   class, function of 30
Metacritical dimension
   of Bhaskar 129
Metaphysical realism 128
Method
   Hegelian 183
Methodological individualism 126, 131
Michels, R.
   and radical elitist theory 35
   and nature of democracy 53
   and bureaucratization 54
   as court favorite of Mussolini 54
Mill, J. S. 162
Monism
   and demands of social reality 138
Monocentrism 26
Mosca, Gaetano 57-58
   and elitist theory 35
   and political elitism 60
Mussolini, Benito 29

Nationalism 40
NeoMarxism 79
   and the state 67
New Left Review 201
1798 Essay 105

O'Connors, James 77
Observations on the Effects of the Corn Laws 109

INDEX

Oligarchic domination
    and transformation of
        personalities of leaders 49
Oligarchy
    and leadership 50
    and the masses 50
    and the organization 50
Ontological realism 129
Ontology
    and the intransitive
        dimension of reality 128
Organization
    as basis for oligarchy 36
    as key to domination 36
    and minority rule 59

Paradigm-shift
    mechanics of 139
Pareto, Vilfredo 58
Paris Commune of 1871 31, 70
Parsons, Talcott 6
Party structure
    and democratization 51
Peace movement 42
Philosophy of Right 185
Pluralism 3
    Weberian, compared with
        Marxian 34
Pluralist relativism 5
Polanyi, Karl 154
Political order
    exclusion of propertyless
        from 65
Political Parties 50
Political power
    and institutional property
        relations 25

Political relations
    as class relations 71
Polsby, Nelson 63
Poor Laws 85, 153
    as form of protectionism 88
Popper, K. R. 149
Positivism 126
    and denial of transfactual 133
    and Marxism 77
    monist variant of 139
Positivist empirics 130
Postcapitalist societies
    power struggles within 32
Postmodernism 69
Poststructuralism 69
Poulantzas, N.
    on Lenin's writings 69
The Poverty of Philosophy 190
Power
    and bureaucracy 25
Power distribution
    Weber's theory of 8
    in postcapitalist societies 35
Principles 105
Principles of Political Economy and Taxation 155
Production 204
    and capitalist enterprise 11
    Property relations
    as determinants of class
        structure 11
Protestant ethic 6
    Weber's thesis on 5
Proudhon, M. 190
Pure labor theory
    Malthus's rejection of 111
Pye, Lucian 75

INDEX

Radical philosophy
  as substitute for radical practice 194
Rationality
  and separation of workers from means of production 20
Rationalization 26
  concept of 19, 27
  and effect on Western civilzation 19
  and nineteenth century European society 18
  and Weber's analysis of capitalism 19
Realism
  Bhaskarian, perspective on human emancipation 137
  as theory of being 123
Relativist/absolutist dichotomy 126
Ricardian laissez-faire
  and the bourgeois state 89
Ricardo, David 83, 150
  and class conflict and labor theory 87
  and class conflict as part of capitalism 120
  labor theory of 119
  Malthus's critique of 94
  theories of political economy 159
  theory of distribution 116
Robbins, Lionel 164
Russian Revolution 12, 186

Saint-Simone's "Council of Newton," 61

Science
  as cloak for private purpose 107
  postEnlightenment view of 145
Secularization
  of social life 19
Self-determination
  and opposition movements 42
Slavery 7
Smith, Adam 30, 115, 150
Social revolution
  Marxian model of 14
Social science
  lack of need for, according to Marx 8
  and the ruling establishment 146
  scientific nature of 146
  as social policy 149
Socialism
  Mosca's revulsion for 62
Socialist theory
  and exposé of social domination 18
  naiveté of, according to Michels 52
Society
  Mosca's conception of 60
  structural delineation of 26
Speenhamland reform
  Malthus's case against 107
State
  as agency of class domination 6
  in capitalist society 71
  changes in function of 71
  as political variable 6

INDEX

and violence 7
Weber's definition as monopoly
  over means of
  coercion 30-31
Subelite, the
  of Mosca's theory 61

Technological fetishism
  and capitalist societies 39
The Theories of Surplus Value 96
Third World 197
  right-wing policy toward 200
Transcendental realism
  challenge to reign of positivist
    intuitions 138
  and critique of Marxism 134
  implications of, for economic
    theory 130
  and the nonidentity of
    thought and being 130
  Roy Bhaskar's theory of 127
Tudor Poor Law 154

Verba, Sidney 75

Vocabulary of Politics 10
Von Mises
  neoAustrian treatise of 164

Warren, Bill 118, 200
Weber, Max 3, 5, 26
  on bureacracy as structure
    of domination 21
  and bureaucratization 13
  and economic determinism 18
  and German imperialism 14
  and historical materialism 18
  and neoKantian tradition 14
  and rationalization 17
  and social enterprise 11
  and value-free concept 17
Weldon, T. D. 10
Western Marxism
  and internalization of European
    bourgeois prejudices 207
  and postwar defeatism 199
Who Governs? 63
Working class
  and the Corn Laws 97

About the Author

Rajani Kannepalli Kanth was educated at the Delhi School of Economics, Columbia University, and the New School for Social Research, with degrees in Economics and Social Anthropology. His teaching career, spanning two decades, began at the Jawaharlal Nehru University, New Delhi, 1971-1974, interrupted by a stint at the United Nations in New York, only to be continued at the State University of New York and then on to the University of Utah, in Salt Lake City where he is currently based. Author of *Political Economy and Laissez-Faire* (1986) and co-editor of *Explorations in Political Economy* (1991), he has held Visiting Fellowships at Oxford University, England, and the University of Bielefeld, Germany. His teaching and research interests include political economy and social theory.